Riding Through the Storm

Riding Through the Storm

ꝏ

GEOFF THOMAS

First published in hardback in Great Britain in 2007 by
Orion Books
an imprint of the Orion Publishing Group Ltd
Orion House, 5 Upper St Martin's Lane,
London WC2H 9EA
An Hachette Livre UK Company

1 3 5 7 9 10 8 6 4 2

A CIP catalogue record for this book is available
from the British Library.

ISBN: 978 0 7528 7614 6

Printed in Great Britain by Mackays of Chatham plc,
Chatham, Kent

www.orionbooks.co.uk

Contents

For Julie, Madison and Georgia

Acknowledgements

I would like to pay tribute to the following people:

My friends and family, especially my wife Julie, my two wonderful children Madison and Georgia, my mum Renee, my sister Kay and her husband Bryan, and Julie's mum Irene and dad George.

The doctors and nurses who helped save my life, especially Professor Charlie Craddock and his team, Dr Shafeek and Dr Frank Taylor.

The many people I have met in hospital wards and waiting rooms over the last three years. You have been a source of comfort throughout.

Cathy Gilman at Leukaemia Research.

The football community, especially Sir Alex Ferguson, Steve Coppell, Dave Bassett, Alan Pardew, Graham Taylor, and a dear old friend, John Pemberton.

My team-mates and support crew on the Tour: Ian Whittell, Robbie Duncan, Matt Lawton, Dave West, Chris Haynes, Richard Chessor, Andrea Smith, Hayley Cullum and Neil Ashton.

Lance Armstrong, for providing the inspiration.

And finally,

Mark Miller, Clare Wadley and Steve Hayden. Your memory lives on.

Prologue

The week Julie and I planned in Majorca at the end of May 2003 could not come soon enough. We were working 15-hour days in our clothing business and needed some time to relax and reinvigorate before the long build-up to Christmas. It had taken more than a year to dissolve our previous business partnership and settle our debts. The last six months had been tough, but we had plans to open another shop in September.

Slowly, ever so slowly, the tide was beginning to turn; but this was just the start – we had a long way to go and we literally had to snatch our week in the sun. When I returned, I had a couple of important meetings in Milan with some fashion houses and we knew this could be the last chance of the year for the family to spend a bit of time together on holiday. The weather in Majorca was wonderful. As a confirmed sun-worshipper I could spend every minute of the day lounging by the pool or taking in a game of tennis on the courts if it was possible.

After I retired from professional football, I had been converted. In a short space of time, tennis had become my new passion and I took regular lessons at my local David Lloyd club. I had played very occasionally during my childhood, but I didn't get the chance to swing a racket during my football career. Now I was learning how to play the game for real and the upper-body strength I acquired playing football had allowed me to develop a pretty fearsome first serve. I just needed to add some polish to the rest of my game.

On the first morning of our holiday, Julie and the children were by the pool and I was on court for a doubles match against our friends Leslie and Rob. This was a chance to loosen my stiff muscles and run off a few beers from the night before. Nothing heavy, just a couple of halves to wind down after the two-hour flight from Birmingham. When I arrived on court, I still felt a little light-headed, but I put it down to the long day's travelling and a change of routine.

I felt fatigued, weary and was struggling to get out of second gear during the warm-up, but I didn't think it could last. My days of training for two hours or more a day on the football field were long gone, but I still considered myself to be relatively young and in fairly good physical shape. This, though, was something different. At one stage, I looked up at the sun and wondered whether I was still dehydrated as I struggled to hold myself together and desperately tried to ignore the discomfort.

We had only just completed a ten-minute warm-up, but already I was struggling to adapt to the pace of the game when it hit me. Straight through the stomach. Whoosh … it felt like a 10-inch knife had been plunged into the pit of my stomach. The pain was immense. I doubled up in agony. It was so sharp I couldn't even find a position to make myself comfortable. I was struggling to breathe in the heat, and the sweat was starting to pour off my face. The excruciating pain, just under the left side of my rib cage, was unbearable and it was a struggle even to make my way off the court.

It was an extraordinary feeling. There was a lump underneath my rib cage, but I didn't want to cause concern. I put it down to a muscle tear. I had suffered my fair share of injuries during my professional career and players can usually detect whether they have done something serious. This would be nothing, a simple muscle spasm and that would be it. A day or two at most and I would be back on the tennis court to teach my playing partners a thing or two.

I also considered the possibility of a recurrence of an old back injury as one of the factors and, that night, I stretched out on the floor of Leslie and Rob's villa and asked Julie to walk up and down my spine to try and relieve some of the pain. Over the next couple of days, I noticed a gradual improvement and that was enough to convince me that my symptoms were nothing serious.

If I'd lost a few pounds over the summer then it was more a reason to celebrate than raise concerns, and if I was looking tired, then it was nothing that a few early nights could not put right. Apart from the constant pain in the side of my stomach, I didn't actually feel unwell. There was no doubt that Julie and I had been devoting a lot of time to our shops, but we were thriving on it.

The pain in the pit of my stomach was a side issue. There were other priorities and, while I was in obvious discomfort, I didn't want anything to sidetrack me from the shops. I believed that my body was in the process of healing itself and that, in time, the pain and the swelling would subside.

I tried to ignore it for the rest of the holiday, but the pain was always there. I couldn't find a position to sit in that was comfortable and I couldn't lie in bed at night without feeling some discomfort, but I was determined to enjoy the rest of our break.

When we returned to England, I threw myself back into the business, but the pain crept up on me again when I made my annual pilgrimage to South London to play in a charity golf day at Purley Downs. It is a tough, undulating course and I had played there many times before when I was a player at Crystal Palace. I'd made a lot of friends in the area and I didn't need much of an excuse to go and see them. I was struggling with the swelling in my stomach, but I still didn't think I should be trying to catch my breath between holes. My three playing partners, Clive Marshall, Ian Alchin and Dave Connolly, are all Palace fanatics and old friends from my time at the club. I was trying not to show any signs of distress, but it was obvious that I had a problem.

I had to pause at regular intervals to try and regain my strength and, by the time we came out of the clubhouse after lunch for the beginning of our second round, I was not sure whether I would be able to carry on. I tried not to show any emotion, but I was only just holding on. My career as a professional footballer had only ended 18 months earlier and now I was struggling to make it up a modest climb. I was gasping for breath, I was nearly on my hands and knees, and all I wanted was some solitude.

'Bloody hell, Geoff,' they teased. 'You've let yourself go a bit. To think we used to pay to watch you play.'

It was only light-hearted banter and that is how I took it. I would have done the same. The dressing room can be a heartless place and when you are with friends, especially on a golf course, there is no escape. I carried on, but I will never know how I got through it. I enjoy playing golf – I'm an 18-handicapper on a very, very good day – but I looked as though I had never played the game before.

An air shot on the 17th compounded my misery and I just doubled up again in agony, hands on my knees, with absolutely no idea what was happening to me. I wanted to curl up in a ball and stay there until someone rescued me. The pain was crippling and I had never known anything like it. I hadn't realised that a ripped back muscle could be so debilitating.

'Look at him, he's all washed up.'

It certainly felt that way.

OO

Our plans for a new shop in Birmingham were well under way and it was scheduled to open in three months' time. I left Julie to look after the business while I travelled to Milan in the middle of June for a meeting with the Italian fashion label Gianfranco Ferré. There was the possibility that they would stock their range in our outlets. I took with me Alan Chatham, a director at the Mailbox Shopping Centre.

Alan had become a firm friend since the days when we opened our first shop in the Mailbox back in 1996 and there was potential to develop our business relationship. Alan takes his fitness seriously and we often swapped notes about our sporting prowess. Milan was in the midst of a heatwave when we arrived at Bergamo – normally the sort of weather that I enjoy. It was almost tropical, 40 degrees or more, but I was puffing, panting, struggling to draw breath and, again, I was dripping with sweat. I couldn't help notice that Alan found it a breeze.

We were due to have a meeting with Amanda Osborne, one of the sales directors at Gianfranco Ferré, and she arranged for us to spend a morning in a swish health spa that had been used by celebrities such as Madonna in the past. I looked at the list of treatments and decided to have a lymphatic massage to try and clear my body of any toxins. Instead, it triggered another severe shooting pain in my stomach.

By the time Alan and I arrived at Amanda's offices, I was wincing with pain and, as I hugged the stair rail, I wondered whether I would be able to make it to the top. I was accustomed to the pain, but not to the embarrassment. After playing sport to a high standard, people naturally have certain expectations of your overall, general fitness, but I was struggling to make it up a simple flight of steps.

It was so confusing. Occasionally I over-indulged with a few pints of Guinness but, even then, nothing heavy, and I was playing tennis two or three times a week. Now I couldn't even walk up a flight of stairs. Each step was a struggle. One foot in front of the other, puffing, panting and struggling for even a few gasps of air. I was so short of breath when I reached the top that I had to pause to recover.

My lungs contracted and the fear that this was something more serious was only adding to the sense of panic. Eventually, I made it to Amanda's office. I couldn't wait to sit down and, when I did, I slouched in the chair, wondering just how much longer I would have to put up with the constant ache. It disturbed my concentration, I couldn't relax and I was deeply uncomfortable.

That night, the pain under my rib cage was so acute that I nearly dialled for an ambulance. The only reason I hesitated was because I did not want to cause any alarm. I have never had cause to telephone the emergency services, but that night it was the closest I'd ever come to it. To try and comfort myself, I curled up in the foetal position watching the film *Gladiator* on my laptop to try and ease the pain, but it was a restless night. The next morning, I congratulated myself on ignoring my instincts to call an ambulance. The lymphatic massage, painful as it was, appeared to have been the perfect antidote to my symptoms and I surfaced that morning feeling fresh.

The massage removed the toxins from my bloodstream overnight and I felt sure that I would continue to improve in the coming days. I still had stomach cramps, but the shooting pains had subsided. I had once had a similar condition so I never thought of getting an expert opinion and I remained convinced that, in time, the swelling in my stomach would gradually disappear. By the time I returned from Milan, though, Julie had realised that my condition was deteriorating.

'Meeting went really, really well. Amanda Osborne was nice. They seem keen to do business.'

'And your stomach pains?'

'Much better. Anyway, about the meeting …'

And then Julie brought it up again. Only this time, she wouldn't let it go. She was like a dog with a bone. I still wasn't concerned, but I told her exactly what had happened in Milan. To me, the swelling was a side issue and there were more important matters to attend to. In less than three months we were opening another shop and I really didn't have the time to be worrying about a problem that was likely to be nothing more than a severe back spasm.

'Geoff, you're going to see the doctor.'

'No, don't be silly. It will be all right, don't worry.'

'Geoff, you are going to see the doctor.'

'Give it a few more days. See if it gets any better.'

'You've been like this for over a month. I'm booking you an appointment tomorrow.'

Reluctantly, I bowed to Julie's demands, even though I was still relaxed about my stomach pains. My sister, Kay, and her husband, Bryan, were staying with us. That night, the four of us sat down for dinner, drank a couple of bottles of red wine and then sat on the sofa and watched television.

We talked, as we often did, about everything. Our shops, our children, family, friends, the future and other household matters. And then we discussed the lump that had been resting under my rib cage for the past two months. I pressed it. Julie pressed it. Whichever angle we probed it from, it hurt like hell. It was uncomfortable, it was agony at times, but I was still convinced it was a torn muscle.

The more Julie prodded, the more painful it became. And that is when I first tried to make light of the situation by referring to the life insurance policies that I'd paid into during my professional playing career.

'Just imagine, Julie, if it was a cancerous growth that could sort all our problems out.'

It was a throwaway remark, instantly regretted, and did nothing to put Julie's mind at rest. She slapped me across the thigh and told me not to talk in those terms. Even then I wasn't worried.

OO

I had not seen a regular doctor since I was seven years old. Regular check-ups with doctors at my previous football clubs meant I hadn't had to and, in any case, I rarely had a problem that required the attention of a doctor. Like everyone else, I had common colds, flu, fevers and other occasional symptoms that might have kept me in bed for a day or two, but they were mild compared to this.

Before, I always battled through, but if I ignored Julie over this, I was sure she would frog-march me to the surgery. Instead, I drove down to Dr Frank Taylor's surgery near our home in Barnt Green well in time for my 9.30 a.m. appointment on 3 July 2003 and waited my turn. It is a date that will remain etched on my memory for the rest of my life. People celebrate Christmas, they celebrate New Year and they celebrate birthdays. This was not a day for celebration.

I breezed into the surgery 20 minutes before my scheduled appointment. As I flicked through the endless supply of magazines in the waiting room, I felt like a fraud. The surgery had a single page of notes with some sketchy details of the tonsillitis I'd suffered when I was a child and I hadn't been back since. Sitting in the surgery, waiting for Dr Taylor's valuable time, I felt sure that the other people in the waiting room were likely to have much more serious symptoms than me.

After all, you only go to the doctor when there really is something wrong with you. Still, I'm here now, I thought, I might as well let him take a look, just for the reassurance. I expected his diagnosis to tally with mine; then he would send me home with some instructions to make sure I got plenty of rest.

I even imagined the probable course of our conversation.

'So, Geoff, what seems to be the problem?'

'Bit of a stomach strain. There's a lump underneath my rib cage that's been causing me a bit of discomfort.'

'How long have you had it?'

'Oh, not long. Few days. Couple of weeks. Maybe a month or so.'

'Bit of discomfort you say? Work busy? Not enough sleep? Yes, just lie down, let me have a look.'

'Bit sore there, hurts when you do that.'

'Hmmmm, yes, you're right, bit of a stomach strain. Bit sore here?'

'A little.'

'Thought so. Take this to the chemist, twice a day for a week, and get plenty of rest. Come back in a week if there's no improvement.'

If only. Instead, I could tell by the anguished look on Dr Taylor's face that there was a problem. He explained that there were five possible reasons for the lump behind my rib cage and he wanted to take a blood sample so that they could rule some of them out. My spleen was enlarged, but he didn't say what might have caused it and, to be honest, I didn't want to ask. He explained that the organ is a filter designed to remove red blood cells when they are no longer of use to the body and that I might have an infection.

Well, that explained everything. I had been retracing my steps over the past few weeks and convinced myself I had a severe bout of food poisoning after my trip to Milan. I was even feeling fairly relieved when he took a blood sample to be sent for analysis.

'It will be two to three weeks before we get the results.'

'OK, fine. Thanks.'

'We'll let you know in due course.'

'Thanks.'

I left for work and did not give my appointment with Dr Taylor that morning a second thought. If it was going to take another fortnight or more before the results were known, it was not likely to be anything too serious. Dr Taylor did. The moment I left his surgery he sent my sample off to the laboratory at the Queen Elizabeth Hospital in Birmingham for an emergency test. The sample had been despatched when I left the surgery and six hours later I received the phone call that I will never forget.

At 3.45 p.m. I was sitting in traffic, cursing the queue of cars heading for the busy junction outside a pub called The Soak in Selly Oak, on the outskirts of Birmingham, when my mobile phone rang.

'Hello?'

'Mr Thomas, it's Dr Taylor at the surgery. I wonder if you could come into the surgery this evening?'

'This evening? Why? Is there a problem?'

'Your test results have just arrived back with us. We need to see you. Are you able to come in?'

My heart rate stepped up a gear. I was crawling towards the lights but it would be another five minutes or more before I made it to the crossroads. I was breathing heavily. I was worried and the tone of his voice left me trembling with fear.

'Back already?'

'There is a problem, but I need you to come to the practice. Perhaps you could come in after work?'

'At least give me an idea – I need to know what the problem is.'

'I don't really want to tell you over the phone.'

'Please, can you just tell me what it is?'

'I would much prefer it if you came to the practice. Could you come into the surgery after six p.m.?'

No, I could not. Not now. I needed to know this second, this moment. I was already panicking. It was clearly something serious. I was sitting in my car and there was nowhere to go. The traffic was bumper to bumper, the lights had just turned red again and the sun was streaming through the windscreen. By now I was shaking, barely audible and could only just compose myself enough to continue our conversation.

'I can't concentrate now. I really need to know now.'

'Are you sure?'

'Yes, tell me now. Whatever it is, I can take it. Just tell me. I need to know.'

And, in the time it takes to read this sentence, came the bombshell.

'Mr Thomas, we think you might have leukaemia.'

If ever my life flashed before me, then it was in that moment. This was not a rehearsal, this was for real. It was too much information. There is no nice way to tell someone they are dying and, conversely, there is no way to prepare them either. I had been given the option. I could have delayed it a couple of hours until I went into the surgery later that evening. Perhaps Dr Taylor would have sat me down, maybe my wife would have been with me to share the burden of the bad news, but I opted for the newsflash.

If you ever want to cut someone down in a stroke, tell them they are dying. So, that's it. I'm 38 years old and I'm dying. I'm 38 years old, I've just been told I'm dying, and I'm sat outside a pub in Selly Oak, sat in traffic and I'm another half an hour away from home. My wife isn't even with me. My head was in my hands. This is happening and it is happening right now. I could not speak, I could not grasp the enormity of it all.

The tears were streaming down my face and sweat was already beginning to trickle down my temples. My father, Gordon, died of cancer in the space of six short weeks in 1993 and I felt sure the same would happen to me. By now I realised I had ignored the warning signs and I was about to pay a heavy penalty. For at least two months I had been living with leukaemia and, big, brave boy that I am, I ignored the symptoms.

The next few seconds went past in a blur but I managed to escape the traffic and pull into the side of the road.

'Mr Thomas, are you still there?'

'Is it serious?'

Is it serious? What sort of question was that? If I heard correctly, this is leukaemia. It is cancer. And it is a killer. Of course it is serious.

I'm as good as dead. Perhaps I just needed confirmation in case, somehow, I had got it all wrong.

'Very serious. We need to establish what stage you are in.'

'What stage?'

'Yes, there are three different phases of the disease.'

'Does this mean I could die?'

'Left untreated ...'

After that, I will never know how I pulled myself together, but I somehow forced a reply.

'OK, see you at six p.m.'

As I sat in my car, I couldn't control my emotions. That morning, I'd left my house at 9 a.m. and headed for a doctor's surgery believing that, at nearly 40 years of age, I was still physically fit and looking forward to living to a grand old age. Seven hours later, I was being told that I had leukaemia. Cancer of the blood. I had to call Julie, but it's hard when someone has just delivered such devastating news.

I was cracking up and I still had to make the hardest phone call of my life: to tell my wife, Julie, that, in all probability, I hadn't got long to live. The tears had long since stopped welling up in my eyes. Now they were running like a river down my cheekbones, so much so that as they dripped off the side of my face, my jeans were soaking them up like blotting paper. I wasn't expecting this. At worst, I was expecting to be told that I needed an operation. No-one expects to be told they have cancer. And now comes the hardest part.

How, exactly, do you tell the one person, the person who, along with your children, you love more than anything else in the world, that you are a dying man? How could I tell my wife, my soulmate, the love of my life and the person who has shared a thousand dreams or more with me, that I have leukaemia? She had already called several times, but I didn't have the strength to answer the phone.

I was a blubbering wreck, but I knew I needed to find the strength to speak with her. She became anxious when Dr Taylor called the house to ask for my mobile telephone number and now I wasn't even answering my phone. The anxiety was escalating.

The phone continued to ring but I couldn't answer. I couldn't even speak. Not to anyone. Not even to my wife. Traffic was crawling past me; cars approached the lights. Finally I summoned the strength to wipe my eyes again, blow my nose and pick up the phone. I dialled our home number and Julie answered in an instant. She picked up the receiver and her voice was trembling with fear from the moment she spoke.

'Geoff?'

By now, I was sobbing again and it was uncontrollable. I wanted to force out the words, spit them out and get it over and done with. I gave myself the time to take in the enormity of the situation and I wanted to say the word. Make the admission. A statement of fact. I told myself that it would be easier to cope with if I told her straight away. Then there is no going back. Then we could make plans, we could decide what to do. As hard as it felt right then, the uncontrollable emotion could not last for ever. Somehow the pain would subside. Unless it was a mistake. Doctors don't make mistakes. They would never tell you something like this unless they were absolutely certain.

Hold on a moment. Dr Taylor said 'might have' leukaemia.

Maybe he was telling me the worst-case scenario. More likely it was still a simple blood infection that could be cleared up with some antibiotics. But I knew Dr Taylor was not beating about the bush. He was just being compassionate and trying to soften the blow. And it is a blow. It is a huge blow; there is no nice way of telling someone they have a life-threatening illness. I put the phone down.

It rang instantly. This time, Julie was crying. She was hysterical. She knew it was bad, but somehow I had to tell her just how bad.

'Geoff,' she asked repeatedly, 'where are you?'

'Julie …'

'What is it, Geoff?'

Maybe 30 seconds, maybe more, passed by.

'Julie. They think I've got leukaemia.'

It was done.

We were both hysterical. Neither of us could speak. I was still sat in my car, I was crawling towards the traffic lights and I was shaking uncontrollably. She was sat at the top of the stairs, trying to digest the reality, and I was still more than half an hour away from our home in Barnt Green. She told me later that she sat there for an age, struggling to take in the reality that her husband, the father of two wonderful children, had a life-threatening illness.

It was ten minutes or so since I had been told I probably had leukaemia. I was still struggling to contain my emotions. I had to get home.

I wanted to be at home in an instant, to wrap my arms around her and feel some warmth. Instead, I was idling towards the lights and fighting against a steady stream of traffic. When I finally made it, Julie was waiting. She had not seen me like this since my father passed away, ten years before. But the tears that tumbled down my cheeks that afternoon more than made up for those lost years. In the hour or so before my 6 p.m. appointment with Dr Taylor, we tried to find out a bit more about the devil we were dancing with.

When we finally composed ourselves, we switched on the computer and keyed the word 'leukaemia' into an internet search engine. There were thousands of websites dedicated to the disease and most of them offered the same do-it-yourself test.

Do you suffer from any of the following?
Breathlessness
Low-grade fever
Loss of appetite
Abdominal discomfort
Night sweats
Tiredness

I could tick every box.

1

Fromentine-Noirmoutier-en-l'Île
19 km Time-Trial

Sometimes, when I can't sleep at night and a thousand thoughts are swirling through my mind, I wonder how I came to ride the Tour de France. As I lie next to Julie in our home on the outskirts of Birmingham, I can picture the pain of the professionals as they ride through 21 days of torture, often in summer temperatures of 30 degrees or more.

Then I visualise them riding through the driving rain of northern France, or past endless fields of sunflowers, deep in the countryside, with only the constant whirr of the wheels spinning at more than 100 revolutions a minute to keep them company. As they crawl up the most arduous and demanding mountain climbs in Europe during the second week, that's when the real fatigue sets in and I can see the agony etched across their faces; I can see the hordes of people lining the route, screaming and shouting, willing the riders to stretch their bodies beyond the limits.

The 189 privileged riders selected to ride the Tour battle against the clock, the heat, the wind and the rain. And then there is the 'broom wagon' that follows the last man in the *peloton* and threatens to sweep him up if he does not increase his speed. I know that the fear of failing in front of the millions of people watching on television around the world is the one thing that stops them pulling up at the side of the road and quitting the most prestigious road race on the planet. These are some of the most finely tuned athletes in the world, but, with their team-mates scattered across the mountains, there is often no-one there to pat them on the back, push them to their limits and pull them through.

I also remember and marvel at the splendour of the *peloton*, the 189 dreamers who glide through the pretty French villages at average speeds of just over 40 kph for three weeks, covering 3,500 km, before the spectacular finale on the Champs-Élysées in Paris.

That is when the real party begins. Under the Arc de Triomphe, those lucky enough to make it to the finish push themselves beyond the boundaries and showboat at speeds of more than 60 kph on the treacherous cobblestones. It is an honour for a professional rider even to finish the Tour, let alone win it, but the finish line is freedom. Freedom from their burning thighs. Freedom from the endless hours spent on the road. And freedom from the most gruelling road race in the world. Cycling is not just about sheer strength. It is a test of endurance, stamina, wit, perception, concentration, dedication and a bit of bravado. And there can only be one winner.

Most of the professionals take part in the Tour knowing that they will never be good enough to emerge victorious. Every year, 21 teams select their nine best riders and, for most of them, the prestige of taking part is payment for protecting their team leader in the seemingly endless, sometimes monotonous, days ahead. The *domestiques* are selected to serve the team leader. They chase down breakaways, shield the main man from the headwinds and crosswinds that sap so much energy, and do everything they can to save their leader's strength for the mountains.

It is in the snow-capped peaks of the Alps or the Pyrenees – where they spend nearly two-thirds of the Tour – that the race is decided. When I was a professional footballer, I would watch the Tour on television each summer and marvel at the bewildering operation of the bunch. I found it fascinating that so many teams could compete against each other and yet each rider would take a short turn at the front of pack to maintain the momentum and keep up the average speed. In my playing days, Greg LeMond dominated the sport; now another American, Lance Armstrong, was the six-time winner of the most demanding race in the world.

Armstrong had survived cancer and gone on to become the most prodigious cyclist in the history of the sport; it sends a shiver down my spine whenever I recall the days that I cycled along the very same roads. As a child in Manchester, my hero was the City midfielder Colin Bell, but, as I fought my battle with leukaemia, it was Armstrong who became a symbol of hope. Even when everything appears lost, there is always something to live for.

Armstrong, who made a full recovery from his illness, retired from the sport after winning the Tour for the seventh successive time in July 2005. I had watched his astonishing ascent of l'Alpe d'Huez during the time-trial in the 2004 Tour and, in my own small way, I wanted to emulate his remarkable achievements. Armstrong began the 14 km, 8 per cent climb two minutes behind the Tour leader Ivan Basso, and finished it three minutes ahead of his main rival. It was an immense display of physical power and Armstrong's extraordinary performance that day has gone down as one of the Tour's greatest moments. Reading Armstrong's book inspired me to battle on and beat leukaemia.

The strength and stamina that served me so well during my football career had been sapped during my treatment for leukaemia, but I was determined to repay the doctors and nurses who gave me another chance. Like so many others who have been in a similar position, I wanted to give something back and to show people that if they stay strong and keep their inner belief, there is always a chance of making it to the other side.

I know that, so far, I have been one of the lucky ones. Most leukaemia patients cannot find a suitable stem-cell donor and they live their life from one day to the next, hoping and praying that the disease does not catch up with them. One day, I hope the experts will find the key and they will be free.

I didn't set out to be a standard-bearer for cancer sufferers. I set out to ride the route of the Tour de France as the former England international footballer who tried to chip the France goalkeeper during a friendly at Wembley in February 1992. It had been more than ten years since that infamous effort and, by the time I was diagnosed with chronic myeloid leukaemia, I was just another ex-professional footballer trying to make a living. My career with seven different professional clubs in England seemed a million miles away.

When I was told, in January 2005, that I was in remission, I knew that I had to begin repaying the people who had helped save my life – I just wasn't sure how. I could only say 'thank you' so many times to the doctors and nurses, family and friends who helped to care for me around the clock. I wanted to do something more, to try and stretch myself to the limits as a gesture of gratitude and to show my appreciation.

The Tour de France idea had been nagging away at me ever since a conversation with Neil Ashton, a close friend and a football reporter with the *Daily Mail*, over coffee in the build-up to Christmas 2004. We met initially to catch up on my progress, but we soon began talking about my future. Throughout my treatment, my sole goal was to give myself every chance of making a full recovery from leukaemia.

I didn't think much about the future. In typical footballer's fashion, I took each day as it came and concentrated solely on survival. When I met Neil in my local pub, the Barnt Green Inn, I was within weeks of being told that I was in remission. Professor Charlie Craddock, the consultant surgeon at the Queen Elizabeth Hospital in Birmingham, had indicated as much when I had last seen him. As we sat in the pub that day, drinking cups of coffee, the talk turned towards my future. I wasn't sure whether I wanted to return to football, my first love, or the retail clothing business that had been closed down when I was initially diagnosed with leukaemia.

In fact, I wasn't sure about anything at all. I needed a focus – I knew that – but I wasn't at all sure what it would be. We discussed the possibility of a charity project, but each time we explored an avenue, someone had beaten us to it. Run the London Marathon? There's no question that it is an extraordinary physical feat, but I also knew that 32,000 other people would be doing it. Ride the Étape, the one stage of the Tour de France that is ridden by thousands of Tour fantatics every year? It was possible, but I wanted to stretch my body beyond its limits and prove to people that even in their darkest hours, there is still hope.

We mentioned Ian Botham's charity walks from Land's End to John O'Groats, but he was a household name and he already had the profile, through his achievements on the cricket field, to raise millions of pounds. I wanted to do something different, something a little bit wild and extravagant, to celebrate my liberation. No-one needed to tell me that I had been given a second chance – I knew that I was one of the lucky ones. With every passing day, I was feeling fitter, stronger and healthier; but for a stroke of luck in finding my sister was a good bone-marrow match, not to mention the skills of the doctors and nurses who looked after me throughout my ordeal, my life would have been slipping away and my family would have been preparing for a future without me.

I don't quite know how we hit upon the idea of riding the Tour de France route. I had only ever heard of the professionals riding it. It didn't seem possible to match their achievements just by riding around France for three weeks. It's a huge commitment and we didn't know if anyone had attempted, let alone completed, the Tour in the same time-frame as the professionals.

'How long is it?'

'Not sure? Three weeks?'

'What about the route?'

'I don't have a clue. They change it every year, but there are a lot of mountains involved. They ride through the Alps and the Pyrenees. All I know is that it always finishes in Paris.'

'How long did you say?'

'Three weeks, I think.'

'I really fancy it.'

'Leave off.'

'No, I do – when does it start?'

'July sometime.'

'That gives me six months.'

'Geoff, don't rush in. Let's have a think about this. Are you sure you're ready for something like this?'

'I don't know, but leave it with me.'

'Do you want another drink?'

'Yeah, I'll have a pint of Guinness.'

It was the last one I would have for a while.

OO

Julie thought I was crazy. She told me so. And so did her friends. 'He nearly died of leukaemia and now he is trying to kill himself by riding the Tour de France.' My wife felt that she had already been through enough and she pleaded with me to put my plans on hold for another year.

'You're bloody mad,' she would tell me.

It was hard to argue because Julie had been my rock throughout my battle to beat the disease. Another year, she felt, would give me time to regain my strength and redefine my goals. Charlie Craddock knew he wouldn't be able to dissuade me from riding the Tour but he warned me that I was unlikely to be able to build the muscle strength in time. Although research had shown that there was unlikely to be any long-lasting damage to my muscles, there had been a certain amount of degeneration during my treatment and I was unlikely to regain the strength that I had during my playing career.

Many people return to sport after their leukaemia treatment, but he had not heard of anyone taking on something so arduous. He certainly wasn't able to put me off the idea, but he did warn me that there was a fairly high risk of failure. Julie became even more concerned when she heard that but, in time, as she watched me waddle through the door like a penguin following another training ride, she became more supportive.

'Geoff, have you not been through enough?' she would say as I stumbled in with my cycling gear soaked through to the skin.

'Not yet, no.'

OO

I was nervous about meeting Paul Kimmage for the first time. He had ridden the Tour three times during his professional cycling career and, although he had long since retired, he knew the pitfalls. He had finished one Tour but he had suffered the indignity of being helped into the broom wagon on the other two occasions. It is the ultimate humiliation for a Tour pro and, although it happens regularly, it is an embarrassing experience.

Kimmage was another Tour statistic in this respect, but he had earned notoriety after quitting the sport by writing a controversial, award-winning book about his experiences as a *domestique*. It had earned him a reputation for fearlessness and, while he had the respect of the cycling community, opinion was divided among the professionals. He had broken an unwritten rule among the pros by breaking ranks and admitting that he had used amphetamines during a race in the latter stages of his career. Kimmage was blackballed by many of his former colleagues as a result, but he had since carved out a hugely successful career as an award-winning journalist with the *Sunday Times*.

He had followed the story about my battle with leukaemia and became interested in writing a piece for his newspaper when he heard of my plans to ride the Tour. It was a bit daunting when he arrived at my home to interview me because I already knew a bit about his reputation. Before we sat down to talk, his photographer asked if we could take a few shots of me riding up a hill to give the piece a bit of colour. At that time, I had only just started training for the Tour and I was puffing and panting each time the photographer asked me to ride up it 'just one more time'.

Kimmage must have thought I didn't stand a chance. I was exhausted just trying to make my way up a slight incline and, to make matters worse, I was being watched by someone who had once done it for a living. I freewheeled back down the hill to where they were waiting for me, outside my house. As I slowed down, Paul began talking to me.

'How did you find that?' he asked.

I tried to conceal just how difficult it had been. 'Oh, not too bad. Getting there.'

'Keep going. You've got plenty of time to ride yourself in,' he said.

I was about to say some more when I suddenly realised that my cycling shoes were still locked into the pedals. They work on a quick-release system that has been borrowed from ski bindings, but if you forget to wiggle your toe to unclip them from the pedals, you fall over when you come to a standstill. That is exactly what happened as I applied the brakes in front of Paul and I ended up in a tangled mess on the drive with a £3,000 Bianchi racing bike (loaned for a photo shoot) lying on top of me. The skin had been sliced off my elbows, my hip was hurting and I felt utterly humiliated. I was trying to create a good impression ahead of an interview that would launch my campaign to raise money for the charity Leukaemia Research, but I was coming across as a rank amateur.

To his enormous credit, Paul didn't laugh. He knew it was one of the hazards of the profession.

'Don't worry, it happens to everyone.'

He wasn't joking. He even claimed it had happened to him. Kimmage had intimate knowledge of the Tour and, although the demands of racing are very different from what I was attempting to do, he had reservations. I couldn't argue with him.

If I took my training lightly, I wouldn't stand a chance and even if I didn't, it would still be three weeks of torture. Kimmage wasn't alone. In the months that followed I met a lot of people from the cycling community and many of them were pessimistic about my project.

As my interest in the sport grew, I started to pick up some of the dedicated cycling magazines and I was disappointed when I read Tony Bell's column in *Cycling Weekly*. He dismissed my chances of completing the Tour route and, although I took his comments seriously, I had a good mind to call him when I read it. Bell didn't know me and he didn't seem to fully appreciate the reasons why I wanted to ride the Tour. It annoyed me, but I understood his reservations. On another occasion, I met David Duffield, the respected Eurosport cycling commentator and a legend in the Tour community, and he told me to prepare to walk up some of the climbs. He didn't expect me to have the physical strength or the lung capacity to cycle up some of the toughest mountain roads in Europe for three hours at a time before we reached the summit.

I had nearly six months in front of me to train and prepare for the Tour and if I didn't complete it, it wouldn't be for the lack of effort or commitment. I had different motivations from my team-members. Aside from providing support for me over the three weeks, the other four riders were taking on the Tour to complete a personal ambition. I had an extra motivation to complete the Tour and I always felt that would override any obvious physical deficiencies.

It took a little while for my children, Madison and Georgia, to accept my challenge. They were embarrassed at seeing their father walking around the house in the bright, lime-green lycra supplied by our kit sponsor, and they were mortified whenever I turned up at the school gates. They didn't like the thought of their friends seeing me and they told me that I was the most embarrassing dad in the world. They were too young to understand the reasons why I wanted to take on this ride, but I hoped that they would one day.

There was no telling whether I would be strong enough in time to prepare to ride such vast distances in such a short space of time. The only person who could tell me was Professor Charlie Craddock. I first met him on the day that I was officially diagnosed with leukaemia and we struck up an instant rapport.

Charlie is also a director of Cure Leukaemia, a Birmingham-based charity committed to raising funds to finance research and treat patients. We met early in January during a routine visit to the hospital to have my blood counts taken. I was feeling positive about my progress and the idea of riding the Tour de France was becoming stronger by the day. I had already started looking at websites and reading up on the history of the most famous road race in the world, so I casually dropped it into conversation.

In the months after my stem-cell transplant, Charlie had spoken to me of his ambitious plan to raise the finance to build a new haematology centre at the Queen Elizabeth. My wife and I had grown extremely fond of Charlie during my battle against the disease. Not only was he an expert in leukaemia treatments, he showed an incredible appetite to find a cure for the disease. He had seen the devastating effects of the disease at first hand and he is part of an era that has seen huge strides forward in leukaemia treatment. He was always attending a conference or a fundraising initiative, and I admired the way he devoted so much time to the cause.

Of course it is his job, but he always showed tremendous sensitivity whenever we sat down in his office. He could be incredibly matter of fact, but he always spoke with my best interests at heart. Charlie has seen the suffering, and he treated his patients with great respect. I always felt that he was more than just my leukaemia consultant because he had such a compassionate side to his nature.

He was surprised to have an ex-England international footballer in his office, but he did not make any special dispensation for me. I imagine he is as friendly and kind-hearted with his other patients as he is with me. We certainly had a great friendship and a real understanding of each other, but I still felt a little uncomfortable when I raised the concept of the Tour.

'How would you feel, Charlie, if I was to ride the Tour de France?'

'What – a stage?'

Charlie was well versed in the sport and he was aware that each year the Tour organises the Étape so that cycling fanatics can follow in the path of the professionals and ride a Tour stage. They pick out one of the toughest stages, or perhaps incorporate some of the Tour's legendary climbs, so that people can get a taste of the Tour. It is a mammoth event and the gendarmes close the roads for the thousands of people who arrive from all over the world to take part in it.

'I was actually thinking of doing the whole lot.'

'What – all twenty-one stages?'

'That's what I was thinking.'

He peered over his glasses, raised his eyebrows and replied: 'Normally at this stage of their recovery, Geoff, people ask me if they can go swimming.'

OO

For the professionals competing in the Tour de France that year, the 19 km time-trial between Fromentine and Noirmoutier-en-l'Île was an early opportunity to flex some muscle and put some distance between their rivals. Cyclists refer to it as the 'race of truth' because it is just the lone rider racing against the clock. They set off, at one-minute intervals, trying to establish an early advantage over their rivals by blistering their way through the course. Even at this stage, staying in touch with the leading times means staying in touch with the race.

Riders who fall behind the race leaders can forget about their chances of winning the race. For me, it was different. I had my doubts about taking on the Tour and I wasn't in France to race. I was aiming to complete a stage a day and, although the 19 km was unlikely to be too taxing, it was a chance to loosen the muscles after so much planning and preparation and find out what the Tour de France is all about.

Fromentine, a pretty coastal fishing town penned against the Atlantic, signalled the end of one journey and the beginning of another for me. Like the professionals who squeeze every last drop of energy from their aching limbs when they climb through the clouds, the fear of failure would add to my determination.

For six months, in between my frequent visits to the hospital for check-ups, I had trained as much as I could on my racing bike in the quiet country roads that meander their way from my home in Barnt Green, but no-one was at the start line of the Tour de France to tell me that I was ready to ride the 3,584 km route in 21 days. Before January that year, I had barely ridden a bike since I was 15 years old. Just before I began my gruelling training schedule for the Tour, I had dusted off an old mountain bike and ridden to the shop and back in Barnt Green. That was no more than a few miles and I returned home exhausted, wondering whether I would ever regain the fitness that was my hallmark when I was a professional footballer.

Now I was determined to ride 3,584 km in 21 days and climb mountains that are so steep that it is impossible to see the summit until you finally turn the corner and, a few hundred yards away, there is one of the support team holding out a cup of coffee or another energy bar. In all, there were 62 climbs in the 2005 Tour, five of them so steep that the organisers deemed them to be 'beyond classification'. We wouldn't need to worry about them over the next 19 km. This was an opportunity to test our teamwork. For six months my team, who were dotted all over the country, trained pretty much in isolation. We often spoke on the telephone but, save for the odd snatched weekend together, we simply trained whenever we could.

Matt Lawton, the chief football writer at the *Daily Mail*, and Neil Ashton, a football reporter at the same newspaper, spent six months preparing in the south of England. They both frequently complained of loneliness as they rode hundreds of miles a week around Berkshire, Buckinghamshire and beyond, but they never shirked a training session. Neither of them were cyclists, but Lawton had been an athlete of some repute in his younger days and was a former London Schools cross-country champion.

In the years that followed, Matt had run the New York Marathon in just over three hours, but a combination of a hectic family life and his commitment to his job meant that he was no longer at his physical peak. He jumped at the chance to ride the Tour, but he was in poor physical condition when he started to train. His weight had ballooned to more than 15 stone, but it began to fall off him when he started cycling again. Matt had cycled around Europe as a teenager and, although the Tour would be significantly tougher, at least he had experience of some of the mountain roads that would be waiting for us when we reached the Alps and the Pyrenees.

Before we began training for the Tour, I didn't know Matt at all. He was introduced to me by Neil Ashton, who was a good friend of his. For Neil, cycling was a whole new world. He had committed his life to football, but he had taken up cycling when he rode the London–Brighton Bike Ride for charity in 2003. That gave him a taste for the competitive nature of the sport and the prospect of finding a way to ride the Tour route had nagged away at him after he read a book (*Riding High*) about an amateur cyclist's unsuccessful attempt to ride the Tour route on the same day as the professionals.

In the north, Ian Whittell, a sports writer and cycling fanatic from Manchester, and Robbie Duncan, part-owner of a bike shop in Manchester and another disciple of the sport, spent hours on the roads around their homes to prepare themselves for the 21 days ahead. Ian is a monster of a man. When he was at university, he completed a marathon in under two and a half hours, but he had long since become a cycling devotee. He was, without question, our Lance Armstrong. He would think nothing of spending six or seven hours out on the roads on a training ride and he was a real tough cookie. He has huge, thunderous thighs and was happy to sit at the front of the pack for hours at a time while we studied every minute detail of his backside from 6 inches behind.

Ian is as strong as an ox and none of us were in his class as a cyclist. He could cycle harder, faster and further than any of us. He would often train with Robbie in Manchester and he became an essential part of the team.

Robbie's experience of road racing was another crucial element. He was 57 and had been cycling for more than 40 years, competing on the road as well as the velodrome in his younger days. Now he was an expert cycling mechanic. Ian introduced him to me when we were working through the logistical nightmare of planning our ride through France. He always looked so thin to me, and his craggy features made him look a lot older than he was. I don't think he knew how to take me at first because, when we crossed over to France on the ferry, I kept asking if he'd brought his coffin with him.

As a team, we had only met on a handful of occasions after our first meeting at Chievely Services on the M4, in January, when we plotted our path around France. From that moment on, I devoted every waking minute of every day to attending meetings with sponsors, to public relations or to riding my bike relentlessly.

When I met the people at Leukaemia Research in their London offices with a view to riding the Tour, I was so excited by their plans for publicity and public relations that I was carried away on a tidal wave of emotion. Sure, I wanted to ride the Tour, but with their involvement it seemed so thrilling that I became totally absorbed by their efforts. The project gave me something that had been missing from my life for the best part of 18 months.

Within weeks, Leukaemia Research had set up a website to tell people of my plans, thousands of pounds were being raised via online donations and I was driving around the country to attend various fundraising events on behalf of my appeal. It was like being caught up in a whirlwind and, despite my doubts about being able to ride the Tour, there was no going back.

By the time Paul Kimmage's feature had been published in the *Sunday Times*, it seemed as if the whole world knew about my adventure. Text messages were pouring in, letters were arriving from friends and football fans, and hundreds of people were logging on to my website every day. Sometimes it would choke me up to 'refresh' the web page that had details of the donations because it would change so rapidly. By the time we reached Fromentine for the first day of the Tour, there were thousands of good luck messages; I just hoped that there would be thousands more at the end of the Tour.

To complete it, I needed the help of my four team-mates and our dedicated support crew. Since they all held down full-time jobs, they had to show enormous dedication and make huge sacrifices along the way. We were thrown together by good fortune, good luck but, crucially, we shared the same intense – sometimes almost insane – desire to complete the Tour route in the same number of days as the professionals. We could not match their speeds, but we wanted to match their miles. Our support team had spent six months plotting the route and poring over maps of France as we contemplated the days ahead, but it was a step into the unknown for all of us.

Dave West, the physio when I was at Crystal Palace, had been recruited as our team manager and Chris Haynes, the head of publicity at Sky Sports, had joined him. I had lost touch with Westie, as he was universally known in the football community, when I left Palace, but we had been very close when I was at Selhurst Park. There was an incredible bond among the players and backroom staff and Westie was one of the key figures at the club.

He was at Palace when we reached the 1990 FA Cup final, and we got to know each other well during my endless sessions on the treatment table at Selhurst Park. Westie had a real dry sense of humour, but it was easy to warm to him and he would have me in stitches with some of his asides. I didn't know Chris at all, but he had been eager to play a part from the moment he first heard about our plans. He knew Ian, Matt and Neil well from his dealings with the media, and he had offered to come out to France and help with the logistics. He had to give up more than three weeks of his annual leave – a magnificent contribution considering that he wouldn't even be riding the route.

Neil's former girlfriend, Andrea Smith, and her friend Hayley Cullum had also agreed to come out as part of the support team. They had only just returned from Australia, where they had spent the previous six months travelling, and were eager to be a part of the team. We also brought in Richard Chessor, a sports nutrition student at Loughborough University, as part of the support crew. He was there to advise us on how much fluid we needed to take in during the day and he recommended what food to eat throughout the day and also in the evening.

They were our own *soigneurs* (carers) and they were there to help us navigate our way around France, pass food and drinks to us from the support vehicles and then locate our hotels every evening. It was a thankless task. While the professionals put down their marker on Stage One, this was a dummy run for us. It was the chance to prove to ourselves that we had prepared as professionally and properly as we possibly could given our respective circumstances.

Those thoughts didn't last long. I don't know whether it was a build-up of excitement, the fear of the unknown or a touch of naivety, but we set off on the first stage like an express train. We didn't expect it to be that way. Our team had only rolled off the overnight ferry three hours earlier, but it was like the match-day experience for me. There was a hint of nervousness as we arrived in our changing rooms – a supermarket car park on the outskirts of Fromentine – but we still couldn't wait to get going.

Bianchi, one of the sport's most famous cycling brands, had

provided us with new bikes for the Tour and also given us sponsored jerseys. Everything was box-fresh and we were excitable as we slipped them on for the first time. It was the moment we had been building up to and we were resplendent as we cycled down to the start line in the town centre. We certainly attracted some fairly strange looks as we lined up at the start ramp that would be used by the professionals a few days later but, after Westie made us line up for a team photograph to mark the beginning of the Tour, we were on our way.

We had calculated that the short trip from Fromentine, across the sprawling suspension bridge that links the pretty coastal town with the island of Noirmoutier-en-l'Île, would take 45 minutes. Instead it took us a little over half an hour to complete the short hop, at an average speed of 38 kph in temperatures that touched 35 degrees.

The heat was stifling, but the breeze that was bouncing off the ocean lulled us and we sped down the dual carriageway towards Noirmoutier-en-l'Île as if we were riding the time-trial for real. When I first started out, I would average under 24 kph; as my strength and technique improved, I nudged closer to 27–30 kph in the weeks building up to the Tour, but there was no way we could sustain these speeds for long.

The professional *peloton* – using the effect of the wind-resistance caused by the riders at the front of the pack – speeds along at an average of 40 kph, but we were not in the same league as them. It was madness but, at the same time, it was so liberating to finally start the Tour after so much preparation. I had spent six months waiting for this moment and, although I knew there would be some really tough days ahead, I was determined to try and enjoy it. It was the start of something special but, at the same time, we had gone off far too quickly.

Everyone was thinking the same, but it took an age for someone to say it as we approached the finishing straight. Robbie, a cyclist with more than 40 years' experience on the roads, was already voicing his disquiet.

'Easy, Geoff, we don't know what's around the corner.'

That's the trouble. We never do.

2

Challans–Les Essarts 181.5 km

The dressing room is not a place for sensitive souls. It can be cruel and heartless and, if you're not strong, you will suffer. I loved the banter among my team-mates almost as much as I loved playing. The endless teasing, the ridicule and the ribbing were never gentle at any of the seven professional clubs I represented.

That's how football is at any level. To my mind, it helped build characters and fostered team spirit. Sink or swim, as simple as that. Different managers have various approaches and various ways of getting through to their players. When I left Crewe Alexandra and signed for Crystal Palace in 1987, we had a raw, but talented young team.

Steve Coppell, our young manager, had tough South Londoners such as Ian Wright, Andy Gray and Tony Finnigan in the side, and they had fairly big reputations even then. They were talented footballers, but they were also street-fighters. No-one wanted to mess with them and, if they did, they would usually end up on the wrong side. Wright, Gray and Finnigan came across as players with a point to prove. Wright had had trials with several league clubs, including Brighton, when he was younger but, incredible as it seems, none of them had taken him on – they felt he was too small. He used those disappointments as a motivational tool when he signed for Palace.

He was at the non-league side Greenwich Borough when Coppell signed him, and Palace couldn't believe their luck. Wright scored on his debut, coming on as a substitute against Oldham, and after that everything he touched turned to gold. Like the others, he worked hard for it. Gray was quarrelsome, but ultra-competitive. He was a great player, but he had not long been signed from Dulwich Hamlet, a decent South London non-league side, when I arrived from Gresty Road.

He was close with Finnigan, who represented London Schools as a young player, and they were forever up to mischief. We were rough around the edges and Coppell would use this to his advantage by deliberately causing friction among the players. The accepted practice at most clubs in their last training session ahead of a game is to have a nice, relaxed six-a-side match between the players. They are usually fun, light-hearted and a way of taking away tension ahead of the following day's match.

Although these matches are always competitive because of the nature of the sport, most managers do not want to risk injuries so close to the game – but it wasn't like that at Palace. Sometimes I got the impression that the players would rather pick up an injury in one of those six-a-side games than come off on the losing side. We would slide around in the mud at our dilapidated training ground in Mitcham and tensions always ran high between the two teams. Just before I signed for the club, Coppell notoriously played blacks-versus-whites in training, but he had to change his approach after Gavin Nebbeling, a tough South African centre-half, head-butted Mark Bright when things got a bit too tasty.

Instead, Coppell's alternative was to divide the teams between players who were born in the north of England and those born in the south. This was like a red rag to a bull and we would go into full-blooded practice matches, kicking lumps out of each other. It was nothing personal, just 12 players pumped full of aggression. That Palace team wanted to win so badly and we had so much determination that nothing would get in our way.

They were fiercely competitive games and they were taken so seriously by the players that we used to keep an aggregate score pinned up on the board at the training ground. Those battles were the highlight of the week. Wright, by far the most skilful player at the club, would try and showboat, but people like myself would be trying to hack him down. There were battles all over the practice pitch and some of the players would come in for some merciless stick.

Neil Redfearn, who signed for Palace in the same summer as me, used to get hammered by the southern lads because of his accent. Redfearn was born and bred in Doncaster and had a broad Yorkshire accent; the rough, rugged South Londoners used to slaughter him for it. They were regarded as Cockneys by the likes of me and Redfearn, and they would put on northern accents to try and wind us up.

'Ere, Redders,' they would say to him and it used to get on his nerves. Some can take it, some can't. Redfearn gave it back, but he had a tough time at Palace. He was also a very good player and went on to have a decent career with Oldham, Barnsley and Charlton, but he suffered on the pitch. Redfearn was talented, but he felt like the world was closing in on him when it came to match days. Wright and Bright were two of the noisiest, most boisterous characters I have ever met in the dressing room and they would hammer Redfearn, who was a right-winger, if he did not serve up crosses on a plate during matches.

When Neil and I joined Palace in the summer of 1987, we were almost treated like outcasts. At the time, there was the old school, such as Jim Cannon and the goalkeeper George Wood, and the young, chirpy South Londoners. Redfearn and I were neither and we had to integrate quickly.

Redfearn's confidence was knocked when he started being substituted by Coppell, seemingly every week. His form dipped and he never recovered. That played a part in his decision to leave Palace and move to Watford; but he gave as good as he got in training, which was just as well because anyone who didn't would be targeted by the rest of his team-mates. Those games were always on edge, but they rarely got out of control when I was at the club. They caused incredible tension and some intense rivalries between the teams but, uniquely, they bound the squad together and we would be united the following day.

Some players you simply have to salute for their resolute characters. Refearn reminded me of my old team-mate Mark Crossley in many ways. Crossley was the goalkeeper at Nottingham Forest when I signed for them in 1997. He was an excellent keeper, but he was something else off the pitch. He was nicknamed 'Norm' because apparently he looked like the former Manchester United and Everton midfielder Norman Whiteside in his younger days. I could never see the similarity myself. Norm was sharp enough to give as good as he got when the dressing-room banter was flying about.

Norm is a big lad and he had a laid-back attitude to everything. Life would just pass him by and he didn't have a care in the world. He was a big character in our dressing room and everything seemed to revolve around him, even if he wasn't always aware of it. He took on the role of sea-faring skipper when we went on an end-of-season tour to Miami to celebrate Forest's promotion to the Premiership in 1998.

With the pressure off, we were determined to have a good time and we all thought it would be a good idea to hire a flat-bottomed boat for the afternoon so that we could cruise up and down the Great Miami River. We were put through a whole safety briefing by the owner of the boat and, as Forest's goalkeeper would be in charge of it, we assured him that his vessel was in safe hands.

'Whatever you do, don't take it out to sea,' were the last words of the owner, as he pointed to the ocean, untied the knot and pushed us off the jetty. Miami was exactly as we expected it and most of the players sat on the deck enjoying the views of bikini-clad women sunning themselves on the back of speedboats while we chugged down the river. It was a beautiful day and I was right at the front, with my feet up on the rail, catching the rays as Crossley steered us down the estuary.

Everyone was feeling fairly relaxed and no-one batted an eyelid when Mark turned the boat full circle. We had spent the last half an hour cruising down the river with the waves gently lapping at the side of the boat, but suddenly the motor sounded a bit more laboured and our speed appeared to be increasing.

Not only that, the wide open space of the Atlantic was dominating the landscape and we were heading straight for it. Speedboats were hurtling past us, comfortably riding the waves, but we were starting to crash straight into them. As we headed out past the breakwater, Mark slipped the lever to full throttle and he looked like the captain of the *Titanic*, Edward John Smith, up on the bridge, as he started ploughing straight through them. Like everyone else, I was holding on to the side of the boat when the inevitable happened.

'Here we go lads, this is the big one,' Mark shouted. And, at that moment, we were all tossed into the sea as the boat capsized, leaving the entire Forest squad bobbing about in the water. He didn't seem to have a clue what he had done wrong. That was a weakness on his part and we didn't need much bait in the dressing room to start laying into him.

It was the same with Matt Lawton in the Tour team. He was far too responsible to capsize a boat, but he could be easily led. Like Mark, no matter how many times you try and knock Matt down, he just keeps coming back for more and I admire that resilience. He took some merciless stick during the Tour, but he thrived on being the centre of attention, irrespective of the situation.

OO

For a brief moment, I felt as though I was on holiday when we arrived at our hotel in Challans later that afternoon. Ian, Matt and Neil booked the hotels at the start of the year and, although we were on a tight budget, I certainly couldn't complain when I found myself sitting on a sun-lounger by the hotel pool – a completely unexpected bonus – after we had completed the first stage.

While the backroom team worked on our bikes, we bathed in the afternoon sun and got to know each other a little better. Unfortunately for Matt, he became the centre of attention. In the six-month build-up to the Tour de France, I did a lot of media work to publicise the event and no-one batted an eyelid when Chris Haynes arranged for Sky Sports News to 'call' that afternoon to arrange a time for a live interview on the telephone.

I was in on it from the very beginning and, bearing in mind that there were three journalists on the Tour, Matt – the chief football writer at the *Daily Mail* – began puffing out his chest when the producers asked if they could speak specifically to him.

At 4 p.m., my mobile phone rang right on cue.

'Geoff?'

'Yes.'

'It's Steve Murray from Sky Sports News. You're live on the show.'

'Oh, hi, Steve.'

I then answered a series of pre-ordained questions. The lads around the pool didn't even look up from their sun-loungers while I fielded the questions they had heard so many times before.

No-one was even paying any attenion until, from completely left-field, I said: 'Oh, I haven't heard the football news so you would be better off talking to Matt about that when you speak to him. He knows all about that side of things.'

That certainly pricked Matt's ears because he had not seen an English newspaper for two days and he knew nothing of any 'football news'.

'What's that all about?' he asked the crew.

Two minutes later, Matt was live on air.

'Welcome back to Sky Sports News. We've got Matt Lawton on from the *Daily Telegraph*, live from the Tour de France. Welcome to the show, Matt.'

'Actually, I must correct you, it's actually Matt Lawton from the *Daily Mail*.'

'Oh, sorry, Matt. It says Matt Lawton from the *Daily Telegraph* here.'

'Well, I can assure you that I work for the *Daily Mail*.'

Our man in London then asked a series of simple questions about the Tour, which Matt fended off, before things really got going.

'So, Matt, you've ridden a hundred and fifty miles with Geoff Thomas on his leukaemia ride today. How are the legs?'

'No, no, that's tomorrow. We've actually ridden the time-trial today which is nineteen kilometres so we've had a fairly easy day.'

'You've ridden nineteen kilometres? How will you ride the three thousand kilometres in twenty-one days if you're only riding nineteen kilometres a day?'

Matt was already showing signs of frustration, but he kept his cool magnificently.

'And, Matt, what do you make of the big football news today?'

'I'm sorry – what is the big news?'

Now he was being told that the *News of the World* had video evidence that Kenyon met Arsenal striker Thierry Henry and midfielder Patrick Vieira in a Paris hotel to discuss a transfer. If it had been true, it would have been one of the biggest stories in football history.

'That is amazing. Absolutely extraordinary. This is sensational stuff. I'm surprised that Henry would want to leave, but this is an extraordinary story. We've known Vieira has been unhappy for some time but this is the story of the summer.'

It certainly would have been.

'Well, thanks, Matt, that's all we've got time for. That was Matt Lawton there from the *Daily Telegraph*.'

'Sorry, I just have to correct you there because it's Matt Lawton from the *Daily Mail*.'

'OK, thanks, Matt. So that was Matt Lawton from the *Daily Telegraph* talking exclusively to Sky Sports News.'

Matt was furious. He put the mobile phone down and started jabbing his finger at Chris Haynes, who is head of Sky Sports publicity.

'Who was that fucking buffoon?' he demanded. 'The man was a fucking buffoon.'

'I think it was Steve Murray – he often does the Sunday afternoon shift,' said Chris. 'Admittedly he's not one of our best presenters.'

'Fucking right he isn't.'

That incident broke the ice among the Tour crew and it certainly helped us relax, but none of us were smiling a day later.

OO

The route from Challans to Les Essarts should have been fairly simple.

The Tour guides, which we spent most of our spare time studying, claimed it would be a flat stage and we viewed it as a chance to break ourselves into the Tour gently. What the guides couldn't predict was just how hot it was going to be.

Running south from the Vendée region, along the French coastline, it then turns sharply inwards and heads east – right into the sun – up the Loire valley. It was an unbearable afternoon – temperatures touched 37 degrees – and, because the roads were so flat and the scenery unspectacular, the stage turned into a slog.

Myself, Matt and Neil were not used to riding such vast distances, and we struggled all day to sit in a paceline behind the more experienced riders, Ian and Robbie. Save for the two days we had spent on a training ride in the Peak District the month before the Tour started, we had never ridden together as a team and it showed. We were strung out along the road – often with several hundred metres between the riders – and the heat was having a huge effect on our ability to ride. Before we broke off for a quick lunch break, the morning session had been a disaster.

We didn't ride as a team and our progress had been so slow that it was obvious that we would still be riding in the early evening. That wasn't how we had envisaged the day progressing when we started out and it was already having a dramatic effect on morale. Instead of looking forward to the first few days of the Tour, we became concerned – and rattled – by the knock-on effect of the likelihood of a late finish. Automatically it meant more time on the bikes to complete the stage, a panic to rehydrate at the end of the day and even less time to recover before the start of the next day.

They were depressing thoughts, but the days were likely get longer and longer if we didn't learn to ride in formation. We knew it would take time to settle into a routine, but the temperatures made teamwork difficult. The benefits of riding in a paceline are two-fold: first, it keeps the team together; but, of far more consequence, it encourages the energy-saving principle of drafting.

The concept of drafting means that the lead cyclist bears the brunt of the air pressure, which has enormous benefits for the riders who are in his wake. The optimum distance to draft, or hold the wheel, behind another rider is around 6 inches and, although it is particularly dangerous for inexperienced riders, it takes the other cyclists 25 per cent less energy to ride at, say, 30 kph than it does for the lead man. Ian was so strong that he often led from the front and, although cycling etiquette dictates that everyone should take a short turn at the front in order to share the burden and save energy, he was often at the head of the pack for long periods.

He loved being there, and I loved him being there too because it meant I didn't have to produce anything like the power output I would need if I was cycling alone. Drafting is the principal reason that the professional *peloton* can ride at high speeds for such long periods of time, but they had far more practice at it than us. They rode like that every day, but we didn't share their experience. They also had the advantage of riding on quiet roads when they trained, and when they competed as professionals the roads were always closed. That wasn't the case for us and it soon became obvious that the Tour route is not on any old roads. Instead, to accommodate the 189 riders and the endless support vehicles that follow the Tour around France, they use main roads and dual carriageways wherever possible. This also means that the magnificent roadside support can watch the *peloton* speed past them at a safe distance; but we didn't have the benefit of the authorities closing the roads for our five-strong team.

As well as concentrating on the wheel 5 inches in front, we spent the day cowering as articulated lorries thundered past us at 100 kph and hoping that the considerable wake this causes – usually sending our bikes several inches towards the roadside guttering – would not cause an accident.

We were especially fearful of the traffic, but it was nothing compared to England. The difference between French drivers and English road users with regard to cyclists is total. Back in England, cyclists are seen as a nuisance. When I was training, I lost count of the number of times that drivers waved their hands in the air in disgust as they drove past me, or nearly sent me into the kerb when they drove too close because they were so impatient. It's shaming, but I have to admit that I had little time for cyclists before I became one. It was only when I started to ride around my home in Birmingham that I realised cyclists had just as much right to use the roads as any of the huge Mercedes, BMWs or articulated trucks that try to dominate the streets.

The difference in French drivers' attitude was apparent as soon as we started the Tour. The majority of the French population live for the Tour and that extends to their behaviour on the roads. They show enormous respect and courtesy to cyclists. Instead of leaving little more than a couple of inches when they overtake, they tend to wait until it is safe before they make their move. It was a refreshing experience and, although there will always be chancers in any country, our first experience of a roadside accident had nothing to do with the traffic.

We were five riders with various degrees of cycling experience and it was difficult to maintain a steady speed, especially in these conditions. By the time we'd reached the halfway point of the stage, the pockets of conversation that pass the time had already run dry and we were just trying to concentrate on finishing. The professionals ride at over 40 kph and they would whip this stage off in four hours; we knew we would be out in the sun for something approaching ten hours and there is no shelter riding through the vast expanse of open French countryside. Instead, we resolved to try and maintain our five-man paceline for the rest of the day and, as we filed into a neat order – Ian, Neil, myself, Robbie and Matt – disaster struck.

The fierce crosswinds of northern France can play havoc with the *peloton* and none of us were used to dealing with the sudden gusts of wind that can blow teams across the road. Our inexperience showed when we were caught out by an unexpectedly strong breeze. We increased our speed after lunch and were riding at around 32 kph – way beyond the target speed we had set ourselves – when Ian and Neil were dragged to the left by a severe crosswind. I followed their path to try and stay in the paceline and on their wheel, but Robbie clipped my back wheel as I moved towards the centre of the road.

Although I wobbled across the road, I remained on my bike, but my two team-mates were not quite so fortunate. As Robbie tried to maintain his balance, Matt had no choice but to clip the back of his wheel and I heard the clash of metal as their bikes collided.

It was a frightening sound and I turned in time to see Matt catapulted from his bike like a crash test dummy. There was a sickening thud as he was sent head first onto the tarmac. It was a horrific sight and I feared for him when the impact sent him bouncing off the road and into a ditch by the grassy verge. The collision also sent Robbie flying through the air and he left his tangled bike behind him as he landed on his side, cracking a rib.

They were both motionless, lying on the road in deep shock. The traffic came to a halt as we tried to assess the damage. Matt was lying in the ditch; the impact had caused his helmet to split straight down the middle. Within a minute, Westie had arrived in one of the support vehicles and was giving him first aid. We were on a single carriageway, traffic was flying past us at 90 kph and we were fortunate that the cars came to a standstill as we cleared the road of debris.

Miraculously, apart from some deep gashes, heavy grazing on his legs and arms, and a fairly big shock, Matt had not done any lasting damage. It is a testimony to both riders' bravery and courage that they ignored Westie's advice and got on the spare bikes to complete the stage. We couldn't believe that they got back on the road – it showed incredible spirit.

Matt was driven by the fear of not riding the Tour in full and that was his reason for ignoring medical advice and getting back on the bike. Robbie, after so many years' experience, was used to roadside accidents. He didn't want to miss out on a single kilometre of trip either. They both showed amazing resolve to get back in the saddle after such a big shock so early in the Tour, but it was a demonstration of their determination to complete the route. The easy option would have been to quit – they both had a perfectly valid excuse to do so after being treated by a physio on the side of the road – but they refused to bow out.

The fall certainly gave Matt the shock of his life and there wasn't a lot he could remember about the stage when he finally got off his bike next to the church in the centre of Les Essarts early that evening, but perhaps it was just as well. The 2005 Tour de France was the first time in the sport's history that the professionals were required to wear helmets at all times, but Neil and I had opted to go without. It was foolish, particularly given our inexperience of riding on the roads in a group, but we were eager to soak up the sun and work on our San Tropez-style tans.

After the crash, we fetched helmets out of our support vehicles because, to my mind, if Matt had not been wearing his, I believe he would have been out of the Tour.

3

La Châtaigneraie–Tours
212.5 km

It's too soon and too early to be getting up. I feel like I have only just shut my eyes, but already there is a shaft of light fighting its way through the curtains. I roll over and wrap myself in the duvet. My muscles are aching; when I stretch my arms and legs across the bed, I can feel the lactic acid that has built up in them overnight slowly, ever so slowly, dispersing. Everything is sore, but it's been like this for days. My muscles are slowly waking up, but they are sure taking their time.

If I shut my eyes again right now, I will be asleep again in seconds. I'm so tired I almost hallucinate as I struggle to keep my eyelids open. I'm weary and struggling to remain conscious. When I poke my toes out of the end of the bed, I can feel the chill and I tell myself that I need at least another five more minutes. I sit up and squint with tired eyes through the curtains to look out of the window. It's bitterly cold, but I know that, in another half an hour or so, I will be back on my bike and battling against the elements.

All I want to do is stay in my big double bed and hide my head under the duvet. It has been raining for the best part of a week, there are leaves on the road, the surface is greasy and snow is forecast soon. Today, like all the other days, will be a day for the wet-weather gear; it means I will need considerably more protection than my figure-hugging lycra. I will bulk up by wearing my long leggings, some thicker socks, an insulated jacket and a rain-cape, but, despite weeks of riding in the wet weather, I still haven't got round to buying some waterproof overshoes. I have been caught nearly every day.

It is nothing more than a simple trip to the local cycle shop in town, but I haven't made it there yet. When I get back in every night, I'm too tired and too wet to make the trip into town. No, the overshoes can wait for another day. That day must surely come soon because, within minutes of starting out, my cycling shoes will be soaked through and I will be able to feel the chill through every pedal stroke.

'Geoff, get up!'

Julie is at the bottom of the stairs. She has long since given up coming into the bedroom to try to wake me up. Even though I know that the kettle is boiling and she will present me with a nice mug of tea the moment I walk through the kitchen door, I pretend I haven't heard. Who wants to get up when the skies are so angry? They have been like this for weeks and the wind is howling so hard that the trees outside are arched back into almost impossible positions. Sometimes the headwind is so fierce that it feels like I am pedalling through treacle and it takes every ounce of effort to complete another rotation. This isn't fun and the fatigue is etched all over my face.

No-one told me it would be like this. Cycling is supposed to be liberating, but it's not in these conditions. I watch the Tour de France on the television every year and the *peloton* is poetry in motion as the cyclists glide through the rolling countryside in a perfectly formed bunch. If they saw me out on the roads, with my legs pumping away in an insanely low gear, they would think I am doing the sport a disservice. It is gruelling and I swear that even my Bianchi bike groans every morning when I wheel it outside.

'Oh, no, not you again ...'

When I got off it yesterday afternoon, it was so filthy that I couldn't face the prospect of cleaning it with an old rag. Instead, I took a hose to it and displaced all the slime that had built up over the day on the rain-soaked roads. When I get off it tonight, when dark clouds are forming and the light is fading fast, that jet will almost certainly be back on again. This isn't fun. Just another five minutes. And then I will be up.

'Geoff, get up!'

All right, all right, I'm getting up. I throw the duvet back and, from the moment I stand on my feet, the hunger knock sets in. It is my body's way of telling me that I need to eat. That little tap on the shoulder tells me that I need some cereal or some toast – fast. After six or seven hours out on the road yesterday, it is difficult to replace the calories that have been consumed along the way. Cyclists burn around 800 calories an hour and there is a lot to replace after a long session. Even after a king-sized plate of pasta and maybe some pizza at night, my body is crying out for more when I wake up the following morning.

And that is another problem. After my shower, all I can see in front of me is a big bowl of muesli, maybe a croissant or a couple of slices of toast smeared with honey, and a nice cup of tea waiting for me when I eventually walk down the stairs. It's the same depressing routine every day and, although I'm a creature of habit, it's no fun consuming a giant bowl of muesli every morning. At one point I was stocking up so much in the mornings I had four or five different cereals on the go to try and vary my diet.

I'm not sure how far we will go today. Maybe we will do a '50' (the common cycling parlance for the number of miles ridden in one session), maybe a 60 or an 80, but it will be some time before I break the 100 barrier. A 100 is the psychological hurdle for a rookie cyclist and it is still a long way off.

Riding 100 miles in a day is an accomplishment for someone new to the sport, but I am still gradually inching towards it and, in time, I will break through the magical barrier. I began my training programme by riding 6 miles around Barnt Green on a mountain bike, but it became far more serious in the days and weeks that followed.

I met Paul Bailey, a renowned coach and semi-professional cyclist, for the first time in February. He was introduced to me when I told Don Goodman, a former team-mate at Wolves, that I was taking on the Tour. Don was keeping his hand in football by working as a match summariser for Radio Five Live and he was already very accomplished, but his personal training company was also thriving. We were very good friends at Wolves and it was an incredible act of generosity on Don's part when he offered to pay for Paul's services while I trained. Paul studied sports science at university and, although he has an academic approach to cycling, he is an excellent coach.

Paul trained young children at the velodrome in Manchester and his enthusiasm began to rub off on me after a few weeks. He never said anything negative and, even on the days when I was really struggling to stay with him, he always encouraged me. It would have been easy for him to criticise me when I was struggling to ride at even a leisurely 25 kph, but he was always full of praise. He probably had his doubts as to whether I would be able to ride the Tour but, if he did, he never showed them. He knew I was determined to do it and I think he had a lot of respect for what I set out to do. There was only a short window to prepare me for the challenge but, in many ways, it probably helped Paul and I focus on the target. Perhaps if we'd had a year, I might not have had the same motivation or drive, but I knew that, with less than six months to prepare, the clock was always ticking.

The first time I went out for a ride with Paul, we both changed in a pub car park. It felt so unnatural and, although Paul put me at ease, I felt incredibly self-conscious and probably a little embarrassed. It took me a long time to get used to having a saddle parked up my backside for hours at a time. Although I was assured that the slimline versions used by the professionals are better in the long run, I used to cast envious glances whenever I saw one of the sponge saddles that are often used on cheaper bikes.

The enormity of the challenge really began to set in when Paul likened the Tour de France to running a marathon every day for 21 days. He was an experienced cyclist and he knew the demands and the rigours involved. It didn't stop me lying in bed for another ten minutes in the mornings, though. Although I know he will be knocking on the door in a minute, I reckon there is just about enough time for a second cup of tea before I brave another day in the drizzle.

I trained almost every day after that first meeting with Paul in early February. He had intimate knowledge of the challenge that faced me and I used his advice to inspire me. If I didn't train, I considered it to be 'down time'. Every minute was precious and I didn't want to arrive in France at the start of the Tour with any excuses. I was determined to make as much use of the time as possible, and that meant riding my bike virtually every day.

It was a slog at first. The first couple of weeks were really tough. I didn't have any experience of riding a bike and I didn't have the energy to turn the pedals for hours at a time. After a while, I could feel the improvements and at times they were quite marked. The days were monotonous, but the fear of failure drove me.

I monitored my progress by keeping a diary; when I look back at it now, I realise just what I was taking on. While the professionals routinely speed along at around 45 kph for a four-hour stage, I couldn't even average half that.

Often it was so windy or wet that I would be soaked through by the time I reached the end of the road, but I always kept the reasons I was riding the Tour in the forefront of my mind. When I started my training regime, I doubt whether I was even fit enough to ride one stage of the Tour, let alone 21. At times I would have preferred to stay in bed and have that extra hour's sleep, but that would be the easy option. Although the first few turns on the pedals were hard, there was always a feeling of exhilaration and a sense of well-being whenever I returned home from a ride.

I was a novice, there was no doubt about that, but in time I learned the rules of the road. I can remember being about 65 km into a training run in early February when I rode over the crest of a hill and saw that there was a huge puddle of water at the foot of the slope. Cars were taking it in turns to ease through it. I should have known better when one of them beckoned me through. As I released my brakes, I could see the whites of the driver's eyes and a wry grin on his face as he began heading towards me. There was no time for me to stop and, as our paths crossed, I became totally submerged in murky rainwater. Those were the moments when I wondered what I was doing out on the lonely roads in early February, but it never put me off.

On other occasions, I forgot my water bottles, or my energy bars, my phone or my house keys, or some spare inner tubes. After a while, I built up a mental checklist before I left the house, but even then I always forgot something.

Whenever those moments arrived, I thought about the reasons I was taking on the Tour. It wasn't a personal ambition. During the course of my treatment, I met so many resilient people. Some make it through. Unfortunately, many don't, but their stories always inspire me.

People react in different ways when they are diagnosed with a life-threatening illness, but I always admired the way some people faced the disease head on. I met a lady called Julie Sanders, who had also been diagnosed with chronic myeloid leukaemia around the same time as me, and she showed immense spirit by raising money for leukaemia research. Julie needed all her strength to fight the illness, but she focused her mind by raising funds in her local pub in Great Worley.

When I look back in my diary, I can see just how busy my schedule became. Leukaemia Research had an excellent press officer, Sonya Corbett, and she worked tirelessly on my behalf. Although she had other projects to manage, she went beyond the call of duty to help our cause and she was forever on the phone with another media request.

She was also instrumental in the organisation of a Leukaemia Awareness Day planned for 5 April. She wrote to every professional football club in the country and asked the players to wear red wristbands that day. The date was poignant for me because Palace were playing Liverpool at Selhurst Park and I will always regard our 1990 FA Cup semi-final over Kenny Dalglish's side as the biggest achievement in my club career. Palace, and especially their chairman, Simon Jordan, were incredibly receptive to our ideas and they invited me to London as the club's guest of honour.

I have always found Simon to be incredibly charming and he can be engaging company. When I first told him of my plans to ride the Tour, without any hesitation at all he just said: 'I will sponsor you – £5 a mile.'

It took me a few seconds to work out the enormity of what he had said, but I eventually realised that was more than £15,000.

'I know,' he said. 'Just make sure you ride every one of them.'

By the time the Palace game came around, I was riding 160 km once a week as part of my preparation. I was getting stronger on the flat and could ride in Paul's slipstream, sometimes at speeds of around 32 kph, for long periods of time. Those were the speeds we were aiming for when the Tour got under way for real, but I was still struggling to find any power in my legs on the climbs.

As soon as I reached the slightest incline, I just fell away and was left lagging behind my partner. At times it was soul-destroying because I couldn't feel any improvement. Even when I powered out of the saddle and clasped the brake hoods, I didn't notice any difference. It depressed me at times because, whenever I watched seasoned cyclists on a climb, they accelerated the moment they lifted themselves out of the saddle.

Those fears were amplified when Paul took me on a training ride that involved a climb up Clee Hill, near the Wales border in Ludlow. It is one of Shropshire's highest peaks, although there would be far tougher climbs waiting for me in France. I averaged 8 kph on the way to the summit. Sometimes I felt like I was travelling so slowly that I was at a standstill. I began to realise that it would take me two or three hours to reach the top of some of the Tour climbs. I didn't know if my body could tolerate that kind of pressure, but I didn't have a great deal of time to think about it.

The clock was ticking and there was so much support for the cause – £38,000 had been raised by the end of May – that I couldn't even think about failure. I was surprised by the level of interest from newspapers, television and radio and I vowed to fulfil every request. I spent a lot of time travelling around the country for various interviews for all kinds of different media outlets and, although it disrupted my training at times, I knew that I was also spreading the word.

When I came home from a training ride, Julie made me a mug of tea and, before I went for a shower, I would log on to my website to check how much money had been raised. After my first interview in the *Sunday Times* and then an appearance on Sky Sports' football programme *Goals on Sunday*, the money started flooding in, even though there was still three months' preparation to go before the Tour. People were incredibly kind and supportive. I spent hours reading the messages and it was touching to know that so many people were backing me. That made it worthwhile and the sacrifices paled into insignificance whenever I thought about the number of people who logged on to my website to donate their hard-earned money.

I used to enjoy being interviewed as a footballer. Coppell didn't like the publicity and shied away from it, but as I was the captain at Palace, he would often send me out to be interviewed by the press after a game. Now the interviews had taken on a different dimension.

OO

In the first few months of the year, I tailored my training rides around my regular blood tests. I was forever in and out of hospital in the early stages to have my 'bloods' taken, but I rarely missed a session. I wanted to give myself the best possible chance of completing the Tour and I knew that it would be too easy to put my feet up in front of the fire for the afternoon.

Instead, I nagged Paul for some company, or I phoned my neighbour John Rawlings to go out for a long ride on a Sunday afternoon. Initially we started riding 40-km loops around Barnt Green, but as our confidence increased we started to go further afield. Sometimes we rode for hours on end and it got to the stage where our families would meet us for Sunday lunch somewhere before we rode home. It helped having a cycling partner from time to time and, even though I felt myself getting stronger, I was still having problems with the effects of my leukaemia treatment.

I was having difficulty with graft-versus-host disease – a syndrome common in people who have had stem-cell transplants – and it was a real issue in the first few months. At first, my mouth would become very sensitive and sore, but there were treatments available to eradicate the problem.

I also had problems with my eyes and they would become very dry when the wind was howling in my face. I wore contact lenses in my playing days, but the radiation treatment had damaged my tear ducts and I couldn't produce enough fluid to keep them moist. Instead, I bought some specially prepared prescription glasses, but I began to have problems seeing the road in front of me. On some days, I had to pull up on the side of the road to adminster some saline solution and, even though Charlie Craddock sent me to see a specialist in that field, they were unable to stimulate my tear ducts.

Riding the Tour also gave me the opportunity to meet some of the people in the sport. Through Bianchi, our bike sponsor, I met the Swedish rider Magnus Backstedt as part of a media opportunity. At just over 94 kg, he is a giant of a man, but he is also an accomplished cyclist. He won the Paris–Roubaix classic, a 260-km one-day race, in 2004, and he was recognised as one of the strongest riders in the Tour. His advice was invaluable and he helped devise my training programme. I certainly needed the discipline because the weather was so bad in the early part of the year that it would have been easy to put off training from day to day.

Kimmage warned me that I was starting at a particularly difficult time, but I figured I would realise the benefit when the weather conditions became more favourable. The roads were still wet, it was dark until 8 a.m. and motivation, even for seasoned cyclists, is tough at that time of the year. They are not the most attractive conditions to train in. But Kimmage had a lot of admiration for me keeping going, considering the weather conditions. He warned me that I would have to prepare properly, or there was the very real prospect that I would fail to complete the route. I didn't take his advice lightly. I knew that, as a former professional sportsman, he knew what was required to get to the top.

Kimmage rode as a professional for ten years and he was dedicated to the sport. Whenever I wanted to stay in bed, or give my legs a rest from my punishing training schedule, I always thought of his final words when he left my home on the afternoon that we met:

'Whatever you do, don't disrespect the Tour.'

OO

I trained hard, but I could never say that I enjoyed the endless hours on the roads in the weeks and months before we reached the start line. It didn't compare with pre-season training when I was a footballer, that's for sure. Most players dread 1 July, because it means running off the summer's excesses with gruelling cross-country runs or endless laps of the pitches. Despite the annual grind, I used to enjoy it. I was noted for my athleticism and stamina throughout my playing career, but pre-season training was still notoriously difficult.

It made me laugh out loud when a newspaper printed a picture of Frank Lampard on a beach a week or so before Chelsea returned for pre-season. Poor Frank was probably only 2 or 3 pounds over his optimum and they were making out that he had been eating ice-cream and drinking beer for six weeks. Summer is the time to indulge after a long season. Sometimes I came back half a stone overweight, but I enjoyed watching it disappear because it showed signs of progress and encouraged me to reach my peak physical condition in time for the start of the season.

When I signed for Palace, Steve Coppell would make us run lap after lap around the pitches at our Mitcham training ground. It was tedious, but it had to be done. Sometimes we went through a 12-minute fitness test designed to improve aerobic capacity, or we would use a training routine using different stations involving a walk, jog and run between each one – but the theme was always the same: running. Coppell put a bag of balls by the side of the pitch, but to this day I don't know why they were there because we didn't use them for the first week and a half after the summer break.

I think he was just trying to heighten our desire: 'Run your bollocks off, lads, and one of these days you might get to kick one of these again.'

It was rare for Coppell to empty that net in the first ten days or so, but I still enjoyed the physical preparation. I thought it was great that we were being paid to be among the fittest people in the country, perhaps the world, and I was determined to enjoy it. I also recognised that being fitter meant standing out more. Towards the end of a game, when other players were struggling to see it through, I was still full of running and it was an important aspect of my game.

As a central midfielder, I was expected to dominate games and, if I was still full of energy in the last 20 minutes of a match – the time when more goals are scored in a game than any other period – I knew that the player marking me would have to be the same to cancel me out. When I was fit, I was flying; I felt almost untouchable in those periods. They don't always last for long but, whenever they arrived, I would take full advantage. I wasn't the type to jump out of bed first thing in the morning and, when I arrived at the training ground, I usually ambled out there still clutching my mug of tea.

As soon as the whistle went, though, I turned into a completely different character. I was laid-back off the pitch but a hustler on it and I loved the physical nature of the game. I worked hard and I could see how much emphasis was being placed on the physical side of the game when I arrived at Palace. Coppell clearly felt that if his players lacked any attributes in terms of ability, then they could compensate by improving on speed and stamina. Towards the end of my career, training methods had changed. When I returned to Crewe in 2001, the balls would come out straight away under Dario Gradi. He had a completely different philosophy and was always interested in learning about modern training methods.

Dario, who has been manager at Gresty Road since 1983, believed we would already be starting with a solid base from the season before. Although players would inevitably come back carrying an extra pound or two, that would soon be trimmed off after a couple of weeks back on the training ground. He knew that we would steadily increase our fitness as we approached the start of the season and I noticed that there were fewer injuries with modern training methods based around a theory known as 'core stability'.

When players are sent on long runs, their muscles are still going through a period of inertia and it takes a couple of weeks for them to warm up again. With Dario's methods, we slowly increased the intensity and there were far fewer muscle strains, aches or pains among the playing staff. I loved training and, once we got down to business, I was as competitive as anyone. I looked forward to going in every day – as much for the banter with so many dressing-room characters as anything else – but I didn't feel like that when I was on my bike.

I can't say I particularly enjoyed wheeling my Bianchi out to the end of the drive every morning. I trained with Paul twice a week but, save for the occasional ride with my neighbour John, I mostly trained alone. Riding a bike for hours on end is a lonely business and there is a lot of thinking time in the saddle. There were so many times that I looked outside at the skies and I didn't want to train, but I knew I had to. By the time April arrived, I had really stepped up my regime and I was following an established routine:

Monday: 8-km recovery ride
Tuesday: 40 km
Wednesday: 65 km
Thursday: 128 km
Friday: 40 km
Saturday: 40 km
Sunday: off.

Although they were nowhere near the vast distances that I would cover when the Tour got under way, the programme was designed to increase my fitness and let my body become accustomed to the demands of cycling. Pedalling 100 revolutions a minute on a bike is very different from the stresses placed on the body by running around on a football pitch for 90 minutes and it took time to make the adjustment. The other concern was the muscle wastage, which was one of the legacies of my leukaemia treatment. Although my legs had never been particularly muscular – Nicky Eaden at Barnsley cruelly nicknamed me 'Flamingo' – I didn't feel that they were getting any stronger.

Once calf muscles waste away, it literally takes a lifetime to rebuild them, and it was always going to be difficult for me to be able to find a way of compensating. Although I could hold Paul's wheel at around 32 kph, the moment we reached a climb I would be 'dropped' and I would be down to my granny gear. In time, there was a slight improvement, but my muscles were not responding. Paul simply pulled away from me whenever there was an increase in the gradient and he would have to wait for me at the top of a climb because I would often be struggling to break through the 10 kph barrier when the going got tough.

It was a real concern because, even though I could ride the miles, I didn't have the speed, and time would become a factor when we reached the Alps and Pyrenees in the second week of the Tour. David Duffield, the respected Eurosport commentator, raised the stakes when he told me to prepare to walk up some of the steeper climbs, and I was genuinely concerned when we went to the Peak District for a training weekend with the rest of the team in May.

Some of the climbs were pretty demanding, but the staggeringly steep 20 per cent rise to the top of Winnat's Pass, which lies deep in the Peak District, was too much. I managed to make my way over the cattle grid at the bottom and ride a couple of hundred yards, but it was simply too steep. Ian and Robbie appeared to fly up it, but Matt and Neil really struggled on that climb too. They inched their way to the summit and it was only when they got there that they admitted to each other that, if one had got off and walked, so would the other. Sheer bloody-mindedness had got them to the top and, even though I had the determination, I simply didn't have the strength. They were dots in the distance by the time I got to some of the steeper sections, but my lungs had contracted by the time I reached my last gear and I knew I didn't have the strength to complete the climb.

I didn't even have a decision: I had no choice but to dismount and make the lonely walk to the top. When I started the climb, some other cyclists puffed and panted their way past me and, even though I could see how tough it was for them, I longed to be like that. I knew, as they knew, that they would somehow crawl to the top of Winnat's Pass and I knew, as they knew, what a sense of achievement they would have when they got there. Roads in England are seldom so steep, but they would certainly be that way when we crossed the Alps and the Pyrenees, and I began to have doubts about my chances of completing some of the climbs. I wanted to be able to complete every pedal stroke during the Tour, but that day on Winnat's Pass placed a huge question mark over my prospects.

I felt I had the mileage in my legs, but the Alpine climbs appeared to be on another level. I made significant progress by riding my first '100' on 18 April and, even though I only averaged 27 kph, it was a huge psychological hurdle to overcome. As the weeks wore on, I even felt I was becoming a cyclist. I committed six months of my life to the project and I was out on the roads virtually every single day.

Out on the road, I even started checking out other cyclists' bikes. Most riders will either wave or nod their head when they pass on the opposite side of the road and almost everyone will have a glance at your equipment. Just by looking at the manufacturer's name, it is possible to tell how seriously someone takes their cycling. I started off riding a £500 bike from Bianchi, one of the most renowned manufacturers in the business, but I used an all-singing and all-dancing bit of kit worth more than £3,000 by the time it got to the Tour itself. Cyclists don't always stop there, either. The professionals have different frames and gearing systems for certain stages of the Tour and their bikes, fully tuned up, are worth nearer £5,000.

I definitely got bitten by the bug. I became a slave to it and I knew I was hooked when I found myself browsing around cycling shops. I had no idea what I was supposed to be buying so I would just pretend I knew what I was doing and then I would scuttle out of the shop before one of the assistants could ask if I needed any help. That was only the start of it. I noticed that whenever I watched the cycling on television or saw someone while I was out on the roads, they had shaved their legs. I went out for a few rides with Ian Whittell and his were as smooth as a baby's bottom. I thought it must have something to do with aerodynamics.

'Er, Whitts, why does everyone shave their legs?'

'Well, there are a few reasons, but if you come off your bike, it makes it easier to clean the cuts if you don't have any hair. It's also a bit more hygienic.'

'Really?'

'Yeah, look at mine.'

He then rolled up his cycling shorts and showed me a deep graze just above his knee.

'That was a particularly nasty one,' he added as he pointed towards the scar on his leg.

So that was the reason. I took me a few weeks to build myself up to it and I didn't even mention it to Julie. She was away on a hen weekend when I finally made the decision. I can remember looking at the hairs on my legs and wondering what they would look like without. With my slender-looking pins, I reckoned I could have modelled ladies' tights, so it shouldn't make too much of a difference if I shaved the blond hairs off. I wasn't sure where to start, so I simply lathered them both before grabbing Julie's lady-shave from the side of the bath and hacking away.

No matter how many times I checked them in the mirror, it still took a bit of getting used to. A lot of footballers wax their legs and even their chests these days, but I was never one for that during my career. Now my legs looked as though they had been polished, but not everyone was impressed.

'Geoff! What have you done?'

'Oh, hi love. Good weekend?'

4

Tours-Blois, 67.5 km Team Time-Trial

The team time-trial is one of the most bewitching spectacles of the Tour de France. Although the stage is short and sweet, it is a demonstration of the professionals' immense physical power. They show an extraordinary capacity to ride at high speed in short bursts in order to keep the pace and power their way towards the finish line. For outfits such as Lance Armstrong's Discovery Channel team, it was a chance to intimidate their rivals with a show of solidarity and strength.

Even Armstrong, who was attempting to win his seventh successive Tour in 2005, admitted that success in the team time-trial was more important to him than the individual discipline. That was some admission because Armstrong was recognised as the best individual time-trialist in the sport when he was racing. The teams wear special aerodynamic lycra bodysuits, teardrop helmets and use bikes adapted specifically for time-trials to try to shave precious seconds off the clock.

They set off at five-minute intervals and each rider will take a turn at the front for around 20 seconds before peeling off and returning to the back of the paceline. It is a drill that is practised for many hours during their training runs, because if a team-mate falls off the back of the paceline when they are travelling at more than 50 kph, it is impossible for him to recover.

Instead, the stragglers are left trailing in their team-mates' wake and they have to wait for their support vehicle to slow down before they dismount, put their bike on the roof rack and jump into the back. The Tour only recognises the time of the seventh rider to finish and that means that a team can only afford to lose two riders en route. This both adds to the drama and increases the pressure on the pros to ride in formation and hold the wheel of the man in front. The 20-second burst at the front is designed to maintain the team's optimum speed before giving the rider at the head of the pack a three-minute breather in his team-mates' draft before he is required to take another brief turn as the lead man. Armstrong was an awesome time-trialist, but the rest of the Discovery Channel team proved they are a machine when they rolled off the starting ramp in Tours.

They set a Tour record when their nine-man team destroyed their rivals by riding the 67 km route in one hour and ten minutes at an average speed of 57.31 kph – 3 km quicker than the record that had been set ten years previously. Although we were not racing, it took our team nearly twice as long to complete the stage. The Discovery team's performance was an incredible sight and, although it was a long-awaited moment for the teams on the pro Tour, it was also one of my mini-targets. I had set various goals along the way and, each time I met one, it meant that I jumped another psychological hurdle.

The 19 km individual time-trial on the opening day of our Tour was simply a case of riding the route, but I knew that the next two stages were significantly harder. They didn't disappoint, but I always viewed Stage Four as a bit of a breather because it was so short and, unlike the professionals, we were not up against the clock. We gave ourselves a bit of a lie-in that morning, but that turned out to be a mistake because our support crew took nearly two hours to find the start line in Tours.

It was a hugely frustrating experience, although we consoled ourselves with endless cups of coffee in a café on the main drag that slices through the centre of town. The stage provided the highlight of the Tour so far. At the time, we were five days ahead of the professionals and we were not party to the buzz and excitement that accompany the teams when they fly through the towns at 40 kph. We were simply anonymous forerunners to the main event. Instead of the lavish ceremonies and endless signing of autographs that mark the start of each stage of the Tour, when we arrived at the designated starting point around six o'clock each morning, there was no starter's gun, no whistling from the crowds and no television cameras monitoring every dip in speed or commentating on our shouts back to the car for yet another bottle of water.

Instead, we were met by lonely country roads; there were no crowds and none of the carnival atmosphere that is so prevalent during the race itself. That changed when the Crédit Agricole and CSC teams flashed past as we were sat waiting for our support crew to find the start line, and we experienced them for real when our five-man team finally eased into action. As we cycled out of Tours and began the short trip along the south side of the Loire, we were overtaken by another two of the pro teams. They were out on a recce of the time-trial route and, even though they were nowhere near top speed, it was awesome to watch at close quarters how they effortlessly turned the pedals.

We were still in awe when we heard the whirr of another team a few hundred metres behind us. There was little warning when the Dutch team, Euskatel, wearing their patriotic bright-orange lycra, began to suck us up. We were riding in a paceline at around 32 kph, but we could hear the wonderful sound of their box-fresh bikes gliding towards us and, within seconds, they had breezed past, chatting to each other and acknowledging us with the thumbs up or a friendly wave, doing a leisurely 40 kph.

They were fast, but they appeared to be putting so little effort into it, which made it all the more breathtaking. They were riding in their big chain rings and barely turning over the pedals as they flew along the Loire. I was mesmerised by the way the team interchanged almost at will. At any time, they could just step up a gear and respond. I didn't have that luxury – every turn of the pedals inflicted more punishment on my battered body; but the boys in the Euskatel, CSC or Crédit Agricole teams are battle-hardened veterans of the Tour.

I watched first-hand when they did step on the gas, though. Iban Mayo, one of the favourites for the Tour itself, stopped in a lay-by to attend to what the French brilliantly refer to as a 'personal need' but his team-mates didn't wait for him. By the time Mayo got back on his bike, they were nothing more than an orange glow on the horizon; but he taught us a new technique when he was paced back to the pack by riding behind one of our own support vehicles. Whenever that happened to us, we would have to pedal like billy-o to catch up our team-mates some way in the distance.

Mayo simply flagged down Haynesy, who slowed down to let him use the considerable effect of the draft created by the huge width and height of the Land Rover support car. Mayo then gestured to Haynesy steadily to increase the speed and they reached nearly 70 kph before he finally rejoined his team-mates. Mayo was barely out of breath by the time he casually rejoined them, but we were. I marvelled at Mayo's power, but he was not even at his peak. He was still riding himself in and it would be several days before he started the Tour for real.

That is when the laughing and joking among his team-mates would stop and the serious business would begin. For us, it had already started, but we were still coming to terms with life on the road. Although we were averaging around 28 kph, Ian or Robbie would go off and stretch their legs from time to time. They were used to riding at considerably higher speeds and I was more than happy to cut them loose now and again. Ian needed little encouragement and no sooner had he broken free of the paceline than he would be pumping the pedals, rapidly disappearing into the distance.

Speed. That was the problem. Back home in Manchester, Ian rode virtually every day and he was far stronger than anyone else in the team. Those occasional blow-outs would do us all some good. I could often tell, just by the slight increase on my speedometer, that he was itching to get away. Matt and I noticed the gradual increase and, unless someone told Ian to take it easy, we were soon creeping up towards 40 kph and we would struggle to hold on to the wheel of the man in front. Occasionally, it could be fun to ride at those speeds. It meant making considerably more progress in terms of distance, but it had to be weighed against the price the likes of Matt and me might have to pay later in the day.

Ian was suffering more than anyone, but it had nothing to do with the long days in the saddle. He just wasn't testing himself. Robbie would often be sat second in the paceline and he would get frustrated with Ian when he noticed our speed increasing. Robbie wanted us to conserve energy, but at times Ian wanted to push us and see just how far we could go. As a non-drinker, Ian's performance was not far short of his peak and he found the endless miles each day little more than a stroll in the park. I often gave him the green light to go and stretch his legs a little. He rarely needed a second invitation and, when he did go, at least he could test himself a little by riding ahead. The only problem was that it would separate the team and our support vehicles and, although this stage was short and sweet, we still had to negotiate our way to Blois.

I would sit in behind Ian and Robbie, tuck my head down, and watch as Robbie got more and more rattled. He was an expert at holding someone's wheel, but the three men behind were novices and we could easily be blown out the back door. We were frequently hanging on to Ian's pace and it was a battle to stay within a foot of the rear wheel in front. I knew it frustrated Robbie and he would get more and more wound up.

He would start by shaking his helmet from side to side, but Ian was oblivious to this. He would just continue to power on and, although Robbie could stay with him, he knew what an effect it was having on my performance.

That's when he would break the silence: 'Watch the bloody speed, Ian.'

That would do it – for about five minutes. Then our speed would be creeping up again and we would be praying that the lights at the next junction were red.

If we rode within our limits, it would save our legs for the mountains. If we pushed ourselves too hard in the early days of the Tour, we might regret it by the time we reached the Alps. Riding for short period of time at 40 kph was certainly fun, but we had no idea what effect it would have later in the Tour. I was worried, as we all were, about the mountains, because none of us really knew just how much those stages would take out of us. I wasn't sure whether the condition of my body would gradually deteriorate as the days rolled on or whether, like the professionals such as Mayo, I would be able to ride myself into the Tour. There was no way of knowing, but it was obvious from the very beginning that Ian wasn't testing himself. We were riding well below the average speed that he would ride at home.

Richard Chessor, our nutritionist from Loughborough University, made sure we were fully hydrated and he kept an accurate measure of how much fuel we were taking on board throughout the day. This meant that he could predict when and what types of food we would need at any time, and he was usually close by in one of the Land Rovers to offer advice. His professional approach, which also extended to mealtimes, ensured that we were as well prepared for each day as we could be. Back home, there is the temptation to have a couple of beers to relax in the evening, or order fish and chips for dinner, but we didn't indulge while we were away. We stuck to a strict regime of low-fat, high-carbohydrate foods – chicken, pasta, rice or pizza – and it had a huge effect on our performance.

We were consuming more than a litre of high-energy drink every hour and, when the bottles ran dry, performance took a dramatic dip. Dehydration sets in, especially in the 30+ degree temperatures we were experiencing; then fatigue takes over and turning the pedals becomes an almighty effort. When our crew were in close proximity, refuelling was not a problem. As soon as the bottles needed to be replenished, we would wave them in the air and our support crew would draw alongside and swap them over without us having to stop.

This was another technique we had learned from the Tour professionals, but when it goes wrong, as it did when the two support cars set off in pursuit of Ian, it has devastating effects. Despite our increasingly frantic phone calls from our mobile phones, neither of the cars answered and we literally crawled towards Blois. With every pedal stroke, we were losing energy and patience. Neil rode ahead to try and find them, but they had already driven all the way to Blois and were waiting for us at the finish line. We caught up with Neil on the outskirts of Blois. It was so hot we were struggling to breathe regularly without any drinks. In nearly an hour, we had not seen our support crew, who had long since abandoned the cars and were drinking cappuccinos on the finishing straight, and we had not passed a single petrol station on the side of the road. Eventually, the penny dropped and they decided to come back and find us.

When they did, Westie was fairly happy with himself, but I didn't share his sense of humour.

'Westie, what's going on?'

'Relax, Geoff. Here, take this.'

And he handed me a full bottle of drink. I was so thirsty that I immediately pressed the drink to my lips but nothing was coming out.

He had covered the opening with sellotape.

OO

Laughter got us through some tough times on the Tour, just as it had helped keep my spirits up when I was first diagnosed with leukaemia. At first, I wanted to keep my illness quiet. I didn't want the attention and I wasn't sure whether or not I would live. My close family and friends knew, but the word had not reached the football community. That all changed when I finally agreed to be interviewed by the *Sunday People* newspaper.

It had been some time since a newspaper wanted to interview me. I was no longer a big name and football has a woefully short memory. It had been 12 years since I played for England and I didn't think anyone would be interested in my story, but when the *People* published the interview on 3 August 2003, it was on the back page and there was a spread inside.

'Geoff Thomas: My Fight Against Cancer' thundered the back page. I was astonished by the coverage, and I was touched that a newspaper thought I was still of public interest. The story led to an avalanche of letters, phone calls, cards and emails from well-wishers all over the country.

My profile faded the moment Baddiel and Skinner battered me on their *Fantasy Football* television programme for that fateful chip against France in 1992, but things changed in a stroke. It was incredible how the football community rallied round, but I didn't want sympathy. I was touched by their kindness, but I just wanted the chance to live. I formed a close friendship with Steve Coppell when I was at Palace and we spoke two or three times a week at first. Graham Taylor, my manager when I was playing for England and later at Wolves, was one of the first people on the phone and he kept in regular touch. I didn't expect people to call but when they did, it was a wonderful gesture – it would make my day when one of my old team-mates got in touch. There were wonderful messages of support but, by then, I had already faced up to the disease and all I wanted to know was how I could beat it.

I kept my sense of humour throughout. When I played, I loved the dressing-room banter almost as much as the game itself. I gave out enough stick and I always felt big enough to take it. Even when I had leukaemia, there was no escape. Dave Bassett, the manager who took me to Nottingham Forest and later to Barnsley, could be vicious at times, and he didn't change when he heard that I had leukaemia. He phoned me up a few weeks after my diagnosis to see how I was and I was explaining the various stages of my illness when he interrupted me.

'I don't like to bring this up, old son, but I just wanted to remind you about those Cup final tickets.'

'Harry' got me some tickets for the 2003 Worthington Cup final between Manchester United and Liverpool and I still owed him about £150. It wasn't a lot of money, but I still hadn't paid it.

'Yeah, what about them?'

'Well, it's just my missus has given me a bit of a bollocking because I've noticed you haven't settled up yet – can you make sure you sort me out before you pop off, old son?'

It was typical Harry and we were both laughing as he demanded that I write him a cheque for £150. The only problem was that Harry's wife, Chris, was listening in the background. She gave him such a rollicking afterwards that she made him phone me to apologise. I didn't mind – it goes with the territory; but he's still waiting for the cheque to land.

Whenever I was injured, as I frequently was during a career that saw me have 27 operations on a variety of injuries, some of the cheeky pros would always pick up my boots and come over to me with them in their hand.

'Geoff?'

'What?'

'If you don't make it back, like – would it be OK to have your boots?'

It's dressing-room humour, but it's the kind of banter that footballers thrive on. Wally Downes, one of the coaches when I was at Palace, came on the phone another time. He was manager of Brentford and he asked me if I would be special guest at their match against Walsall in a couple of months' time.

'Sure,' I said. 'That would be good. It would be great to see you.'

Walsall was no more than half an hour's drive from my home and I thought it would be great to catch up with Wally after so much time.

'When is it?'

Then his voice dropped. 'Oh, sorry, Geoff. It's in October.'

'What's wrong with that?'

'Well, I'm not sure you'll be around by then.'

It sounds cruel, but it's the way the football world operates and it was actually good to be a part of it again. When I stopped playing, I missed the buzz of the dressing room. There were strong characters at every club I played for. At Palace, sometimes you had to shout to get your voice heard. Players such as Wrighty, Brighty, Andy Gray and Andy Thorn always had plenty to say. Thorny was another one to pick up the phone when I was first diagnosed. We played together at Palace and he was a rock-solid centre-half during the Coppell era. He had long since stopped playing, but he was still in the game as Everton's chief scout.

I was at home when he called and he started the conversation by asking if my clothes shops were still open.

'Why do you want to know?'

'Because I'll need a black suit for your funeral.'

Even now there is no escape. It has been more than three years since I was diagnosed with leukaemia, but footballers never forget. Glyn Hodges, who had a brief spell at Palace in the 1990–91 season, was always on the phone with a line.

We managed Barnsley's reserve team for a time and he has since gone on to be a coach under Mark Hughes at Blackburn. One day he phoned from the dressing room and it was obvious that he had set up all the players to listen to our conversation.

'Hi, mate, how you doing?'

'Yeah, good thanks.'

'Geoff, I was just wondering – what's your immune system like these days?'

'It's not great – a bit on the low side.'

'Why, what should it be?'

'Why do you ask?'

'It's just that, well, we're having a sweepstake here on the first person to catch bird flu ...'

5

Chambord–Montargis, 183 km

While the professionals would be feeling their legs after the exertions of the team time-trial, the two-and-a-half-hour trip to Blois reignited my enthusiasm. We arrived in Blois, a town on the Loire in between Orléans and Tours, in the early afternoon and this gave us our first chance to properly relax after three days of late nights and early starts. I certainly needed it.

Although I didn't know Haynesy at all before we started the Tour, I quickly became accustomed to his bizarre little quirks. Matt, Neil and I were with Haynesy in his Land Rover when we set off to the start line from our hotel.

France was already basking in summer temperatures – even at 7 or 8 a.m. it was approaching 30 degrees – and Chris had an unusual way of preparing us for the day ahead. As we made our way towards Chambord, Chris turned off the air-conditioning in the car. It seemed like a fairly strange move to us because we three riders were taking full advantage of it before we stepped into the early morning heat. I didn't say anything because Haynesy was the driver and it is usually his prerogative to choose the temperature or, for that matter, the music inside the cabin. What I didn't expect was for him to start increasing the heating at regular intervals. Although we were dressed in cycling gear, we started to get irritable and I exchanged some fairly puzzled looks with Matt and Neil.

Soon, sweat began trickling down my temples and my arms were covered in tiny little droplets. With the windows on a child-lock system so that we couldn't even open them, we were gasping for some fresh air and, when he turned the dials so that the heating was on full blast, I had to say something.

'Haynesy, what are you doing?'

'Everything OK, Geoff?'

'We're going to boil alive with that heating on – what are you doing?'

'I'm just acclimatising you to the heat so that you don't notice it when you step out of the car to start the stage.'

'Are you mad?'

'I'm just looking out for you guys.'

'You're off your head!'

Although the 183 km trip east from Chambord to Montargis would take around seven hours, I felt remarkably refreshed when I got back in the saddle.

Kimmage had told me that we would ride ourselves into the Tour and I was beginning to appreciate what he meant. When there are no diversions, no telephone calls, no bills to pay and no children to pick up from school, the thought of cycling for seven or eight hours a day becomes a lot more appealing.

I knew I was feeling fresh because, whenever Ian stepped on the gas, as he frequently did, I held his wheel. Ian didn't know his own strength and, when he wanted to up the tempo, he would be 100 yards up the road in no time and we would be off the back, throwing our arms up in disgust and muttering our disapproval. Today was different and, refreshingly, we rode as a team. Perhaps, after four days of living in each other's pockets and moaning to each other about our failure to work as a unit, we were finally beginning to get a feel for each other's capabilities. As our five-man team flashed intermittently through the towns dotted on the Tour route, we drew quizzical looks from the locals. We were three days ahead of the professionals and the locals couldn't work out why we were speeding through their villages with two support vehicles leading the way.

For long periods, we averaged more than 32 kph and even the frequent bursts of rain that left us soaked through to the skin did nothing to dampen our spirits. I felt stronger than at any other time since I had started riding a racing bike six months previously and I began to appreciate the stunning scenery as we hurtled through the country lanes. We were gung-ho and loving every minute of it: so this is what it feels like to be part of the professional *peloton*.

Our speed was increasing but, for once, no-one wanted to temper it. We took advantage of the generous tailwind and we were inching towards 40 kph – the average speed of the pros – and the adrenalin was pumping. It was probably foolish to ride at this pace and, although we knew we were likely to pay for it later, no-one wanted to be the first to say anything. It was fun, it was fast and we were flying. By the time we swept round the corner into the hamlet of Montereau, around 40 km from the finish line, we were topping 48 kph.

I had the shock of my life as we streaked through the centre. To my left, five cyclists, all wearing yellow jerseys, were waiting by the side of the road with their bikes, but we were travelling so quickly that my vision was blurred. As we flashed past, they began shouting my name.

'*Allez*, Geoff! *Allez, allez, allez*!'

'*Allez*! *Allez* Geoff Thomas!'

There was a huge banner on the side of the road which read '*Allez*, Geoff' but I was confused and I only spotted it in a haze. My vision was clouded by my concentration and I was a little embarrassed because we hadn't stopped to see why they were standing there. They had clearly made a big effort to come and see me but, because of the speed we were travelling at, it had barely registered and I had no idea who they were.

'What was all that about?' asked Robbie.

'I don't know.'

'Do you think we should go back?'

We were enjoying the route so much that we were in two minds, but I'm glad we did. As we rolled back down the hill, I recognised my old friend Gio Gonzalez, along with Jan and Clive Marshall, two of my closest family friends from my time at Palace. Gio owned a wonderful Spanish tapas bar in Purley, South London, and we had been friends for more than 15 years.

When I was playing for Palace, I regularly wandered into his restaurant with my team-mate John Pemberton, and Gio used to sit with us for hours while we picked at our lunch. He was a former professional footballer in France and he was wearing one of the Palace shirts that I had given him when I was still with the club. Gio had kept in touch throughout my illness and it was an amazing gesture for him to travel out to France. He had been invited to stay with some of his French friends and they all wanted to ride the last 30 km to Montargis with the team. That afternoon will remain one of the highlights of the Tour. We picked up where we left off and our French friends rode with us at 48 kph as we sped through towns and took turns at the front of our mini-*peloton*.

It was an uplifting experience and it gave me my first real taste of riding in a team. It was exhilarating and, as we approached the finish town of Montargis, they formed a guard of honour to allow me through. As I crossed the line, Gio was waiting for me in his Palace shirt with 'Thomas 8' on the back; and, as we embraced, it brought the memories of my spell at Selhurst Park sharply into focus.

Although I played professional football for more than 20 years and represented seven different clubs, I will always regard Crystal Palace as my team. Whenever I return to Selhurst Park, I consider it to be my home. Sometimes, when I am invited down by their chairman, Simon Jordan, to watch them play, I sit for a quiet moment in the draughty stands and look around the stadium, remembering the success story that Steve Coppell started in the mid-1980s. It has all changed now and the team that Coppell led to an FA Cup final in 1990 and a third-place finish in the old First Division has long since broken up.

That doesn't stop me dreaming, though, and at times I even think about returning there as the manager one day. I can't forget the special times at Selhurst Park and the team that grew up together and went on to represent England at international level. It flatters me when people refer to me as a Palace legend, but I didn't think it would turn out that way when I signed for the club from Crewe for £50,000 in the summer of 1987. Although I enjoyed making my Palace debut at Huddersfield, I remember being jeered by some of the supporters in our second home game because I had taken the place of their favourite, Kevin Taylor.

'Ticker' Taylor was a popular player and a lot of Palace supporters were surprised that Coppell allowed him to leave for the inauspicious surroundings of Scunthorpe. He was a tenacious little central midfielder, an experienced player with an eye for a goal. The Palace fans had never heard of me and the only thing they did know was that I had been released by Rochdale as a teenager and had since played for Crewe. Some of the supporters felt that my acquisition did not match the ambitions of the club and I was initially concerned that I might not be able to fit in with the tough senior players in the team. Back then, they had really strong characters such as Jim Cannon, Gavin Nebbeling and the former Arsenal and Scotland keeper George Wood in the side. It could be an intimidating dressing room.

Cannon was an institution and he was adored by the supporters. When the Palace side that had been christened the 'Team of the Eighties' broke up after Terry Venables left for QPR, Cannon stayed, despite the club's depressing spiral into the lower reaches of the old Second Division. For that reason alone, the supporters loved him and, even though he was from Scotland, he was Palace through and through. The Palace supporters respected him because he remained loyal in a depressing era, when attendances at Selhurst Park plunged from nearly 40,000 in 1980 to just over 3,000 five years later. For that, he had their ultimate respect. He certainly merited it.

Nothing happened without his say-so and Coppell, who was only 28 when he took over at Palace, was considerably younger than the club's captain. He got Cannon on side, though. By the time Cannon left the following season, he had made more than 650 league appearances.

By then, I was partnering Andy Gray in the centre of midfield and the supporters couldn't decide who had the biggest influence in the team. Cannon was a nice man, but he was from the old school and you had to show respect for him. That didn't sit easily with the likes of Wright, Bright, Gray and Finnigan, because they were a different breed and their attitude was different.

As far as they were concerned, they were good enough to be in the team and they were not afraid to tell anyone. They were rough, tough South London boys and they would sooner fight you in the street than give you an inch. I liked Cannon and maybe it was because of my own background that I got on with him, but there were a lot of clashes in the dressing room at the time. There were so many personalities in the team, but it made us fight for each other that much harder when we were on the pitch. The friction rubbed off on the team and the best example of that was my relationship with Andy.

I can remember playing at Reading's old home, Elm Park, one Saturday and the stadium announcer was going through the two teams before the kick-off: 'In goal for Palace, Number 1 George Wood, Number 2 Gary Stebbing, Number 3 David Burke, and Number 4 Andy Gray. That's not the famous Andy Gray by the way, but the Palace Andy Gray.

Well, despite that, Andy went on to make quite a reputation for himself. He was a very good player and, although he was a bit head-strong, Coppell took a chance on him by signing him from the non-league team Dulwich Hamlet.

Andy left for Aston Villa in 1987, but when he returned to the club two years later we made a formidable partnership in the centre of the park. Andy was a real London boy – and could be moody – but we were playing partners on the pitch. Along with Finnigan, they would pitch up at our Mitcham training ground, open the boot of their cars and try and sell us the latest John Smedley knitwear or other designer gear. Andy had a sports shop in Tooting market and, whenever the players needed boots, Andy brought in boxloads to sell at what he assured us were knockdown prices.

They could certainly get themselves into some scrapes. I was in the car with Andy, Finn, Wrighty and Brighty heading for the Kensington Roof Gardens one evening when someone cut us up. After the drivers in both cars began hurling abuse at each other, the Palace lads decided to get out and confront the couple in the other vehicle. It was a mad moment because, as soon as I got out of the car, Wrighty got back in it. Brighty was running round the back and the other two were suddenly running down the road. I didn't fancy my chances on my own against a pretty mean looking lad so I started to inch back towards our car.

When I got there, Wrighty was stretched out across the back seat and Brighty was cowering behind one of the wheels.

'Geoff, get in! What are you doing?'

I didn't have a clue what they were talking about.

'You what?'

'Didn't you see him?'

'See what?'

'He's got a gun!'

I could be pretty naive at times, especially when I was in this kind of company, but no-one expects a gun to be pulled on them. Five minutes previously we had been innocently driving down the street and suddenly I was being threatened with a firearm. It was an extraordinary moment, but I'm glad to say I have never come across anything like that again in my life.

Andy and I rarely talked on the pitch and we certainly didn't have any kind of relationship off it, but when I was diagnosed with leukaemia it was great to be in touch with each other again. Our lives off the pitch were a world away from each other and I believe that our determination to prove who was the better player drove a wedge between us. I can probably count the number of times we passed to each other on the pitch on one hand, but I can count on him as a friend now. At my benefit game at Selhurst Park against Manchester United in March 2006, he was one of the first players to come into the dressing room and give me a hug.

Back then, though, it was all about bravado. Although I was the Palace captain when Cannon retired, Andy and I we were both striving to be recognised as the driving force of the team. Looking back, I have tremendous admiration for his achievements in the game because he was a bloody good player. We were both young, but no-one ever took any liberties with us. Gray was physically strong and I had the legs on most of the midfielders in the division. Our team also had goals, and lots of them, thanks to the partnership of Wright and Bright. Wright was the more talented, but he was raw and had been signed from a non-league team called Greenwich Borough.

Bright, who had been signed from Leicester, was a target man and at the time he was the more polished player, but they both had an insatiable appetite for goals. It was the start of a special era at Selhurst Park under Coppell, but I missed out on the majority of the club's promotion campaign back to the First Division through injury. We won the play-offs, despite an incredible collapse at Blackburn in the first leg of the final; we recovered to win 3–0 at Selhurst Park on a boiling hot afternoon in early June.

I missed the semi-final of the Simod Cup – a second-class competition with a final at Wembley – against Nottingham Forest, but missing the play-off final was a far bigger disappointment. Selhurst Park was bursting at the seams, with more than 30,000 supporters for the second leg and, although I was delighted that we won promotion to the top flight, I couldn't celebrate in the same way as my team-mates.

They won promotion without me and, as the supporters streamed on to the pitch to celebrate with the players, I was an outsider looking in. Wrighty, who scored Palace's third goal, was hoisted onto the shoulders of the supporters and they were tearing off his strip as souvenirs. He left the field in just his jockstrap and I'm sure that if he hadn't been holding on to it they would have got that too. Afterwards, the players partied all night but I struggled to get involved.

Coppell was the same. He was very quiet and rarely indulged. He was quiet to the point where he wasn't really involved in the celebrations after the game. Although he was very astute, he was also very introverted, but he shone out whenever he had a decision to make. There were some fairly big decisions when we were promoted to the First Division in 1989 because taking on the likes of Liverpool, Manchester United and Arsenal was a daunting prospect with a team full of fighters. Of the team that started the season only two of them

– Perry Suckling and Mark Bright – had any experience of top-flight football, but even they had not been considered good enough.

Things were certainly looking bleak the night we travelled to Anfield in September. Liverpool had finished runners-up to Arsenal the previous season but that night they showed us just why they were considered to be one of the best teams of the modern era. They had the likes of Bruce Grobbelaar, Alan Hansen, Steve McMahon, John Barnes, Ronnie Whelan and Ian Rush in the team, and they taught us a lesson.

They beat us 9–0 at Anfield; Tommy Smith, their legendary full-back and former European Cup-winning captain, told Merseyside Radio after the game that we were the worst team he had ever seen at that level. It was a bit harsh because, although we were a little bit gung-ho and more than a touch naive, we were only 3–0 down at half-time. At 0–0 I hit the post, but after the break Liverpool didn't miss a thing. They had about 15 chances that night and scored nine times.

We played without fear, but I won't pretend that it could have ended any differently because they simply annihilated us that night.

Liverpool were awesome, but their supporters were used to them playing like this. I had watched Rush on the television so many times that I knew how lethal he was inside the area, but it was only when I was on the same pitch that I realised just how hard he worked for the team.

I felt sorry for our keeper, Perry Suckling, because he was hammered after that game, but none of Liverpool's goals were his fault. It destroyed his confidence, and his career, but he didn't let us down. Our inexperience let us down that night, nothing else. After Liverpool scored a couple, they sensed blood. Usually, teams settle for four or five and then take their foot off the gas because the job is done, but I think their players knew they were on to something good. I was at rock bottom that night, but I will never forget the Palace supporters behind the goal because they didn't stop singing. It must have been humiliating for them, and they must have taken some fearful stick at work the following day, but they showed incredible humour. They sang their favourite song at the time, 'Stevie Coppell's Red and Blue Army', throughout the game and, even when we went 9–0 down and the pasting was almost complete, they responded by singing, 'We're going to win 10–9.'

That game was like being involved in a school match, but it was a freak night. I was up against McMahon, an established England international who was regarded as one of the best central midfielders in the country, and he gave me a couple of lessons that season. When we played them back at Selhurst Park the following January, I accidentally slipped the ball between his legs and, as I accompanied it with the customary cry of 'nuts', he clotheslined me with his forearm. He nearly cut me in two with it and, as I was lying on the floor, he leant over and jabbed his finger in my face: 'You can do that when you're good enough.'

I took that on board because he was a respected opponent and they had shown incredible restraint at Anfield. The temptation must have been there to really take the piss that night, but they never did. Some felt that was what was happening when their manager, Kenny Dalglish, sent on John Aldridge, who was signing for Real Sociedad the following day, as a substitute to take a penalty, but it didn't bother me who took it. By then, we were 6–0 down and I had missed a penalty of our own. Grobbelaar was showing me to his right, but I had so much anger in me that I wanted to hit hard and relieve some of the frustration.

I can remember Bruce Grobbelaar's spaghetti legs when I took my penalty. It was the routine that famously worked when they beat Roma in the 1984 European Cup final and he seemed to be urging me to place the ball in the bottom corner, but I only had one thing on my mind: I wanted to smash the ball into the net and take Grobbelaar with it – but I was so pent up with aggression that I spooned it miles over the crossbar.

Despite the embarrassment of losing by such a huge margin, I didn't take it too badly in the dressing room after the game. I felt more sorry for the Palace fans who had made the trip. A couple of thousand were on Merseyside; they had been waiting nearly ten years for the club to return to the top flight and they had been looking forward to nights like this. Instead, they watched Liverpool inflict the biggest defeat in the club's history.

It really didn't sink in just how humiliating it was, but Wrighty was in tears afterwards. Coppell was particularly affected by it because he was born in Liverpool and some of his family and friends were sat in the stands while his hometown team ripped us apart. He was a Liverpool fan as a youngster and he told the newspapers that 'this result will haunt us for the rest of our lives'.

It was certainly a tremendous performance by a fantastic side, but I just had admiration for the way they performed. It could have been anyone that night. Liverpool were fantastic, one of the greatest sides in the modern era, and they would have ripped most teams apart in that mood. Defensively they were excellent, but they had so many attack-minded players in the team that it was difficult to keep them quiet when they were in the groove. Some of the other players felt the same. When I got to the dressing rooms, Pembo was just lowering himself into one of the plunge baths. I threw my kit on the floor and, as I made my way to join some of my team-mates in the bath, Pembo turned round all dead-pan and said: 'Christ, that lot will do all right this season, won't they?'

OO

We knew we were not a bad side and we recovered to earn a draw in our next game at Southampton, but the season will always be remembered for our FA Cup run. It started slowly against Portsmouth. I came on as a second-half substitute and scored, then Andy Gray scored a penalty as we scraped through the third round, and, although we comfortably beat Huddersfield and edged past Rochdale in the fifth round, Fourth Division Cambridge were expected to make life a little bit tougher. Everyone thought we were under pressure because their manager, John Beck, had some unusual motivational techniques, to say the least.

At the time, he was notorious for throwing buckets of cold water over his naked players in the dressing room before matches and he would deliberately leave the grass long in the corners to suit their long-ball game. When we turned up at their tiny Abbey Road stadium, some of their supporters were wearing baseball caps with the words 'Crystal Who?' on them. That Palace side had come up the hard way and, if there was a team around at the time who would not be impressed with those kinds of tactics, it was us.

Cambridge were a very good Fourth Division side and, although they were having a good FA Cup run, we were not about to go down to their level. Even though Brighty was injured and keeping tabs on the score from a holiday in the West Indies, I never thought we would lose the game and I scored the winner with a right-foot swinger that bobbled its way past the keeper. The ground was so small that there were only a few hundred Palace fans there, but I celebrated in front of them because I knew then that we were on the way to the FA Cup semi-final.

I attempted to copy Gordon Strachan's celebration from the 1986 World Cup final, when he tried to mount an advertising hoarding after scoring for Scotland against Uruguay, but my attempt was as embarrassing as his. That goal was still enough for us to progress into the semi-finals and we desperately wanted Oldham, considered to be the weakest of the four teams left in the tournament. Instead, we were drawn to play Liverpool and, after beating us 9–0 at Anfield, they thought it was their lucky day.

We had shown signs of improvement since that awful September evening and we were within a whisker of avoiding relegation by the time we faced them in the semi-final at Villa Park in April.

Both semi-finals had been switched to Sunday and it was the first time that the television cameras covered them live. It was a noon kick-off and it was a special moment when thousands of red and blue balloons began cascading down from the Holte End as we walked out to the Palace theme tune, 'Glad All Over'. Coppell prepared for the match meticulously and he had told us not to be concerned if we went a goal down because he felt that we would still go on to win the tie.

It seemed a bizarre thing to say at the time, and a few of the players were privately questioning his wisdom as we approached the game. At the time, if any team conceded a goal against Liverpool, the game was as good as lost. One look at their line-up was enough to confirm that. Just as Coppell had predicted, they went a goal up in the first half when McMahon put Rush through just before time and he went on to finish easily past Nigel Martyn. I can remember the way they celebrated so casually and he just received a pat on the back and a few words of congratulation from his team-mates.

It was as if to say: 'Well done, that's it, we're in the final.'

They underestimated us, because we expected to be 1–0 down. I was so focused for the start of the second half that I didn't even realise that Rush had been replaced during the break. Instead, all I can remember is John Pemberton's run down the right wing straight from the kick-off; when Pembo crossed, Phil Barber's shot fell to Bright and he hooked it into the top corner with his left foot. It was a fairytale moment and you could see from our reaction that it was game on. I remember the fans' celebrations in the stands and it was an incredible feeling to see them jumping up and down.

The game swung like a pendulum until Alan Pardew scored the winner in extra time.

We went back to his house afterwards for a party and I don't even remember waking the next day. In fact, I don't even know if I made it home.

OO

The build-up to the FA Cup final was exactly how I expected it to be as a boy. Eric Hall became the players' official agent and he opened our eyes to the entertainment side. We wore sunglasses whenever we were pictured, we wore stonewashed Burton jeans and certain newspapers were placed under our arms. Although I later wondered whose pockets benefited the most, we had great fun in the build-up. I didn't get involved as much as the other lads and I missed the squad's invitation to the *Blue Peter* studios to sing the Palace fans' anthem 'Glad All Over' because I was at the FA Cup final dinner with the Duke of Windsor.

In those days, it was considered a perk of the job to get Cup final tickets and, after we had given some to our friends and family, we followed a traditional path by agreeing to sell the rest of our allocation to a well-known London ticket tout. The FA have since clamped down and changed the rules, but back then it was the accepted practice for players to sell their tickets. None of the Palace team was earning a lot of money and a few extra quid in our back pockets probably meant we could have a better summer holiday. There was certainly nothing more sinister in it than that and the ticket tout was so grateful to have our business that he invited the squad to the Royal Albert Hall to wine and dine us before he eventually handed over a parcel full of cash.

It was all new to the players and we loved the attention. The pressure was off us because we had avoided relegation and finished 15th in the First Division table. It was an excellent achievement and we had nothing to fear from Manchester United. Although they were favourites to win the Cup with just about anyone living outside the immediate vicinity of Selhurst Park, we had drawn with them in our first home game, when Wrighty scored an equaliser, and we beat them at Old Trafford.

Sir Alex Ferguson's job was under threat when we travelled to Manchester in December 1989, and it was the first time Mark Hughes, idolised by the Stretford Enders, had been dropped from the side. The United fans were furious with Fergie. Whenever Hughes warmed up down the touchline, he was greeted with huge cheers and the fans sang 'Fergie out'. We didn't help his cause by beating them 2–1 and only their FA Cup run, inspired by Mark Robins' goal at Nottingham Forest in the third round, appeared to be keeping him in his job.

Typically, teams ease off before a Cup final. No-one wants to get injured and the star names are often wrapped in cotton wool as part of the preparations, but it wasn't like that at Crystal Palace. In the weeks leading up to the final, Coppell sent us on long cross-country runs and took us to Farthing Downs in Purley – one of the steepest hills I have ever seen – for some extra training.

Coppell had a 100-metre uphill slog marked out and it was a real gut-buster. Players were pulling into the bushes to be sick, but Coppell didn't care a jot. He wanted us to grasp that this was our real chance to create a little bit of history for Crystal Palace. Palace had reached the semi-finals of the competition as a Third Division team in 1976, but then lost to Southampton at Stamford Bridge, and their supporters had waited a long, long time for this moment. Reaching the final against Manchester United was a huge achievement, but Coppell didn't want us to rest on our laurels and let them roll us over at Wembley.

Instead, he wanted us to do our supporters proud by putting up a real fight, and, if we didn't ultimately succeed, it certainly wouldn't be because we were not properly prepared. We had beaten Liverpool, one of the best teams in Europe at the time, to reach the final and this was a real opportunity for us. Although we were close to securing our First Division status when we beat Liverpool at Villa Park, there was no easing off in our league matches, and that was just as well because we faced Wimbledon in our last away game.

They beat Liverpool in the 1988 FA Cup final – one of the biggest upsets in the competition's history – and they were waiting for us at their old Plough Lane ground. Alan Pardew and Dennis Wise were at each other's throats throughout that match and players from both teams were just flying into tackles against each other. It was a real bloodbath, but neither team wanted to give an inch.

Coppell seemed to revel in it and that always surprised me because he was a nimble winger in his playing days with Manchester United and I didn't think he would set his teams up to play that way. He was an astute man, though, and he knew that what we lacked in skill, we would make up for with desire.

I realised what we were up against when I picked up a copy of the *Sun* on the day of the FA Cup final and they had an article comparing the respective captains' lifestyles. There was a picture of Bryan Robson's house in Cheshire and I imagine that even back then it was worth over £1m, and there was the car to match in his driveway. He was not only captain of Manchester United, but England as well, and he had all the trappings and benefits that come with that status.

It was like the prince and the pauper because, across the page, they had my two-up, two-down semi-detached cottage in Beddingon, near Croydon, that was mortgaged to the hilt and worth about £70,000, with a white Ford Orion parked on the drive. I had left my house in Crewe, which was worth about £20,000, and I wasn't earning much more at Palace than I had been at Gresty Road

We left our team hotel to head to Wembley, and the occasion started to hit me when I saw the two sets of supporters mingling as we approached the stadium. There was the usual battle among the players for the choice of music on the coach, but that paled into insignificance when we started to take in the atmosphere. Wembley Way has always been a unique experience; it is a sea of colour on FA Cup final day and it was incredible to see the supporters mingling with each other as they made their way towards the Twin Towers.

Wembley was a magnificent setting and we took the lead when our centre-half, Gary O'Reilly, headed us in front from a free kick early in the first half. The farcical ticket allocation meant that there were only 13,000 Palace fans inside the old stadium that afternoon, but they were all decked out in red and blue.

They were absolutely magnificent and, even when we went 2–1 down, they were in full voice throughout. United were trying to run down the clock late in the second half when Coppell gambled by sending on Wrighty as a substitute. He broke his leg during the 2–0 defeat against Liverpool in January, and he suffered the same injury in his comeback game against Derby two months later. He went to see a faith healer the week before the final and he claimed that her healing hands were part of the reason he was fit enough for the final.

He was our best player, a real stick of dynamite. In the end, Coppell decided not to risk playing him from the start, but, within seconds of coming on as a substitute for Phil Barber, he had turned the game. He left Gary Pallister for dead on the edge of the United penalty area and then struck a low shot beyond the dive of their goalkeeper, Jim Leighton.

No-one could catch him as he ran around the Wembley turf and it took an age before he was eventually buried under a sea of bodies.

His goal took us into extra time and we felt our name was on the Cup when Ian got on the end of John Salako's cross to put us ahead. Wrighty had turned the Cup final on its head, just as we knew he was capable of doing. Before the game, he was telling anyone who would listen that he was 'born for this day' and it certainly seemed to be looking that way. We were within seven minutes of lifting the FA Cup for the first time in the club's 85-year history when Bryan Robson, the United captain, slipped the ball through for Mark Hughes and he lashed home their equaliser.

I felt that we had deserved to win the final and we were still confident that we would have the edge in the replay the following Thursday. We were supposed to go to the West Indies the day after the final for an end-of-season tour, but we had to put that on hold when we drew the first game.

Although we had to prepare for the replay, we still went ahead with our post-match party at our hotel in Hyde Park. It was an incredibly relaxed atmosphere and I can recall sitting in the bath of my hotel room with a bottle of champagne in my hand, dreaming of lifting the FA Cup the following Thursday.

We won the toss to wear our traditional red and blue strip in the first game and that meant United would wear their normal red shirt in the replay. Since our 9–0 defeat at Anfield, we had virtually abandoned the white shirt with a red and blue sash in favour of a yellow away kit, but Coppell wanted something special for the replay.

I loved that white shirt with the diagonal because it reminded me of Manchester City's old strip, but I knew why no-one wanted to play in it. As captain, I had a fairly big influence over the decision and I encouraged our kit manufacturer, Bukta, to design a yellow and black shirt. They were the colours I had worn when I played for my junior team, Littleborough, and we were so good I can't remember ever losing in it. Bukta didn't have much time to make the kit and they only turned up at our team hotel a few hours before the replay, but I thought it was a stunner. Unfortunately, we couldn't match it with our performance. We were criticised for trying to bully our way to victory, but that was never the case.

It was a game that neither side wanted to lose and I think that's why it was so disappointing as a spectacle. We were slaughtered for it afterwards, but I didn't think it was a dirty game.

It was like a game of chess and I always felt that whoever scored first would go on to lift the trophy. When Lee Martin scored, I think we had gone mentally. We weren't prepared for a replay – we'd put so much effort into the first game – and we didn't have the same experience as a team like United.

Robson had been to a replay in 1983, when United beat Brighton 4–0 after drawing the first game, and they could count on big-name players such as Mark Hughes, Neil Webb and Brian McClair.

Ferguson had also changed the complexion of the game by dropping Jim Leighton, their goalkeeper, and replacing him with his understudy, Les Sealey. It was a massive decision by the Manchester United manager and Leighton, who enjoyed so much success under Ferguson at their previous club, Aberdeen, has never forgiven him for it.

There was also a different atmosphere at Wembley that night. Palace had 35,000 supporters at the replay because the ticket restrictions had been lifted; I am still sorry that we didn't put on a performance that could make them proud.

Maybe it would have turned out differently if the referee, Alan Gunn, had given a penalty when I was tripped inside the area by McClair, but he gave a free kick outside the area instead. It was a poor decision and I can remember showing him McClair's stud marks in the area where he slid through me; those were the decisions we needed in our favour. I have seen my protests on a video of the game and, to this day it still hurts, because it was a genuine penalty appeal.

During the 3–3 draw on the Saturday, I felt we could have got back into the game at any time, but the replay was different. United were a bit too streetwise for us and they were better prepared when Wright came off the bench again.

In many ways, I would have preferred to lose the final on the Saturday because we had put so much effort into it. The replay did not live up to expectations and we let ourselves down a little with our performance. We put on a show with United in the first game, but, as soon as we had time to think about the enormity of the occasion, it unsettled us.

We recovered, though, and the following season we flew. Although we finished third in the division, things began to turn sour when we didn't qualify for Europe. We had a great team. Along with Nigel Martyn, Wright, Bright, Salako, Andy Gray and myself, Palace had a team that was full of international players. Eric Young, a Wales international, had replaced Gary O'Reilly in the team, and we had one of the best defences in the league.

John Humphrey – nicknamed 'Tasty' because of his classic good looks – replaced Pembo at right-back and Richard Shaw, another excellent defender, was our regular left-back. Teams were afraid of us, but I started to have concerns about our future when the club failed to match the ambition of the players. We finished third – behind Arsenal and Liverpool – and we should have taken advantage of that momentum, but there were fears behind the scenes that we were one-season wonders. After beating Everton 4–1 at Wembley in the Zenith Data Systems Cup final, we wanted the backing to go on and become a major force in England. Ron Noades, the Palace chairman, was always fairly frugal and, although he had invested significantly in the team during his reign, we were not an established top-flight team.

He had a dream of redeveloping Selhurst Park and building a 40,000 all-seater stadium that could rival Old Trafford, Anfield, St James' Park, Elland Road and Hillsborough for the right to stage matches at Euro 96. Noades was continually frustrated by Croydon Council and it hindered our development. He wanted to build the infrastructure first and the team second, but we were desperate for short-term success.

He had a great manager in Coppell and I had so much respect for him. He took over Palace when he was just 28 and within five years he had moulded a team that had reached the FA Cup final, competing against the best teams in the country.

Coppell gave himself five years to win promotion and he did just

City slicker: I grew up in Arnside Street, in the shadow of Manchester City's old Maine Road. Colin Bell was always my hero; here I am in City's away kit

Outside the family home with my mum and dad, Rene and Gordon, and my sister Kay; my dad with my best mate at Palace, John Pemberton, in 1992

Steve Coppell signed myself and Neil Redfearn at the same time for Palace (*Tom Morris*)

Battling it out with Paul Stewart at White Hart Lane (*Trinity Mirror*)

Royal ascent, after the thrilling 3–3 draw with United and Wembley

Taylor-made: Lining up for England on my debut against Turkey, alongside John Barnes and Des Walker

Going in hard against an Argentinian – I remember he squealed (*Trinity Mirror*)

I gave my all for England – even on a tour of Australia and New Zealand (*Trinity Mirror*)

Thrown to the Wolves: Palace fans were giving me some serious stick on my return to Selhurst Park with my new club Wolves, and I couldn't resist celebrating when I scored (above) – it's still one of my biggest regrets in football. I did love playing for Wolves though, even if injuries meant we never really fulfilled Sir Jack Hayward's ambition (*both Trinity Mirror*)

Winning the First Division in my first season at Forest under Harry Bassett

End of the Road: I scored for Crewe in my last ever competitive game, against Rotherham in the FA Cup. It was a fitting end to my career (*both Trinity Mirror*)

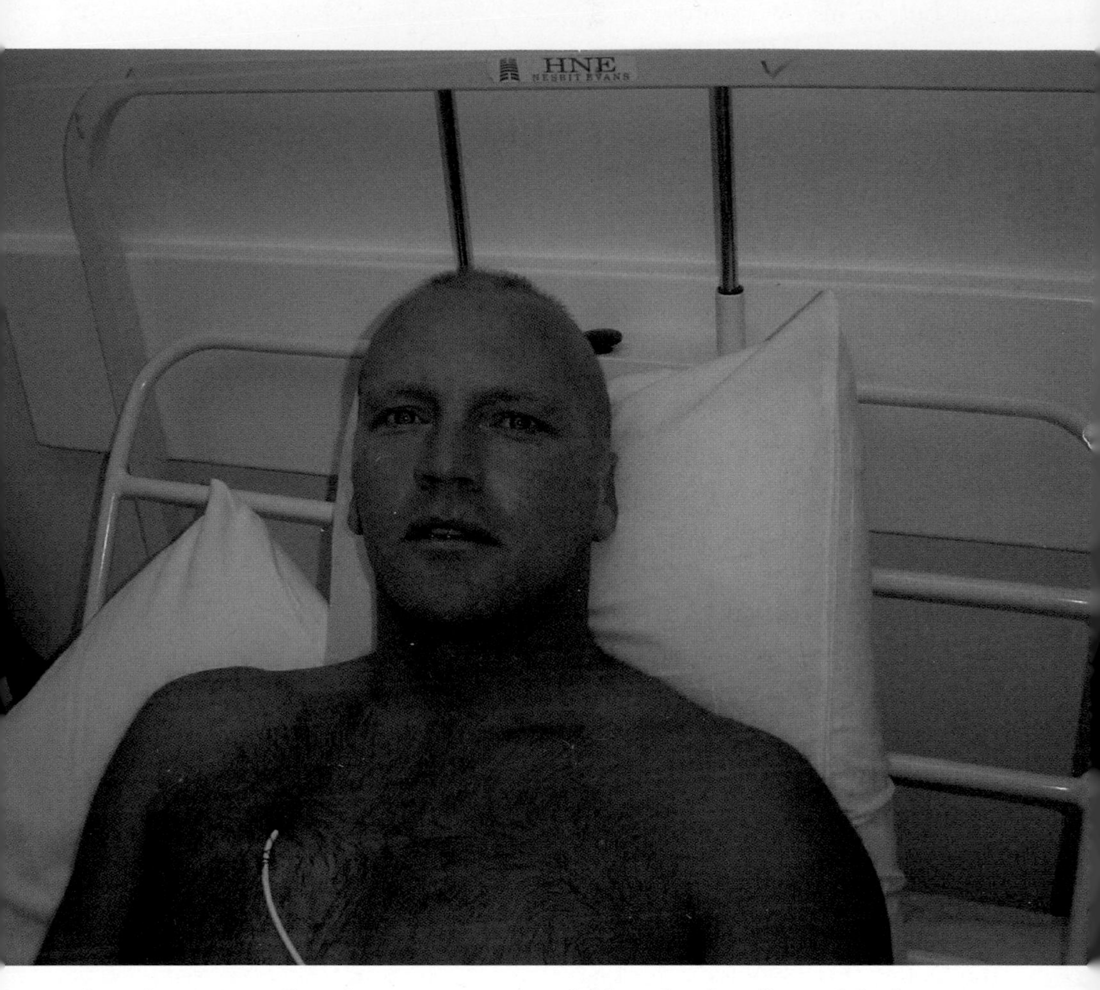

Close shave: I cut all my hair to prepare my children for the effects of the bone marrow transplant. This was just the start of a long road to recovery

that but, in his own words, he created a monster. I don't think he expected the club to take off in the way it did and, although he could handle the characters, I don't think the club as a whole was prepared for life beyond the first couple of seasons in the top flight.

The infrastructure – the training ground, the facilities and the stadium – simply wasn't there, and it was difficult to keep players who were suddenly being thrust into the limelight by playing for England.

Steve always struck me as being someone who was genuine and I never saw a side to him that I didn't like. When I travelled down from Crewe to meet him for the first time, he took me to his house and I met his wife. Although he was very young, he was totally relaxed and in control of his destiny. I admired that and I knew we would be well suited.

At the time, Noades appeared to be keener on the deal than Steve, but they were both very persuasive. They had a very good relationship and, while I don't think they were necessarily good friends, they were the perfect business partnership.

Steve had been schooled in the Manchester United way and he wanted his teams to play with a certain amount of flair. That wasn't really my game, but he knew I had the desire.

I certainly didn't sign for the money because my first contract at Selhurst Park was for £225 a week and, after living in a tiny house in Rochdale worth £20,000, I was suddenly in a house worth three times that amount. I spent my £10,000 signing-on fee on a deposit, but I had the feeling that I wouldn't regret the move. Palace were going places after flirting with the play-offs the previous season and I could see that Coppell had a team in mind that would be good enough to compete for promotion.

Although Steve is naturally an insular character, there is a presence about him that commands respect. He has vulnerabilities, but he rarely shows them because he surrounds himself with strong-minded people. Total transparency and honesty are rare commodities in football. Steve was always up front and if you wanted an answer, you might not like it, but he wasn't afraid of laying his cards on the table. I rarely saw him lose his temper and I always thought his team talks were very effective because they were so simple. He didn't try to complicate what is an essentially simple game and that's important when tensions are running high before a game. At half-time that kind of approach has even more significance because players are tiring, their concentration is not as good as it was before the start of the game, and he understands that.

After Jim Cannon left, he made me captain and that certainly brought us closer together. Until then, I had just been one of the players, but there was a real bond when I became his mouthpiece on the pitch.

He has tinkered with his template at the other clubs he has managed, but I see many similarities with the Reading team that is doing so well in the Premiership. He has filled it with like-minded players who have a point to prove and I am not surprised they have had so much success in their first season in the Premiership.

Wright's decision to leave in September 1991 was the beginning of the break-up. Noades agreed to take part in a Channel 4 documentary charting the rise of black players in English football. He was an obvious person to talk to because Noades and Coppell had been pioneers in that respect. Certainly there were times when I played for Palace when there were more black players in the starting line-up than white, but no-one cared and it didn't matter. All we were interested in was winning football matches and it never bothered me, but Noades created a storm with some controversial comments in the programme.

One of them – 'when you're getting into mid-winter in England, you need a few of the hard white men to carry the artistic black players through' – caused such a stir that some of the Palace lads were threatening to strike. On the face of it, it seemed like an incredible thing to say, but I'm sure it was blown out of all proportion. Noades argued that the editing had been done in such a way that his comments were misconstrued and I can't believe he would say anything like that.

It was a long way from the truth and it's difficult for me to even repeat his comments because they were so ludicrous. To this day,

Noades still has Palace in his heart and I can't believe he would ever say something like that and mean it in that way. In the dressing room, our team was a tight unit, but outside we all had different interests. The black players stayed together off the pitch simply because they had similar tastes – music, clothes, etc. – but there were no other divisions. On a social night out, all the lads got on well and there was never a problem between us. After that Channel 4 documentary, there were splits all over Selhurst Park. It was a turbulent period for the club and it was not helped by Wrighty's decision to leave.

In my entire time at Palace, I never once encountered racism. There were black players and there were white players, but it never bothered me. From a distance, people were trying to stir it up, but there was never a divide among the players. To this day, Ian Wright is still very good friends with Noades. At the time, he lived very close to Ron on an estate in Surrey, and he plays golf once a week with his wife, Novello. For his television programme *Ian Wright's Excellent Adventure*, he even asked Novello to accompany him as he set out to conquer the highest climb in Greenland. It was crazy to suggest that Noades was a racist, but the newspapers gave a lot of coverage to the programme at the time.

Wrighty was the team's talisman and he always offered the team something different. He was an outlet, another avenue for us, but when Arsenal came calling, the temptation was too much. When he first played for Palace in the mid-1980s, he talked of playing in France and there was never any shortage of clubs interested in him. He had a clause in his contract that would allow him to leave if a club came in with a certain amount of money, so when Arsenal offered £2.5m, he could talk to them – but by then it was as good as a done deal.

It ripped the heart out of the club and people lost their enthusiasm when Wright was sold. With him in the team, we were going places. He guaranteed goals and, although they replaced him by spending £1.9m on Marco Gabbiadini from Sunderland, it was an unmitigated disaster. Wright's sale confirmed everyone's suspicions at the club. The players wanted to be competing at the top of English football and we nearly had the team to do it, but Palace could never sustain that success while they sold their best players.

Wright effectively put a gun to Noades' head when Arsenal came calling and very few people could begrudge his big move. I was disappointed that the club let him go, but the moment it happened, I started to think the same way.

6

Troyes-Nancy, 199 km

I'm in the radiation room in Queen Elizabeth Hospital and the tears begin to well up again at the sight of mothers cradling their small children. These children have pale features and bald heads, and they are brave beyond belief, but no-one can say for sure what the future holds.

In playgrounds, in classrooms and in streets all over the country, other young children will be playing with their friends, oblivious to the illness and disease that claims so many precious young lives. These are normal, healthy young children who are enjoying every waking moment. Like my own young daughters, Madison and Georgia, they have seemingly unlimited amounts of energy. They run through the front door when they return home from school and, no sooner have they given their dad a kiss and a cuddle than they are badgering my wife, Julie, for a biscuit or a bar of chocolate.

They scream, they shout and, above all, they smile. It seems like chaos, but for Maddy and Georgia it is all part of growing up and they are oblivious to the other world, where children are desperately ill. Maddy and Georgia shout and shriek through the house, run up and down the stairs; they are there to light up my mornings and greet me with a kiss and a cuddle to mark the start of the day. In a flash, they finish their breakfast, race up the stairs again to dress for school and run out of the door leaving the words 'Bye, Daddy' ringing in my ears for the rest of the day.

Sometimes I stand at the window, clasping my mug of tea, and watch them climb into my wife's car before she drives them to school. On other days, I offer to make the short run up the road and drop them off at the school gates. Then I sit in my car and watch as they spot their school friends, greeting them with a toothy grin, and run up the path towards the classrooms. Later that day, my wife and I decide which of us will pick up the children from school and that's the rub; my wife and I have that choice. It is not like that here, in the radiation room, where hope is the only thing that parents can hold on to.

Their children are suffering from the caustic effect of the chemotherapy and radiotherapy that has battered their innocent little bodies. They know they are sick, but some don't realise just how sick. Their parents sit in silence; they can only wonder about the suffering that their children are going through.

Along the corridor, in the day room, two elderly ladies attached to a drip watch the world go by. They must be 70 or more and the picture of pain on their shrivelled features tells its own story. They sit there, for hours at a time, while a tube transports chemotherapy into their frail and withered bodies. As the chemical charts its way through their veins, their conversation becomes more laboured and they can no longer fight the effects. From time to time, they summon the strength to look up at the transparent bag that holds the lethal substance, and wonder how much longer they will be there.

Maybe another hour, maybe more. In the end, it all depends on the doctors. They sit back in the deep, comfortable chairs and wait for the bag to release its last drop. When that one is finished, a nurse will walk over, remove the bag and carefully mount another. Then the agonising process begins all over again. They do not make a fuss, they show little emotion – they are accustomed to the grind. Maybe they have only been sitting here for an hour, but they have probably been through the same routine twice a week for the past ten weeks.

They are here alone and I can only speculate as to the reasons why.

Perhaps they have already lost their husbands, perhaps they no longer have a family to support them, or perhaps there is nothing more that can be done. As my eyes wander to the other areas of the room, I can smell the sweet scent of fresh lilies that have been placed in vases to try and ease the pain and the anguish of the patients. It is a nice, thoughtful touch, but here the smiles are few and far between. The walls, freshly coated with a lick of light green paint, are suffocated with posters: 'Find a Cure for Cancer,' says one; 'Living with Leukaemia – Patient Helpline' is another.

At the desk in the middle of the room, the administration staff shuffle papers, retrieve patients' files and field enquiries from the endless stream of people who come in. It is peaceful and only the piercing shrill of the telephones on the nearby wards interrupts the silence. To my right, an elderly man, probably 70 years of age, flicks through a magazine rack that contains a well-thumbed assortment of out-of-date copies of *Hello*, *OK!* or *Vogue*. His movements are deliberate and forced; he will have read most of them before. When he finally makes a decision, it is no more than a token effort. It might help to pass the time of day, but very little of what he reads is likely to register. Occasionally, he looks up from his haze, surveys the room and realises that little has changed since he last looked up, all of five minutes ago.

Beside his chair is a 3-foot-high oxygen tank to assist his breathing while his body reacts to another course of chemotherapy. When that one finishes, another will begin. He is here, like me and everyone else in this room, waiting for a nurse to call his number.

'Forty-three? Number forty-three. Anyone with number forty-three?'

When that call comes, the sunken eyes of people dotted around the room will look up, check their tag and realise that it is not quite their turn. Eventually, someone will mutter a response and then, clutching the hand of their wife, husband, friend or relative, they will pull themselves from their chair and shuffle towards one of the consultants' rooms. To my immediate left, a woman is talking to her husband. They have been sat there for more than an hour. They are holding hands. She is well dressed, wearing a minimal amount of make-up and is radiating health. Her partner, a tall man with glasses, is painfully thin and patently very ill.

I know I am being intrusive, but I cannot help looking at him and each time I notice something different. He is pale, he is shaking violently and then I notice a bead of sweat trickling down his temple. It is early summer, the weather is warm and I am dressed in a casual black shirt, a pair of jeans and some light brown loafers; he is wearing a winter jacket with the zip fastened to the top and his legs are crossed to try and keep in the heat. There is fear written all over his face and, if I was pressed, I would say that he is close to the end of his life.

His movements are painfully slow, everything is awkward, including his conversations with his wife, and he is as weak as a kitten. I was still dazed and confused myself but, as I sat beside my wife at the Queen Elizabeth Hospital, I became more and more curious. Dr Shafeek had spoken of drugs to keep leukaemia at arm's length while I considered my options, but very little of it had registered.

I was still being sent to different departments in different hospitals and it was difficult to assimilate all the information. All I knew was that I was very sick. I couldn't take my eyes off the man sitting next to me and I asked my wife whether I should speak to him. She nodded her approval. He was obviously in some distress, but I eventually found the courage to speak to him.

'Excuse me, I hope you don't mind me asking, but what are you suffering from?'

He turned his head ever so slowly towards me and whispered: 'Hi, I'm Adrian. I've got chronic myeloid leukaemia. I've just had a stem-cell transplant.'

So this is where people come to die.

OO

It is 7 a.m., it is already raining and there is 200 km in front of us. A quick calculation tells me I will be in the saddle for at least eight hours and the thought of turning the pedals is turning my stomach. We usually sit outside for breakfast but, as the menacing black clouds continue to roll over the pretty little courtyard of our quaint hotel in Troyes, we take cover. I could put our start time back by an hour, but I can't stop the rain. It is cold, it is windy, and it looks like it is set in for the day.

After five days on the road and some hard riding behind me, I feel flat, jaded and running on empty. I am concerned that there is not enough in the tank today and one look skywards is enough to darken my mood. I should still be feeling fit, but the weather is wearing me down. When the alarm goes off in the morning, I no longer have the energy to get out of bed; now I press the snooze button. Again. And again. And again. It no longer takes two minutes to shower and change into my lycra; sometimes it is so much effort that I don't shower at all in the mornings.

I usually turn on the TV and watch the Tour highlights on Canal+ first thing for half an hour from the comfort of my bed; now I can't even find the strength to focus my eyes and search around the hotel-room floor for the remote control. Even the sight of Andrea or Hayley pouring me another cup of freshly brewed coffee and handing me a *pain au chocolat* to mark the start of the day is not enough to stir me into action.

The rest of the crew have taken shelter from the driving rain, but we can't delay the start for much longer. Today will be the first real test of climbing in the Tour de France. It will not compare with the climbs that await us when we cross the Alps, the Pyrenees and the Massif Central in the coming days, but it will provide a stern test of my progress. As we leave the hotel, it transpires that there is a 200-euro discrepancy in the bill, but, at this time of the morning, it isn't even a toss-up between adding to the fatigue by having an argument in our pathetic French or handing over the cash.

'Just give them the money, Neil.'

'What? This isn't right – they have charged us far too much.'

'Just pay it!'

It is a day for rain-capes, but they can only offer a temporary reprieve. Within minutes, I will be soaked through to the skin. My fingerless gloves offer little protection against the cold and my shoes will be saturated by the continual spray. And then, as the back wheel rotates along the road, it will shoot an endless stream of rainwater up my back and it will seep down my backside. Lovely. No-one wants to ride in weather like this. Certainly not me. Even when there is a temporary respite from the rain, the wind snaps against my face and rattles through my fragile frame.

A change of clothes halfway through the day fails to rekindle my enthusiasm and the thought of the four climbs in front of me sits uneasily. Although they are short and sharp – the longest is 3.2 km – I know I will suffer. I love the descents, but the rain is insufferable. What a way to celebrate the second anniversary of my diagnosis.

OO

According to the statistics, there is a 1:100,000 chance of being diagnosed with chronic myeloid leukaemia (CML). On 4 July 2003, in a consultant's room in Redditch Hospital on the outskirts of Birmingham, I became one of those statistics. I had pretty much known, since my life fell apart in Dr Taylor's surgery the previous evening, that I had leukaemia, but this was the confirmation. Something, somewhere, goes wrong with the DNA in the stem cells and the different abnormalities cause different types of leukaemia. Julie and I sat holding hands in Dr Shafeek's room and revisited the devastation of the previous evening.

That night, I cried into my wife's arms for several hours. We had already learned so much but, in reality, we knew so little. Around 50 per cent of leukaemia sufferers are detected by a routine blood test and the rest as the result of booking an appointment with the doctor. By the time I arrived to see Dr Shafeek in Redditch my diagnosis was a formality. Of far more importance was determining which stage of the illness I was in. There are several forms of leukaemia; there is an adult form – such as acute lymphatic leukaemia, chronic lymphosis leukaemia or acute myeloid leukaemia – and there is also the type that children are susceptible to.

While the success rates for children have been transformed

through highly effective treatments, adults rarely have the same chance to make a full recovery. CML differs from other types of leukaemia because it replicates so many white blood cells that infection is not the dominant feature. With other forms of the illness, such as acute myeloid leukaemia, there is not only a high number of white blood cells, but also a problem with their ability to divide into red blood cells or platelets. Eventually, the bone marrow will fill up with the cells, which can't properly mature, and this eventually leads to bone-marrow failure.

Dr Shafeek didn't beat about the bush. It's black or white and matter of fact. They save the compassion for your family. Every day, the doctors treat people like me and their job is to save lives, not listen to sob stories. His assessment was brutal. The disease has three stages – chronic, accelerated and blastic – and the earlier it is diagnosed, the higher the chance of survival. There are several types of leukaemia and mine – CML – is one of the most distinctive. As I listened to Dr Shafeek's analysis of my condition, I began to realise that I had been suffering for quite some time. He explained that leukaemia is the result of a break between chromosome 9 and chromosome 22.

Julie and I sat there, barely able to accept the situation, let alone understand it. We were struggling to comprehend what he meant. I'd like to be able to say that I absorbed all the information that day, but when someone tells you that you have a life-threatening illness, the only thing you want to know is: 'That's all very well, but am I going to live?'

As Dr Shafeek gave Julie and me a crash-course in chronic myeloid leukaemia, we sat holding hands, a pair of blubbering wrecks. The break in the chromosome causes an abnormal gene which researchers refer to as the 'Philadelphia chromosome', after the city where the breakthrough was first made, to populate the bone marrow. That creates a new gene – 'bcr:abl' – which has the capacity to replicate the number of cells in the body. Dr Shafeek likened it to someone pressing down on a car's accelerator. The effect was a massive replication of white blood cells – which are primarily responsible for fighting infection – and that was the principal reason why I was often drenched in sweat.

My high blood count meant that the white cells often ended up in my spleen, which explained why it had become so sore and swollen over the past few months. Red cells carry oxygen around the body and, because they were being suppressed by the large numbers of white cells in my system, I was frail, pale and anaemic.

White cells are primarily responsible for fighting infections; without them, there is a higher risk of illness and that can prove fatal. Stem cells also have platelets, to stop cuts, bleeding and bruising. After the confusion of the previous day, Dr Shafeek's analysis started to make sense, but he was still not sure which stage the disease was in. The incubation of the disease can be very long and some people have it for months before they start to feel unwell. If I hadn't done anything about it, almost certainly I would be dead within three to five years.

My symptoms – night sweats, nausea and tiredness – suggested that I might still be in the first stage and, although I'm not deeply religious, I've never prayed for something so much in my life. The chronic stage is fairly indolent, but somewhere between one and five years, the disease would become more active.

That is when it would move into the accelerated phase and it would be much harder for the doctors to control my blood count. If I reached this stage, it would only be another six months or a year before I reached blastic and then I would be virtually untreatable. The third phase of CML is terminal and Dr Shafeek told me that I was unlikely to live for more than two or three months if the disease reached that stage.

We sat in a draughty hospital corridor while I waited to be called in for a blood test to establish the history of the disease. By the time I was taken in for a lumbar puncture, the pain inside my mind was so intense that I even passed up the offer of an anaesthetic. Julie couldn't bear to watch but I could hardly feel a thing as Dr Shafeek skewered the huge, hollow corkscrew into my back. As they finally began to unwind the lumbar puncture, I could feel the fluid draining out of the gaping hole in the base of my spine. It was horrific, but by then I was in another place. The blood tests the previous day had confirmed that I was suffering from leukaemia, but the spinal tap is designed to give the experts a more accurate reading.

By taking a bone-marrow sample, they would be able to determine how many leukaemia cells were active. The bone marrow usually contains a high number of fat cells, but with CML patients there is very little fat present and the bone marrow is usually filled with leukaemia cells. I didn't have to wait long for the results. They told me that the blood count for a normal, healthy person should be somewhere between 4 and 10. Mine was 237.

OO

No-one knows why I got leukaemia. It's just bad luck, a break in the Philadelphia chromosome, and then the chances of survival are in the delicate hands of the surgeons who commit their lives to finding a cure. There is a link with high doses of radiation and there had been a large number of reported cases among the survivors of the atomic bombs that were dropped on Nagasaki and Hiroshima at the end of the Second World War.

That is when I began to question whether the hospital scans that I was sent for throughout my playing career had anything to do with it. I had 27 operations to my knees, legs, ankles and back during my football career, and was sent for hundreds of scans in hospitals to determine the extent of my injuries. I began to think that perhaps the radiation from all the x-ray rooms was partly responsible, but I will never know.

Research shows that there is no apparent link with family members who have been diagnosed with the disease and, in any case, there was no-one in my immediate family who had suffered from it. What they do know is that the risk of being diagnosed with the disease increases with age. The average age of a leukaemia patient is 50 and, as the years progress, the condition becomes more difficult to treat. Now I was being told that I could die: the natural history of the disease means that if I did not take drugs to keep the leukaemia from progressing into the accelerated phase, I would most likely be dead within three years.

The short-term treatments are highly effective, but the majority of adults still die from the disease. Even now, the statistics still frighten the life out of me. In the UK alone, 750 people will be diagnosed with chronic myeloid leukaemia each year and it is the biggest cancer killer among teenagers to 35-year-olds.

That afternoon, I met Professor Charlie Craddock, an expert in leukaemia treatment, for the first time. He told me that the short-term goal was to keep me in the chronic phase while I considered the various options open to me. They were fairly limited. A new drug, Glivec, had just come onto the market and shown that it could change the natural history of the disease. But there were no guarantees. It is a target therapy drug and works by disabling the abnormal bcr:abl gene. Glivec had produced excellent results during clinical trials in the United States, and in many cases it helped to control the disease and keep blood counts normal. Professor Craddock referred to Glivec as 'magic bullets' and it was fairly evident that it was the only realistic alternative to a stem-cell transplant.

Glivec would prolong my life, but it did not offer a cure: in 90 per cent of cases, the doctors would still be able to detect some leukaemia. It would be a problem, though, if I did not respond to the treatment because then nothing can be done. Even if I responded well to Glivec it was such a new drug that the long-term results were unknown. I wasn't sure if I wanted to take a drug for the rest of my natural life and I could see there were concerns over the potential side-effects. The alternative was a stem-cell transplant, but that depended on factors outside of my control. They would have to find a suitable match and, even then, the procedure is fraught with difficulties. While the transplant itself is a relatively simple procedure, the course of chemotherapy and irradiation treatment building up to it is so potent that it can kill. The more they give you, the more leukaemia cells they kill, but they have to limit the amount because otherwise it starts to attack the normal bone-marrow cells.

The majority of people do not have the choice of a bone-marrow transplant and, even when they do, there are no guarantees of survival. If I had a stem-cell transplant, radiation treatment would wipe out my existing cells and they would be replaced by cells from a donor. If I could find a bone-marrow match from a member of my family, a stem-cell transplant would give me a 70 per cent chance of living for the next five years. The transplant raised the stakes, but it would give me a better chance of survival in the long term. It could damage my heart, though, and there were other possible side-effects.

For example, graft-versus-host disease (GVHD) occurs when the immune system that has been transplanted from the donor recognises the patient's skin, liver, mouth or eyes as foreign and mounts an inflammatory reaction. In the first three months following the transplant there would be a significant risk. Jaundice can set in, the risks of diarrhoea are high and rashes are commonplace. There is an increased risk of cataracts, an under-active thyroid gland, the possibility of secondary tumours in the skin or mouth, problems with joints and muscles, and the chance of a relapse.

It was enough for me to be thinking about. Everything seemed to be based around statistics. Around 50 per cent of people who have a stem-cell transplant will suffer GVHD and in 10 per cent of those cases it will prove fatal. I was fortunate to even have that glimmer of hope. The radiation treatment that precedes the stem-cell transplant is so dangerous that the doctors will not treat people over the age of 50.

If possible, I wanted the chance to be cured. I wanted to take the bull by the horns and say 'bring it on'. The treatment would make me infertile, but Julie and I already had two wonderful children and we had no plans to extend our family.

Although there was a 30 per cent chance that the stem-cell transplant could kill me, it also represented the best chance of killing off the leukaemia cells. I was fortunate that I was 40. Another ten years down the line and a transplant would not be an option.

If I could find a suitable match, I would be in hospital for around four weeks. I would spend a week having radiation treatment, another two weeks waiting for my blood count to return to normal and then another week responding to the treatment. It was fraught with dangers. Straight after the transplant, my mouth would be very sore because all the cells would have been wiped out through the chemotherapy and radiation treatment. I would feel sick, I would have stomach cramps and I would lose my hair. I would feel rough – as if I had been beaten up – but this was a chance of survival.

'Go home and have a think about it. You can always put off the decision for a while,' said Professor Craddock.

'OK, thanks.'

'There is no rush. Book an appointment for a couple of a weeks' time and we'll go from there.'

'OK.'

'And while you're thinking about it, take these four times a day.'

7

Lunéville-Karlsruhe, 228.5 km

There is some kind of mystical, hidden charm about the Tour de France that ensures its enduring quality. The wondrous sight of the huge roadside support as the *peloton* speeds through French villages is part of its attraction and there is a certain romance about racing. That allure has turned the Tour into one of the biggest sporting attractions in the world and it seems a shame that the organisers sacrifice some of that magnetism for the sake of making money.

The route is planned several years in advance of the annual event and the towns lobby the Tour organisers for the right to host a stage. It is big business, because there is so much prestige and publicity associated with being an official Tour town, and the local councils pay big bucks to secure a stage. Although the Tour was once ridden exclusively in France, the organisers dip into other countries from time to time in order to spread its global appeal. England has previously hosted stages, so have Ireland, Holland, Luxembourg, Belgium, Germany and Spain.

In 2007, the Tour starts in London with an 8 km Prologue in the city centre before heading into the Kent countryside for Stage One, crossing via the Channel Tunnel and heading into France. It is thought to have cost the British government more than £1m to secure the two stages, as part of a drive to encourage more people to ride bikes, but the publicity that will be generated and the estimated extra £50m generated for the economy ensure that it will be money well spent. I can't say that after our journey into Germany.

The roads leading out of France were set against a backdrop of mountains around 200 km away in the Alsace region and we enjoyed a steady morning's work towards the border. There was a tingle of excitement as we headed towards Germany because some of the French towns along the route were taking their involvement very seriously. Flower beds had been arranged in such a way that they resembled the *peloton* and banners greeted us along the way. Although the professionals will speed through in a matter of seconds, I had a little while longer for it all to sink in. Bicycles – from old bone-shakers to more modern racers – were strategically placed on roundabouts, some were hanging from trees and others were sitting on the side of the road. It had a romantic edge to it and we were all buzzing as we flew toward the German border.

We continued the journey towards Germany with a 3.5 km climb through the Black Forest and a descent that led us to within an hour of the border. I was carefree whenever the team rolled over the top of a summit and, despite the relatively short drop to the foot of the Col du Hantz, I recorded 65 kph on the way down. It was some way short of the 100 kph that would be expected of the professionals, but I was still learning my trade and there would be plenty more opportunities to close in on their speeds when we reached the Alps and Pyrenees.

That cheery outlook did not last for long because, the moment we crossed the Seine via a wonderful old railway bridge, the day soured. The quaint French signage that prevailed earlier in the day was swapped for something that was eminently German. For reasons best known to themselves, they diverted the Tour from the traditional rambling roads that have been associated with it for more than 100 years and sent us towards Karlsruhe on an autobahn. There was no warning of this. A single road became a dual carriageway and, as we cycled over the crest of a steady climb, we were suddenly accompanied by an unlimited supply of BMW and Mercedes drivers flashing past us at 120 kph.

The German drivers sounded their horns from the moment they spotted us on the horizon until they were several hundred metres down the road. It caused a symphony of different sounds from passing motorists and we eventually stopped on the hard shoulder wondering what to do. Although this was undoubtedly the Tour route, it was no place for five cyclists. It was infuriating and, after six hours in the saddle, tempers were beginning to fray. Robbie called the support crew from a mobile phone.

'Haynesy, are we on the right road?'

'Yep, you're definitely on the right road.'

'Are you sure?'

'Yes – just keep going.'

'What, on this road?'

'Yes, that's where the route has taken us.'

'But this is a fucking autobahn!'

Neil wanted to continue riding the official Tour route all the way into Karlsruhe but Ian, Matt and I were concerned by the dangers. It was like being stuck on the M1 somewhere between Luton and Hemel Hempstead but, for once, luck was on our side. As we eased down the hard shoulder, we spotted another cyclist on the other side of the barriers. We closed in on him and realised that there was a cycle path running right alongside the autobahn that took us all the way into the town centre.

OO

Riding a bike down an autobahn is bad, but it doesn't compare with chemotherapy. From the moment Professor Craddock sat me down and explained my options, I knew that I would have a stem-cell transplant if I could find a suitable bone-marrow donor. My sister, Kay, was sent for blood tests four days after I was diagnosed, but it would take eight weeks before we got the results.

There was only a 20 per cent chance of her being a suitable match and I knew that if she wasn't, my hopes of surviving would dramatically recede. While I waited for the results, Charlie put me on a course of chemotherapy to reduce the large number of white blood cells that I was producing. At first I was given Hydroxyurea, a pink and green capsule that I swallowed four times a day. I didn't even realise it was chemotherapy until I read the box a week later. Although chemo made me more prone to infection, it was essential to keep the disease in its first stage. Within a few days, the number of white blood cells decreased and Charlie expected that my levels would return to normal within a month.

At first, I didn't feel any different. The tablets worked well and, although I occasionally felt tired and a little nauseous, I generally felt good. In fact, I responded to it too well and there were concerns that my immune system might be at risk if I continued taking it – one of the hazardous side-effects of Hydroxyurea. I was moved on to Interferon, a far more potent drug, and that is when I really felt the effects of the chemicals circulating around my body. Although Interferon is gradually being phased out because it is such a toxic drug, it is still used to treat people with kidney cancer, malignant melanomas and various strains of leukaemia. It stimulates the immune system, but it had a dramatic effect on my lifestyle. While I was taking Hydroxyurea, I still led an active life but that changed when I began taking Interferon.

The syringes full of Interferon were kept in a package in the fridge and, within days, when it began to wear me down, I would open the door each morning and greet them with the words 'Come on then, you little bastards.'

I administered it by injecting the solution into my stomach each day and then waited for the effects to kick in. I could barely count to ten.

I hated injecting myself each morning, and again each night, but I knew it was part of a long-term strategy. From August until the end of September 2003, I injected myself with Interferon twice a day, every day, and my condition deteriorated with every passing hour. Sometimes I could barely look at the boxes when I opened the fridge door, but I knew that they were for a purpose. It is a severe substance and I would initially feel rough before the nausea, the muscular aches and the soreness set in. I felt terrible. But the thing that kept me going was the prospect of finding a suitable bone-marrow match.

The eight-week wait for Kay's results to come back were among the most difficult of the whole ordeal because so much rested on them. I knew that I would have a transplant if there was a chance. That decision was down to me, but people would occasionally put seeds of doubt in my mind. One night, Julie and I held a dinner party for our friends Caron and Andy Cooke. Caron is a micro-biologist and as the red wine flowed, the conversation took a twist.

'Geoff, it's like having Domestos running through your veins,' she was saying.

She spoke with such authority that it sent fear flooding through my body, but I was still determined to go through with it.

'Geoff, do your research. There are alternatives. You don't know what you are going to put your body through.'

I had already been through enough and I knew that the worst was still to come, but I remained resolute. Her concerns came at a time when friends were putting negative thoughts in my mind and I would lie awake at night wondering what it would be like to die. The transplant didn't offer any guarantees and people were always reminding me of that. If I went down the road of taking Glivec, I could have a certain quality of life, but the downside was that the doctors could not offer a cure.

Maddy and Georgia had been wonderful and, although Julie and I told them I had leukaemia, they were coping brilliantly. I don't think they really understood, but we told them as much as we thought they could manage. We wanted to wrap them up in cotton wool when I was diagnosed.

Maddy was ten at the time, but she was incredibly grown up about it all. She is a very lovable kid, but she rarely showed her emotions. She is a lot different to our younger daughter, Georgia.

Maddy is a quick runner, but she doesn't have a competitive bone in her body. At school sports days she leads from the front, but then waits for the others to catch her up. That is the difference between her and Georgia. Georgia has inherited my competitive edge and if she takes part in something, she wants to win.

I know some people cannot tell their children, but we wanted to be up-front and honest with them from the very beginning. We told them that I had a blood disease and that it meant I would be in hospital for some time, but it was difficult to explain the precise nature of the disease because Julie and I weren't even sure ourselves.

They knew that I was very ill, but they would act normally around me. The nature of the disease was brought home to them one night when we sat watching television. Central TV came to our clothes shop in Birmingham to interview me and they flagged up the feature with the words that 'ex-England international footballer Geoff Thomas is fighting cancer'. We had never mentioned the word 'cancer' because of all the connotations. The girls sat, transfixed by the television interview and then Georgia turned to me, with tears in her eyes, and said: 'Daddy, I didn't know you had cancer.'

OO

I was in the Mailbox Shopping Centre when my mobile phone started ringing. It was Professor Craddock.

'Hi Geoff, how are you?'

'I'm fine, thanks. You?'

'I'm very well, Geoff. Are you alone? Are you OK to talk?'

I stepped out of the shop I was in at the time and went out to the mezzanine.

'Yes, I am. I'm fine. Go ahead.'

'Geoff, I have some news for you.'

There was tension in his voice. He always had a calm, relaxed air about him, but I could tell that he was excited about something.

'Is it good news?'

'Well, I would like to think so.'

There was a momentary pause before he said: 'Kay's blood test results are back. She is a very, very good match.'

I had not cried since 4 July, the day of my official diagnosis, but there were tears in my eyes as he told me that she was suitable for a stem-cell transplant. He briefly outlined the procedure and the ramifications, but I was already in another place. This is what I was hoping for and now I knew exactly where I was in my life. I knew there was a chance that it would not be successful, but I preferred to dwell on the positive: there was now a 70 per cent chance that I would live. My mind had long since been made up. To me, it was an opportunity that I had to take.

There was another bonus because, when I went to see Charlie, he told me, would need to be clear of chemotherapy for three months before I had the transplant. It meant that I had injected my last dose of Interferon. There would be no more early morning greetings and there would be no late-night visits to the fridge for the final injection of the day. I was concerned that my white cell count would rise, but I was assured that it would not be at a dangerous level by the time I went into hospital.

With CML, there is a constant threat that the disease will suddenly fly out of control, but Charlie was confident that I would still be in the first stage – chronic – when I went into hospital in January.

When someone tells you that your life is in the balance, everything else pales into insignificance. Julie and I closed our retail clothing business in Birmingham in order to concentrate on beating the illness. It broke our hearts to close the shops, but we had been under a lot of stress. I had a long interest in the fashion industry and it made sense, when I was approached during my career at Wolves, to invest in a clothing business. I wanted to explore the possibility of another career when my football career finished and this was an opportunity. Although I harboured ambitions to stay in the game, perhaps as a coach or a manager, it would mean a lot of upheaval for my family if I changed jobs.

We were settled in Birmingham and we had two young daughters – both happy at their schools – to consider. That made me look at other options and Julie and I were committed to building a portfolio of designer clothes shops in the Midlands. Looking back, I invested without too much thought because the shops I poured money into didn't perform at the level required to remain solvent. I opened my first shop in 1996, two years after I signed for Wolves; by the time I was diagnosed, we had three.

It was a real battle to keep them afloat and, because the bills were so colossal, we were seeing a lot of money disappear. Although I earned a decent income from football, I didn't earn enough to sustain the lifestyle that my family had become accustomed to during my career. The three shops were another drain on my already dwindling resources. When I was diagnosed, the first thing I did was check my insurance policies. I wasn't sure whether I would be covered because I had reduced my premium when I stopped playing. At Wolves, I was paying around £1,000 a month, but I didn't have that kind of money coming into the house when I retired. Instead, I reduced the payments to a more manageable level – around £250 – but it is just as well that I kept the policy.

The first thing I did when I got back home from Dr Taylor's was to fish out the documents and it was an enormous relief when I scanned through the list of illnesses covered and found that leukaemia was one of them. Until I saw the money from the insurance company, I still didn't really believe that I was properly covered. I had huge financial responsibilities to our businesses and it was a very traumatic time.

When we knew we had that money coming in, it was a massive relief. By this time, I was taking legal advice on the business and, given the circumstances that we were in, I had to be careful that we were not running an insolvent partnership.

I poured around £300,000 of my own money into my business when my playing career ended and I haven't got any of it left. Not a penny. I had personal guarantees with the bank but when I was diagnosed with CML, Julie and I knew that the fight was over. Part of me wanted to struggle on, but I also knew that the stress involved in keeping them afloat would affect the odds of me beating the disease. It took several months to dispose of the business but I knew it was the right decision.

By the time Kay's results came back, I was talking regularly to patient support groups by telephone and on the internet. I had made the decision to have a transplant, even though there were some positive stories about Glivec: the fear of the unknown had pushed me away from that path. Although the results for Glivec had been excellent, I knew that once patients slip into the accelerated phase the disease is terminal. If I took Glivec, I had to accept that eventually that could happen to me. It could be as little as six months away or it could be 60 years. No-one knew. Once my blood count was stable, I started to feel better, but the transplant was always nagging away at me.

'Am I doing the right thing?'

I knew that people in the same position as me were very wary about making the decision to have a transplant; but I was so focused on beating the disease that I didn't want it to hang over me – that's why I wanted to go for it. I even compared it to a game of football. If there was a chance of winning, I always wanted to go for it. If it was half-time and we were drawing the match, I didn't want to settle for a point, I wanted all three. My mind was made up but, to this day, Julie still feels that I was selfish when I made the decision to have a transplant. But it had to be my decision. She understood.

I could have had the transplant in December, but Charlie told me to go away for Christmas and New Year. Julie and I knew that time was running out and we sat down and made a wish-list of all the things we wanted to do in our lives. As an ex-professional footballer I know that I have been given a privileged lifestyle and we were financially independent. But, even though I played in the Premiership with Nottingham Forest for a season, I didn't earn anywhere near the vast sums that are paid now.

My family's future was my priority from the moment Dr Taylor told me I had leukaemia. It was such a relief when the cheque arrived from the insurance company because it meant that Julie and the children would be looked after if the worst came to the worst. It also meant that I could step back for six months and spend some precious moments with my wife and family.

If there was an opportunity to do something, we would just do it.

We drove to Cornwall in our convertible just after the school holidays in September. We had always taken our holidays abroad, but some friends recommended Bedruthan Steps, a National Trust area deep in the countryside, and we spent four wonderful days there. Leukaemia had taken over our lives, but we never talked about the worst-case scenario. Instead, we concentrated on enjoying ourselves. We took the children to France but they hated EuroDisney so much that we moved to Paris ahead of schedule.

We took them round the sights, sat in the cafés that line the Champs-Élysées and showed them what life in Paris is all about. In that six months, everything became so much sharper, so much more real. I would drive around in my car with the roof down in the middle of winter and the music on full blast. I would pull up at a set of traffic lights and there would be someone making a comment in my direction because they thought I was being ostentatious, but I was oblivious to it all. Friends would see me in the street and we would stop for a chat. They would tilt their head, frown with concern and ask: 'How are you, Geoff?'

I'd just throw it back: 'I'm fine, thanks. How are you?'

It wasn't all plain sailing before my stem-cell transplant because we had another family crisis in October. My mother, Renee, was staying with us for a few days when she had the classic symptoms of a heart attack. She has a history of angina so when she felt numbness in her arm, Julie phoned for an ambulance immediately. At the time, I was at Redditch Hospital for different reasons. Her condition seemed to be under control to begin with so I left the hospital for a business meeting in Birmingham. As I was getting changed, I received a phone call from the hospital telling me to come back straight away.

They asked if my mother had any close family apart from me and, when I asked the nurse what she meant, she warned me that my mother might not make it through the night.

Incredibly, she pulled through and she looked a hundred times better the following day. 'Look at you, you attention-seeker,' I said.

Fortunately, she made a recovery, but it was quite surreal being back at the hospital where I was diagnosed. We even bumped into Dr Shafeek.

'Hi, Geoff, how's things?'

'I'm fine, but my mother's on her death bed ...'

When she was finally released from hospital, I took her out in my car in November. I had the roof down, we were flying through the lanes and we had Frank Sinatra on singing 'My Way' at full blast.

It was a hectic period and it was hard to keep my emotions in check at times. I had a date looming at Selhurst Park on 13 December – when I had been asked to lead out the Palace and Forest teams for their league fixture – and I wondered whether it would be the last time I ever went to the ground.

I remember standing in the tunnel next to the Forest skipper Des Walker before the referee emerged from his dressing room. I was as nervous as I have ever been at a football match. It felt strange to lead the teams onto the pitch in a suit, but I can't forget the reception I received from both sets of supporters that day. It filled me with genuine warmth and I glow when I shut my eyes and listen to the echoes of the supporters singing 'There's only one Geoff Thomas' inside the stadium. I was an honest professional and I think the Palace and Forest fans recognised that. I didn't want sympathy, but it really was some feeling to be stood in the centre circle with an entire stadium wishing me well.

Of course I had split loyalties that day, but Andy Johnson scored after 12 minutes to win the game for Palace and it started a run that ultimately led to the club being promoted back to the Premiership. That was a special day at Selhurst Park and it eclipses everything that happened there during my playing career. That day gave me the chance to say thank you to the supporters from both teams and show my appreciation to the two clubs. I didn't know if I would ever be back, but it put me in good spirits as I prepared to take Julie, Maddy and Georgia away for Christmas.

We went to Mauritius for two weeks over Christmas and New Year and we had a wonderful time. It was always in the back of my mind that it could be the last Christmas I would spend with my family and I wanted to make it really special for them.

Although most people stay on the east coast of the island, we chose to stay on the less commercial west coast in the Hilton. It was a fantastic resort and I was determined to make the most of it. Time was running out before my scheduled bone-marrow transplant in January and, although there were a lot of things going through my head, I wanted to enjoy our two-week break. We spent the first few days alone, but then I struck up a conversation with a guy I met by the pool one day. He was on a sun-lounger reading a book about Manchester City and we got talking.

He introduced himself as Rob Frais. He was a big Jewish guy and we hit it off straight away. We talked a lot about my illness and then we started talking about football. He had played to quite a high standard and was telling me about some of the games he had been involved in when he was younger. He was obviously quite a good player and then he turned to me and said: 'What about you, Geoff – do you play?'

After that, we would spend time with him and his wife and we spent New Year's Eve together. That holiday in Mauritius brought my illness into focus. Seeing Georgia and Madison's faces on Christmas Day was a magical experience and it was enhanced because we were so far away from home. They couldn't believe how Father Christmas had got all those presents to Mauritius and, when I saw the credit card bill, neither could I. I think my senses were heightened during those two weeks and I wouldn't have swapped it for anything.

When we returned home, I did an interview with the respected Radio Five reporter Pat Murphy. After we told him all the things we had done in the last six months, he turned round and said: 'I suppose you're just buying memories really.' It was a touching thing to say and it certainly brought everything home. Julie and I didn't know what the future held and I was within days of going into the Queen Elizabeth for my stem-cell transplant. Charlie had told me that I would lose a lot of weight when I had my transplant so I deliberately over-indulged. By the time we came back to England, I was tipping the scales at more than 15 stone, but I wasn't concerned. Julie even said she quite fancied me, which made a nice change.

I was due to go into hospital on 19 January 2004. I shaved off my hair so that the children would be prepared for the effects of my treatment.

8

Pforzheim-Gérardmer, 231.5 km

So this is it, Geoff. Kill or cure. These are the four weeks in front of me that will either save my life or close the curtains on it. It is 5.45 a.m. and I know it will be a difficult morning. I don't have to be at the hospital until 9 a.m. but already I am nervously pacing around the house. My bags are packed in preparation for the four weeks that I will spend in isolation at the Queen Elizabeth and, even though I have already checked them several times, I check them again. And again. And again.

I have packed Maddy and Georgia's PlayStation, a portable television and several books, but I have ignored the hospital's advice to bring some pyjamas. I have never worn them and, even though I'm likely to be confined to my bed for several weeks, I am not about to start now. It chokes me when I say goodbye to my children and, when I turn to the two mothers in my life – Renee and Julie's mum, Irene, – I can't say for sure whether I will ever be back. I have already been warned that the next four weeks will leave me so weak that on some days I won't even make it out of bed.

The consultants told me that my body would be battered by total body irradiation to kill off the cancerous cells, but I can't begin to imagine how that will feel. This is bad enough. But what could be worse than leaving your house and not knowing whether it will be the last time you ever see your children?

In around a week, they will harvest the stem cells from my sister, Kay, and decant them into my body through a Hickman line that will be attached to my chest.

Then all we can do is hope. That is what it has come down to.

OO

It was 9 a.m. by the time Julie and I found the Bone Marrow Transplant unit at the Queen Elizabeth. We had fears, but I also knew that the long wait to begin my fight against leukaemia was over. The reality hit home the moment I signed the yellow consent forms that allow the doctors and nurses to alter the course of nature and try to save my life. Over the next few weeks, a continuous cocktail of drugs would be decanted into my body and I didn't have to wait long for it to start: within half an hour of my arrival at the hospital, I was sent to have a Hickman line fitted.

Despite the gravity of my situation, I arrived at the hospital in a positive frame of mind. I was determined to beat leukaemia, but I was shocked by the attitude of the porter who took me down to have the Hickman line fitted. Although I still felt perfectly healthy, he insisted that I sat in a wheelchair. I thought it was ridiculous because at that time I was still perfectly capable of walking to the ward myself. He was caught up in hospital protocol but his bedside manner was appalling. I was shocked because I was trying to stay strong and the porter was trying to belittle me. It shook me because I had only been in hospital a matter of hours. In the end, I gave in, sat on the bed and was wheeled down to the unit to have the line fitted.

The device would be used to transport chemotherapy and other drugs into my system over the next few weeks and it was fitted straight into the blood vessels in my chest. The procedure is gruesome, but it meant that the doctors and nurses would not have to keep injecting me with syringes or drips. Instead, they could just feed the drugs straight into my bloodstream. It is relatively straightforward – they would just open up the cap, connect the tube to a syringe, and pump me full of chemicals to prepare me for my stem-cell transplant.

Later that day, I was sent for an appointment with a radiographer. They calculated my body mass to work out how much TBI to administer before the transplant. The procedure is designed to kill off all the bone marrow so that I could no longer produce any cells and prepare my body to receive Kay's stem cells. Radiotherapy would reduce the level of cancer in my body and the more they could give me, the better the chance of the transplant succeeding. The flip side is that TBI (total body irradiation) would leave me without an immune system and my body would be prone to infection for the next few months. That was why I spent so much time in isolation over the coming weeks, because if I picked up anything – even something as innocent as a common cold – it could kill me.

It was a depressing morning. While I was talking to the radiographer, I was warned about the possibility of developing cataracts and tumours as a side-effect of the treatment and it led to a lot of tension between Julie and me. My wife seldom swears, but we were under enormous strain and I told her off when she realised that she didn't have any change for the car park. I knew instantly that I was wrong and I offered to walk her to the car park, but she just turned on her heel and said: 'Fuck off.' I apologised, chased after her and we quickly kissed and made up. It wasn't the time for arguments.

OO

There were signs of a normal day when the nurse brought me cornflakes and a cup of tea the following morning. It didn't last long. I was given a concoction of pills to swallow and, by 8.50 a.m., I was in the radiation room for my first treatment. It had certainly been some time since four pretty young girls had invited me into a darkened room, and things were looking good when they directed me towards a black leather chair in the middle of it. When they told me to remove my trousers before I was strapped into the chair, I really thought my luck was in.

Instead, they left me in the room while a big bright light came on and there was a series of rapid clicking noises. It lasted for seven minutes, then they came back to turn me over so that they could 'bake' the other side of my body. I was happy just to survive the experience. Julie arrived with my mother later that morning and we went to the canteen for a cup of tea. That afternoon I went for some more radiation and, as I got up to leave, the nurses reminded me that I hadn't been 'cooked' on both sides. Damn. I didn't feel too bad until the third day, when I began to feel the effects. I had another double session of radio and, as I listened to the Aston Villa v. Bolton match on the radio, I started to get stomach cramps which had nothing to do with the quality of the football.

The treatment was starting to kick in and, although I was given some medication, I knew that far worse was on its way. I was still waking up early in the mornings and on the fourth day depression really set in. All sorts of questions were flying through my head:

'Should I have let the cancer take its course, which might give me five to ten years, or even less?

'Have I made a mistake?

'Does it get worse than this?'

I watched a documentary on television the week before I came into hospital, about a patient who had taken Glivec instead of having a transplant. He responded well and the programme even showed pictures of him playing football. He was radiating health but there was a sting in the tail at the end of the programme. As the credits rolled, there was a haunting addendum: the poor guy had a relapse shortly after the programme-makers had finished filming and, in a last-ditch effort to save his life, he underwent a transplant. It had no effect and he died a short while later. It terrified me and my mother was straight on the phone questioning the wisdom of a transplant.

Even though I knew the risks, that programme had actually reinforced my decision. It's not in my nature to let things happen and I always wanted to attack the illness. Despite that, I was already losing my strength. I wanted an end to the uncertainty and I was only four days into my treatment. I was feeling down and things were beginning to creep into my mind.

There was a nagging doubt: 'What if I don't make it through this?' I thought about it while I was having my morning blast of radiotherapy and my eyes just started to well up. I wanted to be positive, but my body was so weak that I was struggling to hold on. My attention was no longer there. People would talk to me, but I was in another world – I was a zombie. The nurses smiled sympathetically at me as I walked down for the last dose of radiation.

OO

Whenever one of our support cars was out of sight, it was almost always a cause for concern. We had already ridden 40 km too many so far during the Tour but, until now, our support crew had largely got away with the occasional map-reading mistake. When we didn't see them for a while, it usually meant that they were struggling to work out the route. We were always on their backs because, whenever they weren't sure if we were on the right road, they let us carry on cycling and stayed out of sight. They were surviving on less sleep than us and there were always likely to be mistakes. After our evening meal, we headed to bed, but the rest of the crew planned the following day's carbs and pored over the maps.

Andrea and Hayley were two superstars and they brightened up my days. I don't know how they did it, but they always had a smile on their faces. My two little angels would stay up at night making our snacks for the following day and then they would be up an hour before us in the mornings to prepare our breakfast. They were slaves to the cause but, despite their remarkable efforts, there was no hiding place for the support team during this stage. I thought that the 228.5 km slog into Germany had been bad but it did not compare to the 231.5 km coming out of it. After starting the stage in driving rain at 7 a.m., we struggled to find the right road to lead us out of town.

In previous days, we all converged around one of the Land Rovers to try and work out exactly where we were. Sometimes that involved turning the map the right way up for them. It was frustrating for everyone, but we didn't have the advantage of the roads being closed or the dozens of arrows that are attached to signposts when the Tour inches closer. There are so many souvenir hunters among the legions of supporters who are drawn to the Tour de France every year that the race officials only put up the arrows the day before the race. Although the chances of the *peloton* taking a wrong turn are small, it has happened in other professional races. This was just another kick in the backside to add to the long list of others that had already confronted us.

The crew were tired and so were we, but this time we were so fatigued we simply left them to it. We had only been on the road an hour when they missed a left-hand turn towards France and that was enough for us. As the two support vehicles constantly crossed each other trying to find the correct road, we got off our bikes and sat in the rain waiting for them to find the route. It was a proper sit-down protest and I know that it put them under even more pressure, but we were so tired and cycling in the wrong direction would simply sap more of our precious energy and desire.

Our protest lasted more than half an hour and the crew did little to put our minds at rest. In previous days, they pulled up alongside us and Westie would wind down the window.

'Everything OK, Geoff?'

'Are you sure we're on the right road?'

'Oh, yes, quite sure,' he would say with a satisfied grin and then he would drive off into the distance.

It was a constant theme with Westie because even though Hayley was sat beside him in the car reading the map, we often had to follow them round roundabouts several times before they finally selected the right exit. Sometimes we even went back in the direction we had come from and that would wind us up, but they appeared indifferent to their mistakes.

We were on a relatively straightforward 1.9 km climb which shouldn't have presented any complications as we made our way back towards France. A climb like that should take no more than 15 minutes and the girls were waiting with coffee at the junction around 1 km into the climb by way of apology for a disastrous start to the morning. It was unusual for us to stop at any stage of a climb, but we were so demoralised that we were easily seduced. As we cupped our hands around the mugs, we asked Westie which way we would be heading. To our left, the road continued up the mountain. To the right, there was a beautiful descent through the early morning mist and the promise of some sunshine in the distance. If we made steady progress, we could be through the cloud cover inside an hour and we would be able to enjoy the sun drying out our rain-sodden lycra outfits.

'Westie, where now?'

'That way,' and he pointed to the left with his customary authority.

I was actually laughing at him because he could be so comical. He also spoke with such confidence that it was difficult to challenge him. So we set off.

'Westie, how much left of this climb?'

'Around another kilometre, I would say.'

'Are you sure?'

'Quite sure, Geoff.'

No-one batted an eyelid. We just groaned. We were so cold and tired that we were past the point of caring. Arguing meant spending energy and most of us were already riding on the bare minimum. We left it in their hands. They had sat on that bend for 15 minutes while they waited for us and, with the mood we were in, they would have cross-checked the official Tour route with the road map a hundred times before they sent us to the left.

'Keep going and in about a kilometre, we will be waiting for you there.'

'Are you sure we are going the right way?'

I was actually teasing him because I *knew* he wouldn't dare make a mistake this time.

We set off in the rain and didn't see them again for the best part of an hour. Whenever I climb, I head for another place and I would just keep turning the pedals over until I reached the top. Sometimes I wouldn't even look ahead because it could be so soul-destroying. Today was one of those days. We just pedalled in the rain. It was so cold that our rain-capes were zipped up to cover our ears and we stood out of the saddle, hunching our shoulders to protect our faces, praying for the sun to slip through the clouds. Instead, the rain was bouncing so hard off the surface that it was jumping in the road.

This isn't how it was meant to be. This isn't the Tour. This is torture and this climb is only supposed to be 1.9 km long.

'How much longer?'

'Can't be much further – this must be two km by now.'

When you climb, it is easy to lose track of time. The gradient is the opponent, not the clock, and I simply concentrated on making it to the next switchback before starting the debilitating process of pedalling all over again.

'Westie, what's going on?'

'Don't worry, Geoffrey, it's all in hand.'

'We've been riding up this hill for ever.'

'No, Geoff, I'd say it's about forty-five minutes so far.'

'Well, what's going on – have we ridden too far?'

'Oh, I'd say you've ridden about seven km too far.'

And then he raised the electric window and sped off up the mountain to find somewhere to turn around.

We should have taken that right.

'Westie?'

'Yes, Geoff?'

'Wanker.'

'Thank you, Geoff.'

OO

Matt inadvertently lightened the mood as we made our way out of Germany. It was still raining hard and we had an 80 km stretch in front of us along a busy main road as we made our way to the border. It was absolutely belting it down and we were already riding into a strong headwind. It made sense for us to all ride together and take advantage of what little comfort we could from the draft behind Ian's back wheel.

The route turned south and there should have been some excitement because, in a couple of days' time, we would be taking on the

Alpine climbs. Instead, we just wanted to get through the day. The road was slimy and we just tucked in behind Ian for some protection. Each time a car passed us, it would spray water directly into our faces and there seemed to be no end in sight.

The road was busy so poor Matt, still nervous of riding on the roads after his brush with death on Stage Two, decided to ride on a cycle path that was off the main drag. 'Over here,' he was shouting, but he was having to pedal like crazy to keep up with us. We looked at him as if he was mad. To keep up with our four-man train, he was having to pedal into a fierce headwind in the freezing-cold rain, but he couldn't see the advantage of riding with us.

Poor Matt was riding manically to keep up with our paceline. It kept our spirits up to watch him cycling alone, but he eventually saw sense and rejoined the pack. We still had the 16.8 km climb to the top of the Col de la Schlucht to overcome, but little could stand in my way after this experience. It was a second-category col and, although the average gradient was only 4.4 per cent, it was 7.30 p.m. by the time we reached the 1,139-metre peak 13 hours after we started out. It took another hour to reach Gérardmer and there was a chill in the air as we made our way down the other side of the mountain. Then again, it was nothing compared to the chill that our support crew received that evening.

OO

By the time Kay arrived at the hospital for the transplant procedure, I was in another world. The radiotherapy left me struggling to even sit up in bed and holding a conversation for more than a minute would sap my strength. There were concerns among the medical staff that Kay was not producing enough stem cells and she was given some drugs to take overnight to try and stimulate growth. She had been a nervous wreck in the months leading up to the transplant and she had only produced a tenth of the 7 ml that would be needed. The outlook was far more positive the following day and the doctors decided to proceed. The cells were distilled through the Hickman line and, as promised, it was a relatively painless procedure.

Although the doctors explain the procedure in great detail, no-one can be fully prepared for what comes next. Over the next few weeks, Kay's stem cells would kick in and take over my immune system. It left me battered, but not beaten. The drugs were so debilitating that there were days when I was so weak that I couldn't even lift my withered frame out of bed. I used to look forward to my cornflakes and a cup of tea first thing in the morning. Not any more. I didn't even look forward to waking up in the morning, but at least it told me that I was still alive.

I was woken by nurses handing me a cup of water and all manner of tablets to take. My morning diet consisted of 200 mg of an anti-viral drug called Aciclovir; 50 mg of Fluconazole (anti-fungal); 480 mg of Septrin (antibiotic); 30 mg of Lansoprazole (to settle my stomach); 6 mg of Nozinan Levomepromazine (anti-sickness); two tablets of magnesium oxide; 100 mg of Cyclosporin (anti-rejection); and 250 mg of penicillin. It left me feeling constantly sick and I was doped to the gills on morphine to try and mask the pain.

Undoubtedly, there were times when I wondered whether I would be able to make it through. Some days I felt better and then, on others, I would be given an almighty smack in the face. Someone told me to think of chemotherapy as a friend and it will look after you, but it is some friend. I would look in the mirror after being sick for the tenth time that day, when I just couldn't be sick any more. My face was dry and I was gaunt – I couldn't even recognise myself. I thought I looked about 90 years old. It scared the hell out of me.

9

Gérardmer-Mulhouse, 171 km

I pushed myself hard at first. Too hard. The doctors wouldn't let me out of the isolation unit until I had weaned myself off morphine, but I was determined to return home as quickly as possible. Morphine is another part of the treatment and I was warned how difficult it would be to wean myself off it. I just didn't realise how difficult. Although it is principally used to mask pain, it has dramatic effects on the rest of the body. My mouth became sore and sensitive through the radiation treatment, but the drug sent me into a trance-like state. Sometimes I didn't know what day of the week it was, or even know the time. I could sit in my hospital bed for hours and I wouldn't even be able to move. I was oblivious to the pain and had little recollection of the events of the past few days.

On one occasion I lost about four hours when I sat in my room in the isolation unit. I had one leg stretched out on the bed but I was lost in my own little world and I couldn't do anything about it. I knew I wanted to move but somehow I couldn't. It was unnerving, but there were positive effects. Without the drug, I would have been in enormous discomfort as my body reacted to Kay's stem cells. Instead, I had a pleasant feeling of euphoria, and while I was taking morphine I didn't have any fears or anxiety about the future. Instead, I sat in bed with the television on and life became a blur. Julie came to visit two or three times a day, but I didn't have the attention span for a conversation.

She could ask me questions about something we had talked about the previous day, and I would look at her quizzically.

'You what, love?'

These days she just rolls her eyes, but back then she was far more concerned. She saw me through the worst of the illness, but she also wondered how much longer I would be like this. Besides disabling the central nervous system, morphine also effects mental and physical performance. It is easy to become dependent on it, but I was determined to beat it as soon as possible. I wanted to go home and spend time with my family, but Professor Craddock wouldn't allow me to leave until they were sure I had beaten it. Within days of starting to reduce my dosage, I was craving it. It's highly addictive and it activates the reward systems in the brain: the more you have, the happier and more content you are.

I wanted to be out of the comfort zone of the hospital, where I had a button beside me and a nurse on call 24 hours a day, and I wanted to see Maddy and Georgia back in their own surroundings rather than from the end of my hospital bed. If that meant lying on my own bed at home, then that's what I wanted to do. The withdrawal from morphine would not be easy, but I was determined to resist the temptation. I was warned that the first three days without it would be the hardest part and they didn't disappoint.

Convincing the brain that it no longer has to rely on the euphoric effects is something else and I knew I had to combat those feelings. I knew that the morphine craving could last for many months, but the worst part was the first few days. It would be so easy to reach out and demand another dose, but it becomes a battle of wills. I imagine it's like smoking cigarettes in many ways. You can put off the next cigarette for another few minutes or so, but that just heightens the desire.

When the cigarette is finally taken from the packet, the fulfilment is amplified because the elation of that first puff has been delayed for that little bit longer. I wanted to delay it for good, but the first few hours are tough. It made me prone to mood swings and the slightest things made me irritable, but I was driven by my desire for independence. Charlie had offered me a deal and if I wanted to keep my side of the bargain it meant finding a way to overcome the cravings.

It was two and a half weeks before I finally emerged from the Queen Elizabeth and it was the first time I had seen daylight since I went into hospital for the transplant on 4 January. To see the sky again, no matter how miserable, was a wholly liberating experience but I wasn't able to fully appreciate the moment. I was still too poorly and I needed Julie's help to get into the car for the half-hour drive home.

Leaving hospital was a significant moment for me in the battle to beat leukaemia. If there was a timeline for my treatment, I think of the moments when I was told that Kay was a suitable stem-cell match; the decision to have a transplant instead of taking Glivec; the moment I entered hospital to have the transplant; and then the moment that I was given my freedom back. I was still continually monitored by the hospital and I had to return regularly – maybe once or twice a day – for detailed analysis of my condition and to check my recovery rate.

That was the price I was happy to pay if it meant I could return home. This was another milestone and it meant the world to turn the key in the front door again. Three weeks previously, I couldn't say for sure whether I would be able to do something like that again. It sounds such a trifling, insignificant thing to do but it was a personal triumph to be able to do it. No matter how bad I felt, it was a relief to be back in my own bed. In the isolation unit, the incessant shrill of the telephone played tricks on my mind. I hated the piercing noise that accompanied each call and there were times when I wanted to rip it out of its socket and throw it down the hallway.

That phone would ring constantly, day and night. It was worse when the duty nurse was away from her desk because the person on the other end knew, just as I did, that someone eventually had to answer it. The caller knew that the nurse was probably with a patient and, sooner or later, she would be back. I used to turn over and roll up into a tight ball to try and escape the noise, but there was no solitude. Even when the phone wasn't ringing, my mind was telling me that it was and I would wake up thinking I could hear it.

OO

The last thing I expected when I came home was to walk straight into a row, but that is exactly what happened. Not with Julie, but with one of our neighbours. I literally crawled upstairs to the bedroom and, even though the heating was on, I was fully clothed and wearing a bobble hat to keep warm. Even then I was still shivering. But I was concerned when I heard raised voices in the garden. I could recognise Julie's voice, but I didn't know who she was talking to and eventually I decided to make my way downstairs.

It took me an age to reach the kitchen. When I walked out of the patio doors, Julie was in the middle of a heated argument with one of our neighbours.

She was horrified. 'Geoff, what are you doing? Go inside, I will sort it out.'

It was too late. A neighbour was unaware of what I had just been through. He was accusing us of moving our fence at the back of the garden and encroaching on his boundary lines. Julie was trying to tell him that we hadn't done anything of the sort. He felt that we had taken some of his land and he lost his temper. He had gone too far and I told him not to speak to my wife like that. It was a terrible experience. I only just made it back to the inside of the house when I came over all nauseous. My body was reacting to even the slightest movement and it certainly wasn't prepared for a full-scale argument so soon after my transplant.

The neighbour didn't realise (and later apologised), but it was upsetting. I needed peace and tranquillity but I walked into a battle zone. I made it up the stairs on my hands and knees, and as soon as I got to the bathroom I was violently sick. I would throw my head back and then just cough up all sorts from the pit of my stomach. I felt like that for so much of the time that I wondered whether my condition would ever improve.

I was incapable of doing anything and I couldn't even hold conversations. Friends often visited, and, after they had spoken to Julie in the kitchen, they came upstairs to see me in the bedroom. I didn't have the strength to get out of bed to say hello. Instead, they tip-toed up the stairs and, after a gentle knock on the bedroom door, they would walk in. Looking back, I felt like the queen because all I could muster was a pathetic wave from the duvet. I was barely able to move my head. The pain and the effort were too much. My eyes were sore, my ears were ringing and it felt like I had an intense form of flu.

My muscles ached, sometimes my stomach was unsettled and I didn't have any energy. Our friends would go back downstairs and comment on how bad I looked, but this was nothing compared to how I felt when I was in hospital.

At least I was back at home. I knew that it would take time before I started to regain my strength, but I never lost my spirit. I knew that the answer was rest and that is what I did. I just slept through the night and slept through the day. I had long since resolved to do whatever had to be done to overcome the illness and time was on my side.

There was no pressure to get back to work and, although we were not exactly on a sound financial footing, we didn't have any immediate worries. If I had to spend three months in bed, then that's what I was prepared to do. It nearly was that length of time before I started walking around the house again. When I started to feel a little braver, I went downstairs and sat in the lounge wearing my bobble hat and dressing gown. Julie would potter around in the kitchen and I could muster a grunt whenever she asked me something.

My immune system was still low and Charlie had warned me about some of the potential problems waiting for me after the transplant. I was so susceptible to infections that there was a possibility that I would be gripped by one of them and I wouldn't be able to fight my way out of it.

When I mentioned to Julie that my back was itching to the point where it was causing discomfort, I immediately thought I might have shingles. Shingles is an attack on the central nervous system; it can be a killer. I was lucky because I recognised the signs straight away. It quickly developed into a rash and that was when I checked myself into hospital. Part of me didn't want to go back to hospital and stay over for days on end while they tried to control it. I felt like I was climbing one step and taking two back. I associated the hospital with my transplant and I wanted to be back at home and recovering with my family by my side.

The moment I went into the hospital, I was put on a drip with a cocktail of antibiotics and I spent another four days there while they monitored my progress. I'm scarred physically from it and I have lost the pigment in the skin on my back, but at least it was caught in time.

I knew that if I was allowed home, then I must be making good progress. There was always a chance of a relapse, but I knew that I was responding well to the treatment. If I had to go through it all again, I would. I imagine people can go through more painful experiences, but I've never come close to anything like this. I've spoken to people who are about to go through the same procedure and I try to be honest, but it's very difficult. It would be easy to put people off because it's such a terrifying experience, but I don't want to do that. Ultimately, it's down to them.

OO

The team had been isolated from the events back at home for nearly two weeks, but we were left shocked as news filtered through to us about the 7 July bombings. We had been riding through driving rain for yet another long stint in the saddle when we were told of the London bombings by our support crew.

Although they had first heard of the horrific events back home first thing that morning, they decided against telling us immediately. Instead, we cycled in ignorance through some of the most stunning scenery in the Tour de France.

The stage began on the edge of Lake Gérardmer and followed a continuous uphill stretch through the Vosges region. This was the real Tour. Despite the relentless rain, we marvelled at the panorama as we made our way up the 21.9 km climb to the top of the Grand Ballon and shrieked like children as we freewheeled down the other side at speeds of 60 kph.

Then it was on to the Ballon d'Alsace, which has its place in Tour folklore. The 9.1 km climb, at an average of 6.8 per cent, was the first mountain pass in Tour history and it carries iconic status as a result. Exactly 100 years after the first Tour, the professionals made the arduous journey through Alsace and climbed this historic mountain in the 2005 Tour. We beat them to it, but not by much. By the time we reached the steepest sections, the climb was populated by dozens of camper vans decked out in the colours of Jan Ullrich's T-Mobile team.

They crossed the border to show their support for the German powerhouse in his latest attempt to challenge Lance Armstrong for the right to wear the yellow jersey in Paris. As we rode Stage Nine, the professionals were already on Stage Seven and Ullrich was already more than a minute and a half down on the American. By the time they finished in Alsace, he was nearly two minutes down.

Ullrich was immensely popular with Tour fans. He is a beast of a man but, more importantly, he was viewed as the only realistic challenger to Armstrong. He won the Tour in 1997, but since then Armstrong had gone on to assume the title as the greatest cyclist in the sport since Eddy Merckx. Ullrich was talented and that's why the Germans stuck by him. They flew T-Mobile flags outside their camper vans, they had his picture in the windows and they wore his pink T-Mobile cycling jersey in support.

They still had to wait a couple of days for the *peloton* to pass through, but they entered into the spirit of things as we made our way up the gruelling climbs by clapping or waving me through. I don't suppose they had too much of an idea who I was, but they were incredibly sporting. They offered plenty of encouragement as I struggled to make it to the top and I will always cherish those moments because they kept me going.

These were the first real climbs of the Tour, but I knew that they would get tougher as the days wore on. At least there was some respite from the constant rotation of the pedals on the way into Mulhouse. From the top of the Ballon, the finish line was around 50 km away and I was determined to make the most of it. I always looked forward to the descents and on this one I barely had to turn the pedals over.

Despite the filthy conditions, the 50 km flew past. It was only when we crossed the finish line in Mulhouse that we were told of the events in the capital. Details were still sketchy, but we knew that bombs had detonated on three London Underground trains and the roof of a bus had been ripped off by an explosion as it made its way around Tavistock Square in the heart of the capital.

We didn't know how many casualties there were, but the number was obviously going to be high. It left us feeling empty and helpless. I set out on a fundraising mission in January to try and find a way to help save lives, but some people are hell-bent on ending them. It made no sense to me and we were appalled as we watched the news on French television that evening.

For once, our conversation around the dinner table was about something other than our ailments, aches and pains.

10

Grenoble-Courchevel, 192.5 km

This was the start of a journey into the unknown. For the professionals who have been training for months in the mountains, this is the chance to make their move. For nine days solid, the *peloton* has been riding in a tight pack and only a matter of minutes will separate the leader from the backmarker, the *lanterne rouge*, by the time they arrive in Grenoble. That will all change by the time they negotiate the brutal mountain passes of the Cormet de Roselend and the climb to the finish at the world-renowned ski resort of Courchevel.

The Alps are where the Tour de France really turns into a spectacle and, by the time the leaders have rattled off the stage in just under six hours, the pack will be split and the fatigue will be setting in. The strongest, such as Armstrong, would compete for the stage win but the stragglers will trail in half an hour, or maybe more, behind the race leader.

For me, as well as Matt and Neil, this is new territory. I decided against a recce to the Alps as part of my preparation for the Tour because I wanted to stay positive throughout my training, but there was no avoiding them now. I knew the Alps would be considerably tougher than anything I had attempted before and I had wanted to maximise my training time in England. I felt that experiencing the Alps before I took on the Tour could demoralise me if I couldn't complete some of the climbs. David Duffield's comments had been nagging away at me for weeks and I knew that the two climbs involved – the 18 km hike with an average gradient of 6 per cent to the top of the Cormet de Roselend and the 22 km climb to the finish line at the heliport in Courchevel – would test me to the very limit.

I was excited about the mountains and I was always in awe whenever they appeared on the horizon. By the time we finished the stage, we would be lying deep in Alpine territory. Courchevel has a fantastic reputation as a winter paradise for skiers and snowboarders, but it was notorious among the seasoned Tour veterans. It is a tough, uncompromising climb and it is deceptive because the renowned '1860' resort creates the false and misleading impression that it is the summit. In fact, the road winds on for another 5 km before reaching its conclusion in a barren, wind-swept car park next to the heliport that is reserved for the rich and famous who touchdown during the ski season.

When we planned the Tour, a couple who owned a hotel, the Jump Bar in 1860, had approached us to offer accommodation and an evening meal after we finished the stage. It was a magnanimous gesture and two of the people involved with the hotel, Jim Bell and Charlie MacKay, offered to act as tour guides and ride with us between Albertville and Courchevel. We readily accepted the offer of their company, but we had an uninspiring start to the day.

The previous evening, Haynesy checked the official Tour guide against his map and concluded that we would turn right out of the hotel, even though the riders felt that we should be turning left onto a dual carriageway. We were so tired that we were rarely in a position to argue. When the crew told us to ride down a road, we just eased into automatic pilot and pedalled wherever we were told to go.

That morning, just after 7 a.m., we wasted more than an hour in the rain as we cycled up and down the same road before the crew finally worked out where we were. They were just as fatigued as we were, but whenever we were lost, it was a deflating experience. There were a lot of miles to cover every day and somehow we would either add to them or waste time trying to work out the route. Our support crew were often blamed, unfairly, for our plight and it was easy to forget that they were surviving on less sleep than us.

After Hayley or Andrea brought us a cup of tea in bed late at night, the two girls headed for their hotel rooms to begin preparing enough food to get us through the following day. That didn't mean just a few rolls and snack bars. They were preparing for five riders burning more than 800 calories an hour on the bikes for around ten hours a day. They also prepared lunch for the support crew, as well as themselves, and although they eventually developed a production-line system to cut corners, they rarely went to bed before 2 a.m. In another room, Richard Chessor, our nutritionist from Loughborough University, prepared dozens of litre bottles of high-energy drink for us to use the next day. He was also in the unfortunate position of being nominated as the Tour accountant and he spent his evenings stapling receipts into a ledger book. Often it was an amateur operation, but we did the best we could with a skeleton, but incredibly diligent, support team.

The Tour took its toll on our support team at times. They put up with us being grumpy, irritable and withdrawn for hours at a time, but they always greeted us with a smile in the morning. The professionals can take advantage of the dozens of support staff on hand when they finish their ride to make life as comfortable as possible, but we didn't have that luxury. When the professionals jump on their bikes each morning, the team's mechanic will have serviced every one of them through the night and they will be as good as new when they begin the stage. Worn parts will have been replaced, gears checked and brakes adjusted. That is a professional operation at work. We had Robbie, who doubled up as our mechanic, checking each of our bikes each night. Elsewhere, Westie and Haynesy would be plotting the next day's stage. Although the Tour organisers publish the route months in advance of the actual race, it is not given in any great detail, which makes navigation extremely difficult. Although travelling along the main roads is fairly simple, plotting our route through the towns and villages proved extremely difficult. We often came to a standstill, sometimes for half an hour or more, while the support crew worked out the correct route.

While the road out of Grenoble, an industrial town in south-west France, was fairly unspectacular, the straight line led directly to the mountains in the distance. The Cormet de Roselend was the first challenge. We met our new friends, Jim and Charlie, in Albertville, home of the Winter Olympics in 1992. They were seasoned cyclists and, although they had ridden the col many times, they warned us of the two climbs to come. The Cormet de Roselend is a quite magnificent ascent. The winding mountain road circumnavigates a stunning lake about halfway up and, although progress was achingly slow, I made it to the top in just over two hours.

The rest of the team, along with Jim and Charlie, were waiting at a small tea hut at the top. Matt was in exceptional form and, even though our two friends were strong, he had kept up with them riding in their slipstream all the way to the top. He had found his mountain legs and was going great guns. All of us were surprised at the speed of his progress and we were giving him plenty of stick because he usually sat off the back of the paceline when we were riding on the flat.

'Hey, look at Lance go!' we teased.

'Put him in with the pros!'

He was walking around the top station with a wicked grin on his face and his now legendary pot-belly all puffed out. It was brilliant to see him in this kind of mood because, of the five of us riding the Tour, Matt had been clinging on for a couple of days. His confidence had been low, but this had been the shot in the arm that he needed.

He made a late decision to ride the Tour. It is fair to say that Matt was not in the best physical condition when he began training in February, but he was used to disciplining himself. He was the London Schools cross-country champion in his youth and, for a time, he even considered a career in athletics. He was used to endurance events. In 2003, he ran the New York Marathon in just over three hours. Matt likes his food, though, and he had indulged after coming back from America. He had barely trained since the marathon and he tipped the scales at more than 15 stone when he made the decision to ride the Tour. He was up against the clock because he had only left himself four months to train.

He had not enjoyed the long sessions in the saddle and he was on the phone to his office in London whenever he had the opportunity. There was a lot of talk at the time of the Liverpool captain Steven Gerrard's potential move to Chelsea and Matt was fielding an endless stream of phone calls about it during the day.

Gerrard's decision to stay at Anfield coincided with an upturn in Matt's fortunes. With the weight lifted off his shoulders, he finally found his zest and he was in fine fettle as he flexed his mountain muscles. It was an exceptional effort and I only caught him up because I was fearless whenever we made a mountainside descent. I loved the thrill of the chase. Ian and Robbie barely touched the brakes on the way down and I had trouble keeping them in my sights at times. Matt and Neil were far more apprehensive and they took their time, but I was carefree whenever we set off on a descent. Matt was haunted by the fear of his brakes failing, losing control or having a blow-out, because if that happens your life is no longer in your own hands. Neil was still scarred after a high-speed accident on a descent when he was much younger.

For me, these were the moments I could enjoy myself without worrying about another agonising climb. I set a new personal best of 77 kph on the way down, but I was still some way behind Robbie, a cyclist with vast experience of the Alps, after he topped 84 kph. We still had the hard part to come – the climb up to Courchevel – and we rode into a fierce headwind for nearly 40 km until we reached the foothills. I hated riding into a headwind. They were the bane of our lives when we crossed northern France and they provided a nasty reminder of those days as we trekked across the Alps.

I loved taking advantage of the tailwinds that can whip up off the roads, but cyclists spend 75 per cent of their time on the bike battling against either crosswinds or headwinds. It is a hazard of the roads and they come without warning. On a straight road, we often battled against them for an hour at a time and I would always seek protection behind some of the stronger riders whenever we were riding into one.

That meant Ian being despatched to the front and either Robbie or Neil would sit in behind him to provide a protective shield for Matt and I. Headwinds dented progress and, when we were really tired, our average speed fell to just under 20 kph. Those headwinds were so frustrating – I can just remember wanting to scream out in anger whenever we were faced with them for long periods of time.

Our spirits were lifted when we made it to the foot of the climb to Courchevel because we were met by a small army of people who would ride to the top of the 22 km climb with us. Charlie's wife, Gina, was waiting there with a number of friends. I was daunted by the prospect of riding to the top of one of the world's toughest climbs. Courchevel is home to the world's largest skiing area and the jagged, snow-capped peaks of 1860 and beyond seemed like hours away when we started to make our gritty ascent. It was an unnerving experience because I was beginning to get an idea of just how tough it would be to complete all 62 of the Tour's climbs. The road to Courchevel starts with some gentle switchbacks on the lower slopes and, as the energy in my legs began to dwindle, the gradient became steeper.

There is no respite and I knew from the outset that it would test me. I wasn't alone. Matt, Westie and myself had complained of mild stomach cramps earlier in the day. We put it down to the fact that we had, perhaps foolishly, all eaten carpacccio in our hotel the previous evening. Matt, though, was suffering more than anyone. His face was pale and the sweat was pouring off him by the time we made it to the start of this particularly arduous climb.

As usual, we climbed at different rates. We had long resolved that it was 'each man for himself' on the climbs. As long as someone rode with me to keep me company and offer words of encouragement, I was happy to let the others go ahead and wait at the top with a nice cup of coffee. Ian and Robbie had been looking forward to the climb for days and they were soon out of sight. The hairpins are often hazardous because they are so tight and it is easier to ride around the edge where the road is not as steep. I knew Matt was in difficulty because we kept overtaking him. He could be slow, but he was never that slow. I was struggling to make any advances on 10 kph but Matt was capable of much more. Neil kept riding back to him to check on his progress, but he was in a terrible state and he looked so exhausted I didn't think he would be able to make it to the top. Every so often he put on a mini-spurt and came past Neil and me, but we soon clawed him back.

He was so nauseous and so tired that he couldn't even speak to us. We frequently asked if he was OK, but he couldn't answer. His eyes were sunk into his cheekbones and he was looking frail and gaunt. By now, he should not have even been on his bike, but he was on auto-pilot and just kept turning the pedals over. Neil was in two minds over who to ride with. I always needed someone with me to offer me moral support, but Matt was in a far worse condition than me. He beckoned one of the support vehicles to summon Ian or Robbie, but they were already too far up the mountain to bring them back.

Matt insisted he was fine, but we kept an eye on him for more than half an hour until one of the support vehicles finally came back down the mountain to check on our progress. It is hard to stay with some-one when they are moving so slowly as it is more tiring to ride at a slower pace than you are capable of, so we left him in the hands of our support crew.

Even at the height of summer, Courchevel is a pretty barren place and as we made our approach to 1550 – the ski area's mid-station – temperatures were beginning to plummet. We were at high altitude and, as the air gets thinner, the temperatures begin to drop. We left the sunshine at the bottom of the mountain, but even our arm and leg warmers were not keeping out the cold. We often put them on at the bottom of a climb because, no matter how hot it felt at the foot, it was always cold when we approached the top. It was no different on the climb to Courchevel and, by the time we approached 1850 an hour later, snow was beginning to settle on the ground. We didn't know where the heliport was but, as we turned the corner, we saw the girls outside our hotel. They were waiting with jackets, ready to load our bikes onto the cars.

We asked a local French girl where the heliport was and, when she pointed down the mountain, Neil and I both believed that we had passed it. It was bitterly cold and we couldn't get off our bikes quick enough. As the girls took them from us, Matt made a heroic entrance.

He was struggling to turn over the pedals, but the fact he was still on his bike was far more than we ever expected. We had discussed his situation on the way up and we both felt sure that he would abandon the climb and get into the safety and warmth of the Land Rover with a blanket wrapped over him. When Neil went to check on him on the lower roads, he felt sure that he would keel over at any time.

When Matt arrived at 1860, he looked terrible. He was pale, thin and gaunt. It was only when we got inside the hotel it emerged that we had not reached the summit – we were actually still 5 km from the top. By this time Matt was oblivious to anything going on around him. He was in a world of his own and he was clearly in a lot of distress.

We knew Ian and Robbie were probably waiting up there and, although we were just about to start thawing out, the stage was not complete. Neil and I had a decision to make, but it took no more than eye contact for us to make it. Although we had already tacked on an extra 50 km to the Tour's official route during the previous nine days, we knew that the stage would not be complete until we reached the heliport.

Beyond 1860, Courchevel is a soulless place but we vowed to cycle on. We unloaded our bikes from the racks and started the journey to the heliport another 2,004 metres up. Dusk was setting in and snow was settling on our fingers as we made our way up the final 2 km. When we finally got there, Ian, Robbie, Jim and Charlie were shivering in the car park, where they had been waiting more than half an hour. It was a special moment for all of us. We had conquered one of the most arduous climbs in the Tour de France and even the professionals were unlikely to encounter conditions like this.

They set off around 11 a.m. each day and finish in time for it to be televised live on the French evening news. This means that, invariably, the mountain stages are still bathed in sunshine when they reach the summit, which only adds to the appeal of the world's greatest cycle race. At 8 p.m., that is certainly not the case. It was a surreal experience. At the height of the ski season, Courchevel is a bustling, thriving village full of life. In six months' time, the whole mountain would be covered in a blanket of snow and the pistes would be packed with skiers and snowboarders. When we were there, it was a deserted, desolate place, like something out of the Wild West. There was a haunted look about it and we couldn't get off the top quick enough.

During the climb, my heartbeat was high – maybe 160–70 beats per minute – and this ensured that I had plenty of insulation on the way up. As soon as I stopped cycling, my body stopped pumping blood and the chill began to set in. My heartbeat returned to normal – perhaps 50 beats per minute – and I began to feel the cold air biting against my battered bones. The 5 km drop in the rapidly settling snow only took ten minutes, but the wind and the biting cold sapped my energy.

My hands were so cold I could barely feel the brakes through my fingerless gloves on the way down. The roads were treacherous and I was worried that my pencil-slim wheels would slide on some ice and send me crashing into the pavement. I never expected these conditions when we set out and I was annoyed that Haynesy had driven down the mountain and back to the hotel the moment we arrived at the summit. It was freezing by the heliport and I expected that we would load our bikes onto the racks and get in the back of the car to warm up, but he just shook our hands and drove down to the hotel.

Perhaps he didn't realise just how cold it was but, if I had been given the chance, I would have told him. Things took on a different perspective when we finally arrived at the hotel in 1860 and we were told that Matt had been taken straight to bed. The crew told him he had reached the summit but he barely acknowledged his remarkable feat. He had struggled up the climb to Courchevel for three hours and all he wanted to do was curl up and sleep. At the dinner table that evening, the discussion centred on Matt. He was fast asleep in his bedroom and was unable to eat. Some mistakenly believed that he had 'bonked' – cycling-speak for running out of steam – on the way up to Courchevel, but I wasn't so sure.

Bonking occurs when the glycogen stores in the liver and muscles are depleted, which results in a massive dip in performance. I experienced it a couple of times in my training rides and I once rode all the way back from Stratford-upon-Avon – around 65 km away from my home – after bonking. Speed is dramatically reduced and the only way to come through it is to get plenty of rest. On the Tour, that wasn't possible. When Matt went to bed that night, he had around eight hours' sleep before he was back on the bike and that wasn't anywhere near enough time for his body to recover.

On average, the body stores around 2,000 calories of energy and, with regular feeding, that is continually stocked up. Even though we were burning around 800 calories an hour, as long as we replaced it at regular intervals throughout day, theoretically we shouldn't have suffered. The problem is when you fail to consume enough calories. There are only so many ham and cheese sandwiches you can eat in a day before you start crying out for something else. I lived on the high-energy gels that simply slipped straight down my throat and were absorbed straight into the bloodstream. At times I opened up a packet, each of them containing around 80 calories, just to relieve the boredom of spending so many hours on the bike. Sometimes the girls passed me a handful of jelly babies, but after munching through a packet in the space of a couple of hours, I wanted something else for a bit of variety. It was the same in the evenings. Our staple diet consisted of a starter of a (main course) pizza followed by a plateful of pasta. On other days I would have a (main course) bowl of pasta as a starter followed by a pizza. There was no getting away from it.

They were both rich sources of energy and there were few foods that could provide us with so many carbohydrates in such small portions. Even if we weren't hungry, we forced it down because we knew that bonking the following day could put an end to our hopes of completing the Tour. That was the principle of carbo-loading – maximising glycogen levels before we got on the bikes – to safeguard against the nightmare scenario. Unless we ate while we were riding, our glycogen stores would be depleted within the first couple of hours and this was a constant threat throughout the Tour.

The effects of the bonk are horrific. It happens to everyone at some stage or another and even Armstrong hit the wall during the 2000 Tour on the way to the summit of the Col de Joux-Plane. It was rare for Armstrong to be dropped, but the Frenchman Richard

Virenque and the German rider Jan Ullrich both left him behind with 22 km of the climb still to go. He admitted afterwards that he had not eaten or taken enough fluids on board.

We wondered whether Matt's body had shut down – physically and mentally – in much the same way. Matt had been in a similar situation before. When we rode in the Peak District on a training weekend, Matt had suffered exhaustion at the end of the first day. I had taken a wrong turn and, when I eventually joined up with the rest of the team half an hour later, he was asleep in some long grass. He was so tired, but he got back on his bike and rattled off the final few miles. When he finished the stage, he was feeling terrible and he wasn't sure if he would be able to ride again the following day.

He was driving Neil to our hotel when he began complaining of sickness. Neil offered to drive his car so that he could get some rest in the passenger seat, but he didn't even respond. Without even indicating, he just drove his car onto the verge by a zebra crossing and got out.

Those were two tough days, but the Tour was something else. At times we found it difficult to regulate our feeding. We were consuming thousands of calories each day and we had to be sure to eat before the hunger knock set in. Matt was suffering after his climb up to the top of the Cormet de Roselend earlier in the day but his condition was deteriorating by the minute. He had clearly lost a lot of energy, but there was far more to it than that. Even Ian was worried.

'I have a feeling he will have a decision to make in the morning,' he said.

11

Courchevel–Briançon, 173 km

For six months, our team lived a dream. Day in, day out, we trained as professionals and we were all approaching the peak of our personal fitness when we set out from Fromentine on the opening day of the Tour. Back then, we shared a mutual determination to complete every kilometre of the Tour's testing route, but today we would be a man down.

Hayley came into my room to tell me that Matt was in tears because he could not carry on. She sat down with him on his bed and he told her he was so ill he would not be able to continue.

Westie had diagnosed him with a stomach complaint and he had been up all night with a combination of diarrhoea and sickness. He wasn't the only one suffering because my stomach was already churning, but Matt was unable to continue. He hadn't bonked. He was weak and had barely slept; Westie, his favoured room-mate, had been kept up with his frequent visits to the bathroom. Now Matt had to try and come to terms with a massive decision. He believed, wrongly, that he had let down the team. We knew that we all had enough will-power, but he no longer had the energy to turn the pedals. He had not been able to eat for more than 15 hours and that was no preparation for getting on a bike at 7.30 a.m. and riding until 9 p.m. Although it was rare for any of us to be particularly cheery first thing in the morning, it broke my heart to see Matt in such a terrible condition. He told me he intended to hang a huge picture of the team against a backdrop of the Tour route when he returned home and frame it in his living room. He was telling me that he was going home. He sat on his hotel bed, with his head in his hands and told me he felt so ill he could not carry on.

'It's over for me,' he said.

'Are you sure?'

'I feel terrible – I can't get on my bike today.'

He believed that he had failed, that he had somehow let me down, but I reminded him of his heroic efforts the night before. I experienced plenty of highs during my football career. Leading Palace out at the FA Cup final was one of them, but I also had plenty of dark days. I experienced some real troughs and I never felt more depressed than the times I was injured. I had 27 operations throughout my career and, although I made more than 550 appearances as a professional footballer, I missed another 300 or more through injury. Watching your team from the stands is no way for a professional footballer to spend a Saturday afternoon. I knew exactly how Matt felt.

If he carried on in his condition, he would probably have finished up in a hospital but there was no way I wanted him to go home. He talked of getting a flight that afternoon. For Matt, he felt the finish line at the Champs-Élysées would not be the same, but I assured him it would mean just as much to me. We were a team and this was a team effort. We were there to support one another and that's what I was doing. When we uncorked the champagne bottles in Paris, I wanted him to be just as big a part of the celebrations as anyone else. When the Tour professionals quit, they catch the next flight home and bury their heads in the sand for a couple of weeks. I didn't want Matt to do that. His unique sense of humour had already kept me going and he was so entertaining at the dinner table in the evenings that he always lifted our spirits.

There was a long day ahead of us and I had a camera crew in my face before I even had a chance to pour myself a cup of coffee. The team from *Futbol Mundial*, a weekly magazine programme on Sky, had joined us for the day and they thrust a microphone in front of me when I sat down at the table. When they finished filming, a chap from Radio Courchevel walked into the hotel and asked, ever so politely, if he could interview me. I couldn't refuse, but this felt like an intrusion on a very private moment between the team. It wasn't his fault, but it was difficult to deal with. It had just gone 6 a.m. and I was still struggling from the previous day's exertions. The girls were chasing around, trying to get the cars loaded with our equipment in time for the start, and there was a strange atmosphere hanging over us.

The decision not to ride that morning was probably the hardest Matt had made in his entire life and, even if it wasn't, it was certainly the bravest. He felt empty and his spirit was crushed. When we finally set off that morning, it broke my heart to see his face pressed against the window of the Land Rover as we set off, shivering in the early morning cold, from Courchevel. It was still early in the morning and the agony of the start line was prolonged by a television crew, this time from ITV, insisting on ten separate shots of us setting off.

This was the stage we feared but, at the same time, we all looked forward to the challenge. The 173 km trip to Briançon was the Tour's signature day and included the epic climbs up the Madelaine, the Telegraphe and then the final, brutal, ascent to the top of the Galibier. Matt knew it would be another momentous day.

There was snow on the side of the roads and, in Matt's condition, I doubt whether he could have lasted an hour on a bike. His illness had kicked in again and the support crew had to pull up at the side of the road every ten minutes or so as he tried in vain to cope with the diarrhoea and sickness. We saw him holding his stomach and dashing to find the nearest bush with a toilet roll in his hand.

It is always hard to celebrate with your team-mates when you have not been a part of a success story. Over the previous ten days, we had formed a unique bond. Some of us barely knew each other before the Tour, but now we were together 24 hours a day. Each morning we set off at the start line together and, no matter how hard the stage was, we always shook hands when we got to the other end. Getting to the end of a stage was another minor victory and, without fail, we always patted each other on the back.

'Nice one, lads. Good effort,' we would say. They are simple words, but they mean so much. It reminds me of every time I see Arsenal score and Thierry Henry beckons his team-mates to form a group hug. It is a show of unity and Matt knew that he would not be part of that on this stage. Those thoughts would be eating away at him all day and I knew just how disappointed he was. The Tour was a once-in-a-lifetime opportunity and missing out on a stage meant missing the chance to complete it in full. He was inconsolable.

It was such a shame because he was in really good shape. When he went on a training ride with Ian before the Tour and was introduced to Robbie, our most experienced rider, it's fair to say that Robbie wasn't impressed. He told Ian that he had strong reservations about Matt being able to take on the challenge of the Tour. Robbie was amazed the next time he saw Matt, though, because he had lost nearly 3 stone. One of Matt's greatest qualities is his ability to bounce back. No matter what you say to him, or how much ribbing he gets for his unusual mannerisms, he always comes back for more and he loves that side of life. That was exactly what happened when Ian relayed Robbie's comments to him. He trained more and trained harder. He ate better, he stopped having even the occasional glass of wine and looked leaner and fitter as a result.

When we arrived in France, he looked like a different person. He was fit, strong and raring to go. Very few people ever have the chance to take more than three weeks off from their careers and my team were determined to make the most of it. If you break down in a marathon through injury or illness it is devastating, but there is always the chance to run another. My team-mates are unlikely to ever get the chance to ride the Tour again. It wasn't just three weeks of their lives: they had given up six months of their time to prepare for it. We planned the event as a team and it was on our minds 24 hours a day. Matt went out on his bike at 7 a.m. for a couple of hours before he started work, and then he sometimes went for an hour in the evening. On his days off, he would ride alone, or sometimes meet with Neil, for six, seven or even eight hours. It was a huge commitment and, in some ways, the discipline was perhaps harder than riding the Tour itself. It never left our minds. Training took up an awful lot of our time, but we were all driven by the fear of not being prepared to reach the finish line.

Matt's climb to the top of Courchevel is the stuff of legend as far as I'm concerned and he knows that. I'm still full of admiration whenever I think of him punishing his battered frame up the final 22 km. It was inspirational. That night, he had the option of pulling over into the side of the road and putting his bike on the rack, but he refused to give up and those are the qualities that make a man.

OO

My mood wasn't helped by Haynesy dashing around the hotel. He was outside in the snow washing down the cars so that our branded vehicles would look good for the television. After the emotion of the previous day and Matt being sick all over the hotel, I didn't give a damn what our cars looked like, but Haynesy was out in the cold with a bucket and sponge, washing down the alloys, scraping the mud off the wheel arches and covering himself with soap suds. I couldn't believe it.

Haynesy knew exactly how it would come across on a television screen if our Land Rovers were all battered and bruised after 12 days on the road. He made sure they looked as though they had just been driven out of the showroom. It was last on our list of priorities, but Haynesy was obsessed with their appearance. He comes from a public relations background and that was probably the reason why he paid so much attention to detail. He has years of experience working for Sky television and he knew how important our image was, but that was the last thing on my mind. Haynesy had our best interests at heart and he always meant well, but it wasn't always agreeable. He is a kind-hearted, warm man, and he was only looking out for us but he didn't always show it in a way that suited the team.

On one occasion, Matt, Neil and I were locked in the car with the air-conditioning on when we had finished the stage. We were literally locked in a sealed unit inside the Land Rover while Haynesy started checking us into the hotel.

'Don't move,' he mouthed through the glass.

'Well, where can we go? You've locked us in!'

He was doing it for our benefit, but we sat in the car like naughty schoolboys. He was so well organised it was untrue, but he forgot to tell the rest of the team how they should operate. We had so much equipment with us on the Tour that Haynesy colour-coded our bags. Each rider had their own individual colour attached to their personal effects but, while we knew what colour we were, the support crew – Haynesy aside – had no idea. He even had little stickers on the dashboard so that he could identify each rider's gear quickly if they asked for something. It was a system that worked for him, but no-one else.

I often asked Westie, or one of the girls, to look in my bag for something and they would stop the car and rummage around the boot, looking through all our gear before they finally found it. According to Haynesy, it was a simple system, but why we couldn't just have stickers with our names written on them in a black marker pen I will never know. That was Haynesy – and for the most part, we learned to ignore him when he was being a pain.

When I heard Matt was not riding, I wondered whether my own stomach cramps would get worse. Westie, who had also eaten carpaccio, was struggling and we wondered whether our condition might deteriorate during the day. Westie had just about survived Matt's frequent visits to the bathroom overnight and he only had a few words of advice when I asked him what precautions I should take. His advice had only one interpretation.

'As soon as you think you can get rid of it, unload!'

Typically, that call came as we started the long climb up the Col de Madelaine, but there were contingency plans in place. As soon as I threw down my bike by the side of the road, Richard drew up in one of the Land Rovers and passed me a fresh toilet roll. I dived into the woods at the foot of the Madelaine, but it wasn't the last time. When Westie spotted me crouching by the side of the road a short while later, he turned to the rest of the crew and said: 'Look at him, he's got a taste for it now.'

It always took me a couple of hours to wake up in the morning. Often, my legs were leaden and it took me an hour or so for the burn in my thighs to wear off. Today was different. From the moment we set off in the fresh snow in Courchevel to the moment we completed the stage after 14 hours on the road, I suffered. The Madelaine, a beast of a climb, was simply a precursor to the main event. The endless grind to the summit was broken up by the spectacle of another rider overtaking Ian. It didn't last long. The Madelaine is a long, winding climb and the trick is to ride within yourself.

For this poor soul, he had the incentive of spotting Ian in front of him and he called it on. The trouble is, when you do that, you have to see it through and that was all the motivation Ian needed. He let our new companion gain a 100-metre gap before he pushed hard down on the accelerator and caught him in a matter of seconds. He didn't stop. He just blistered his way past and carried on alone all the way to the summit. When Robbie, Neil and I arrived at the top station, we couldn't resist. 'How did you get on with your mate?'

'Taught that fucker a lesson,' was his typically forthright reply.

Ian isn't the sort of person you take on lightly. If anyone goes past him on a climb, it's game on and, even if you get ahead, he will reel you back in. Neil paid the price for his competitive edge a couple of times when he went past Ian on some of the long climbs, but Ian always had the speed and the stamina to claw him back.

I flew down the other side of the Madelaine, but the conditions closed in as we made our way to the foot of the Telegraphe. When we entered the village of Saint-Jean de Maurienne, it was monsoon-like and we decided to take refuge in a café until the storm clouds cleared. The trouble is, they never did. We were always conscious of the clock and as we set off on the 12 km climb to the top of the Telegraphe, we did so in the knowledge that we would not be able to escape the rain for another couple of hours.

Although the Telegraphe is a tough climb, I was more concerned by the Galibier. It is such a daunting ascent that it breaks even the professionals. It has a fearsome reputation and I knew I was in for a long day when we made our way off the back of the Telegraphe. As soon as we began the 22 km climb to the summit, I beckoned one of the support cars and asked for the iPod. The support crew had downloaded Kraftwerk's legendary *Tour de France* album and it helped stimulate me on the way up the climbs. It also helped me take my mind off it because I knew this was likely to be one of the toughest days of the Tour.

The first kilometre is quite steep but it levelled out after a while and Neil and I made solid, but slow, progress on a long, steady drag. We were often cheered on by Tour fans from their camper vans parked on the side of the road and I was quite surprised when I thought I heard one of them say: 'Well done, you've got over the hard bit.' In hindsight, I think he actually said: 'Well done, you've got the hard bit to come.' The number of camper vans parked on the side of the road is always a good marker. They arrive several days in advance of the professionals and pitch up at the steepest parts of the climb. That way they get to see the pros at their lowest ebb. As we turned the corner to make our way into the steepest sections, there were literally hundreds of camper vans fighting for space on the side of the road. I knew then that, with another 10 km until we reached the top, it would be torture. It was made worse by the fact the Kraftwerk album had finished and had been replaced by some of Richard's punk rock music. I was so angry I wanted to reach into the back of my jersey to change the track, but I was cycling so slowly that I would have fallen off my bike if I had tried to take it out.

The higher we got, the colder it became. The wind was howling and my jersey could no longer absorb the rain. My skin was so cold and so wet that it was puckering. I was surrounded by the snow-capped peaks of the Alps and I could only imagine the weather conditions at the very top. Neil and I made our way up, first in rain and then in sleet, until we approached the final few hundred yards. By that time, it was so cold that I could barely feel my toes and my fingers were freezing cold. It got worse as we inched towards the top of the Galibier and I really wondered whether I would make it. It couldn't compare with what I went through when I was lying in a hospital bed fighting for my life – nothing ever will – but I was so confused. There were voices in my head causing so much conflict.

'You won't make this, Geoff – you'd better get off.'

'No, Geoff, keep turning the pedals – you'll get there in the end. Come on, keep pushing.'

Then there was David Duffield: 'Geoff, you'd better prepare for walking up some of those climbs.'

'Remember why you are doing this, Geoff. Come on, only another couple of hundred yards to the top.'

It had been raining so hard on the way up that it had been bouncing off the roads, but, as we approached the summit and temperatures fell below freezing, snow was beginning to settle. My leg warmers had slipped down by my ankles, but I was going so slowly that I couldn't pull them up.

The road to the top of the Galibier was the only time I felt it might be too much. The snowflakes were falling so quickly that I couldn't even look up and I was just staring at the slush spraying off the front of the wheel. I could hear one of the Land Rovers labouring behind me and I eventually ground to a halt just before one of the bends. Westie got out of the car and came running over.

'Geoff, are you OK?'

'How much further?'

'It's just round the next bend.'

I was exhausted, but I got back on my bike. The road is so steep towards the very top that he had to give me a push start and for a split second my legs felt normal. As soon as he released his hand, that dull aching pain set in again.

When the professionals wilt, the roadside support often gives them a helping hand by propelling them up the mountain and, even though it is a breach of the rules, the riders are rarely punished. I wished I had that kind of assistance. As I turned the final corner, the only thing that kept me going was the sight of the camera crew waiting at the top. The team had been teasing me all day about their presence.

'They're only here to watch you fail!'

'You've come on the right day, lads. If he's going to get off his bike, today's the day!'

That spurred me on. There were lots of thoughts swirling around my mind and I know that if I hadn't been riding the Tour for personal reasons, I would have got off my bike a long time ago. I only had those feelings a couple of times, but the fear of failure drove me on. The snow masked it, but I was very emotional when I finally made it to the very top. I was breathing heavily and I only had enough energy to high-five Neil after another epic climb. The finish line was 40 minutes away, but it was downhill all the way to Briançon. The problem was that the heart rate drops as soon as we stopped pedalling and now the wind chill was battering our bodies.

Neil started to make his way down the mountain in torrential rain. He only noticed that I wasn't behind him when he stopped after half a kilometre. I had realised after about 50 yards that I would not be able to survive in these temperatures. It reminded me of a school football game when I was nine years old – I was shaking violently in the showers afterwards. I took refuge in the Land Rover and Haynesy tried to thaw me out by turning up the heating. He gave me some extra clothes because he was so worried that I would get hypothermia. Neil couldn't see what was going on at the top and he had tucked himself against the rock face to try and protect himself from the elements. After about 15 minutes, he decided to ride back up the mountain to find out why I had stopped. When he arrived, he was genuinely worried about whether it would be possible to cycle down in these conditions. The Tour has, on occasion, been forced to abandon stages, but for me it was never an option. Westie had made some room by getting out of the car and he looked like Gene Kelly in *Singin' in the Rain*, with an umbrella up and that bloody smirk on his face. It was no laughing matter for us, though, we were still shivering. Westie and Haynesy took off their socks so Neil and I could put them over our hands.

'Whatever you do, don't let us stop.'

OO

There was no option but to go through chemotherapy. I simply had to do it. It was part of the process. There is no way of preparing yourself for the ordeal, but I knew there was no other choice. Being on a bike for hours at a time, climbing mountains when you can't see the peak until your head finally bursts through the cloud cover as you approach the summit, is arduous. But there is no bigger challenge than chemotherapy.

I was close to hypothermia and my body was on the brink of exhaustion. When I completed every other climb on the Tour, I was always elated but the conditions on the Galibier that day were so bad that there was no time to enjoy it and survey the views. In fact, there weren't any views. We couldn't see through the mist and visibility was less than 20 metres.

Briançon was a long way into the distance and, until we ducked under the cloud cover, we had to brave the temperatures. The socks on our hands protected our fingers but the sweaty feet smell was disgusting. We took it easy at first as the roads were covered in a greasy film, but as soon as we broke through the clouds, we were bathed in sunshine again. The rain cleared, the roads were dry … and we could abandon our mittens. That was the cue for us to let our hair down and enjoy what was left of the 40 km descent into Briançon. We flew down, barely touching the brakes on the way, and that is when it started to sink in exactly what we had achieved that day.

When it was snowing on the Galibier, and Neil and I sought refuge in one of the support vehicles, I told Westie that there was no way we would be driving down. I know Neil didn't see it that way when he stood against a rock half a kilometre down the road with the snow falling in his face, but I know he doesn't regret it now. The long haul to the top of the Galibier took almost everything out of me physically. People who climb mountains put their bodies under extreme stress and they know that if they make one mistake they can slip off the edge, but they also know what the rewards are for reaching the top. I'm convinced cyclists enjoy the challenge of reaching the top of a climb so much because of the physical and mental strain they put themselves under to get there. Whenever I got on my bike, I was so focused on the day ahead that I went into trance-like states at times. Often I didn't even take in the scenery and I continued to push the pedals for hours at a time until someone relieved the boredom by telling me that we were stopping for coffee or a mid-morning snack.

On the climbs, particularly the Galibier, my body constantly nagged at me to pull over at the side of the road and admit defeat, but my mind told me to carry on. It is impossible to prepare for the conditions that we encountered in Courchevel or at the top of the Galibier. It was mid-July and we expected to be wearing short-sleeved shirts most of the time; instead we had several layers of clothing on and were protected by rain-capes.

The Galibier was a monumental day because, after getting through that, I didn't think there was anything else that the Tour de France could throw at me. It was a defining moment, not only to reach the top, but to cycle down the other side in the freezing conditions. That ten-minute descent, when I followed the slush that was fizzing off Neil's back wheel until we burst through the clouds and suddenly felt the sun beating against our backs, is unforgettable. We left the clouds, the freezing fog and the snow behind and replaced it with the stunning views of the scenery below, freewheeling into the town for the best part of 20 km. Without doubt, it took me back to the dark days when I was first diagnosed with leukaemia and the days immediately after my transplant, when I wondered whether my body would survive another night. Bursting through the cloud cover was like a new beginning. I felt I had left everything else behind and that it was time to make a new start in life.

It was a fantastic descent and was made even more memorable when we stopped at some traffic lights on the approach into the town. A couple had been waiting for us all day and it turned out that the lady was a nurse on a cancer ward. She told me how frustrating it was that so much research was going into the disease but things were not progressing quickly enough for the patients. I was touched by her gesture and I haven't forgotten her words. It was fitting to meet someone like that at the end of such a gruelling day and her views simply reinforced the reasons for me riding the Tour.

It was an emotional moment when we arrived at our hotel. Ian and Robbie had crossed the finish line more than two hours previously and they hadn't given us a prayer of completing the stage. There was a hint of snow when they crossed the top of the Galibier and they felt sure that conditions would deteriorate by the time Neil and I got to the summit. They expected us to arrive at the hotel in the back of the Land Rovers. When we got off our bikes outside the hotel, the girls came flying out with huge smiles on their faces and wrapped their arms around Neil and me. It was a special moment for us. It is at times like that when I realise there is a real bond between people.

At the top of the Galibier, we barely had time to shake hands. We just wanted to get down as quickly as possible. When we broke through the cloud cover and flew down the other side, we began to appreciate what we had been through. We could easily have got off our bikes that day and taken refuge in the car – no-one would have thought any less of us – but I was determined to cycle every kilometre of the Tour. After all, I wondered if this might be my only chance.

12

Briançon-Digne-les-Bains, 187 km

I witnessed some fairly spectacular dressing-room rows during my playing career. Football is such a demanding sport and, with so many characters involved, there is always likely to be tension among team-mates. Although clubs share a common goal, there can be divisive elements. In the heat of the moment, anything can happen. At Palace, Wright and Bright used to hammer our young winger John Salako. They were a double act on and off the field and they would feed off each other's enthusiasm. Salako was a young lad of 17 when he broke into the Palace first team and he was under a lot of pressure to deliver. Although he was tender in years, he had a lot of talent, but when he didn't serve up crosses for Wright or Bright, they slaughtered him.

They looked after Salako by giving him cast-offs of their clothes, but they gave him a hard time on the pitch. He was a little bit different from most footballers because he was well educated, and, because he had come up through the academy system at Palace, he had to work a little bit harder to earn the respect of the other players. He told Coppell that he was good enough to play for England when he was just breaking into the side, but the manager doubted whether he had the desire to do it. He made his name when he went on loan to Swansea and scored for them in the European Cup Winners' Cup, but he was always going to play for Palace.

He was a confident lad, but that was tested many times because of the abuse he used to take off Wright and Bright. He was a very talented kid and although they used to tell him he was hopeless, they didn't really mean it.

Sometimes things can be taken a little further. At Wolves, Don Goodman and I had a fearsome row with the manager Mark McGhee after we drew at QPR towards the end of the 1997 season. Mark and his assistant, Colin Lee, set the team out to man-mark a couple of their danger-men throughout the game. Keith Curle, our centre-half, was detailed to shadow QPR's John Spencer and Darren Ferguson was assigned to Gavin Peacock. It was a system that made no sense at all to the senior players in the side and we were railing against it before the match kicked off. Keith was telling anyone who would listen that he was not the man for the job and no-one in the team disagreed. Darren was noted for being a ball-playing midfielder and it was ludicrous to expect him to shackle Peacock. Wolves were a team battling for promotion and the opposition should have been more worried about what we were up to. It was a disaster waiting to happen.

As expected, Peacock and Spencer gave us the runaround and they both scored within the first half-hour. Keith was in a bad mood and he simply couldn't contain the pair of them. I was a substitute at Loftus Road, but I came on for Steve Corica when Rangers scored their second. Don scored for us just before half-time and, even though Keith equalised late in the game, there were fireworks in the changing rooms. We were busy patting ourselves on the back for making a comeback when all had seemed lost. We had shown a lot of determination to get back into the game, but Colin Lee flipped with Darren Ferguson. He was shouting at him, claiming that he had not carried out his instructions and blamed him for Rangers ripping us to shreds.

Don and I couldn't believe what we were hearing and I waded into Colin. 'If you had played the right side in the first place, we wouldn't have been in that situation.'

Colin was out of order and anyone could see that Darren should not have been playing that role. Mark McGhee didn't even get involved. He was very quiet, but obviously there were some words between them later because Don and I were called into his office the following day. We expected a bollocking for starting the row in the dressing room but instead McGhee told us we were right and that training was cancelled.

OO

Football is a sport that is so passionate that there will always be disagreements, but I didn't realise cycling could compare with it. That view certainly changed after we completed the 187 km trip from Briançon to Digne-les-Bains. After 11 days on the road, we all got on surprisingly well. There had been the occasional disagreement, especially between the support crew and the riders, but nothing serious.

That changed in a car park at the end of the stage. Matt was still suffering and he was sitting in silence in the back of a Land Rover as we took on another tough stage. Our spirits were lifted when Andrea and Hayley surprised us by painting our names on the roads in true Tour tradition, and we marvelled as we rode around the perimeter of Lac de Serre-Ponçon, but we suffered in the extreme heat – we were relying on determination alone to carry us through the stage. Our spirits were lifted temporarily by Haynesy. He had a habit of driving on ahead and he radioed back to our other support vehicle to tell them that there was a tunnel ahead and that he was waiting for us at the entrance.

He was safety-conscious to the point of being obsessive and he wanted to drive with one Land Rover in front and one behind our mini-*peloton* all the way through the tunnel. Admittedly, it made some sense and we all lined up at the start of the tunnel until he was ready to lead us through it. Haynesy could be a bit of an old woman at times and this was one of them. He wound down the window and spoke to us as if we were five-year-old children crossing the road.

'I'm just going to switch on the lights to the Land Rover so wait there,' he said.

We were totally bemused. 'What's he going on about?' we muttered.

'Right, everyone take off their sunglasses.'

'You what?'

'I don't want anyone's vision to be impaired in the tunnel.'

'Are you joking, Haynesy?'

'No, take them off. It's dangerous.'

We shook our heads in disbelief, but we did as we were told and took them off.

'Right, follow me. Take it easy.'

We need not have bothered because as we began to crawl forward, we realised that the 'tunnel' was less than 50 yards long.

I nearly fell off my bike laughing as we made our way through it and gave Haynesy the now customary hand signals as we pedalled past them when they pulled up on the side of the road to allow us through. It improved our morale but there were some minor irritations when we entered Digne-les-Bains. Instead of making our way to the finish line, the Tour organisers took the *peloton* on a 50 km circuit of the town – including a couple of tough climbs – before we finished. It was a real kick in the teeth after our exertions in the Alps and I was really struggling towards the end of the stage. Ian and Robbie were nowhere to be seen and they left Neil to draft me into Digne-les-Bains. He was struggling in the heat and against yet another headwind; we were riding at less than 10 kph in places.

We were wilting in the sun and we needed to sit on Robbie and Ian's wheel for half an hour to get some respite. After two days of climbing in the Alps, we were both deep in the red zone. Mercifully, the last stretch was downhill and we eventually came grinding to a halt in a car park in the town centre. Neil had already resolved to talk to Ian and Robbie because their going ahead so often was clearly affecting the number of hours we had to spend on the road each day.

'Listen, mate, we're not going to get through this if you don't wait for us. We need to ride together as a team so that we can each take a turn on the front.'

'No problem, you should have said something before. Don't let it fester.'

'Yeah, I know.'

'No worries.'

And that was that.

Matt, though, had been waiting his turn and his blood was boiling. Neil had been writing a Tour diary for the *Daily Mail* and he usually wrote it within minutes of getting off his bike. The *Mail* was publishing his despatches to coincide with the stage that the professionals were about to embark on and that meant that today's edition of the paper would have the story of the climb into Courchevel. That proved to be the root of the problem. When Neil got off his bike in Courchevel, he had written that Matt had suffered the dreaded 'bonk'. That was his belief at the time and, although he had also described him as a hero for completing the stage considering his deteriorating condition, Matt didn't see it that way. As Neil and I approached Digne-les-Bains that afternoon, Matt made a call into his office in London.

'Hi, it's Matt.'

'Ah … the bonker!' replied Steve Cording, the sports news editor.

'You what?' asked a rather surprised Matt.

'We've just had some copy filed by Neil and it says you're a bonker!'

Steve then read out Neil's piece over the telephone.

As soon as Ian had finished talking with Neil, Matt jumped in and began jabbing his finger in Neil's face.

'Did you write that I bonked on the climb up to Courchevel?'

'What?'

'Did you write that I bonked in Courchevel?'

'Matt, you're my friend, have you read it? I've made you out to be a hero.'

'No, you said I bonked.'

It was explosive – one of those moments when time stood still. Andrea and Hayley were so scared that they retreated to their cars. I didn't know where to look, neither did anyone else. Neil and Matt were close friends, but they were laying into each other and I was worried that they would end up coming to blows in the car park. They had known each other a long time, but they never exchanged a cross word between them. Now the stress of 12 days on the road and everything that had happened over the past 24 hours or so was coming to a head.

'You're out of order.'

'Matt, you're not listening ...'

'What you've done is out of order.'

Eventually, they turned their backs on each other and walked off. There was a reservoir by the side of the car park and Neil went over to it, threw his water bottles into the water and tried to cool down. He called his office, but they were lapping it up. I got the impression they didn't mind if the story inflamed the situation. I actually thought it was quite funny to watch the two of them jabbing their fingers at each other, but it wasn't the time to laugh.

By now Westie and the girls were loading the cars with all our equipment, but there was no sign of Haynesy. His car was parked across the road and he was calling us on the radio every five seconds. Things were tense enough as it was and people were nervously circling the cars. I had a feeling something was about to explode.

I sympathised with Matt because I knew what he had been through, but his office were obviously giving him some merciless stick. He was already feeling low enough and he felt that Neil had deliberately set out to undermine him. I don't think that was the case, but Matt wasn't letting it go. By now, Neil was sitting by the river and Matt wasn't prepared to give him an inch. And Haynesy was still crackling away on the radio.

'Can anybody hear me, over?'

Silence. No-one wanted to speak.

'I'm in the car park across the road if everyone can come over.'

By that, I took it that Haynesy wanted us to cycle over to another car park, but I had already taken my shoes and socks off and put on my flip flops. It was clear that no-one had any intention of joining him. We were mentally and physically exhausted after our 12th day in the saddle and things were really coming to the boil. I liked Haynesy, but he had a certain way of working that could be extremely irritating – particularly if we were tired and not in the mood for talking.

'It's Chris, over.

'Can anybody hear me, over?'

We all could, so I reached into the cabin and got on the radio. After all the arguing over the past 10 minutes, I felt it was my turn to let off a bit of steam.

'Haynesy?'

'Yes, Geoff.'

'We've just done two days in the mountains, we've just ridden a whole day into the wind and we aren't going across the road just to suit you.'

'I appreciate that, Geoff, but—'

'Haynesy?'

'Yes?'

'Fuck off!'

13

Miramas-Montpellier, 173.5 km

There are some things in life you simply never forget. I will never forget 4 July 2003, when I was officially diagnosed with leukaemia, or the day – 28 January 2005 – when Charlie Craddock told me, as I walked through the Mailbox Shopping Centre in Birmingham, that I was in remission. And I am damned sure I will never be allowed to forget 19 February 1992, when England played France in a friendly at Wembley.

Neither, it seems, will anyone with more than a passing interest in football. For me, it signalled the start of the most depressing year of my entire football career.

I was the proud captain of Crystal Palace and my performances over the past couple of seasons had helped me force my way into Graham Taylor's England squad. Wrighty became the first Palace player to represent England in more than a decade when he played against Cameroon in January 1991, but I wasn't far behind.

Nigel Martyn, the goalkeeper, went on to play for England 23 times; Salako won five caps; Gray played once; and Bright, who deserved more recognition, made it into the 'B' team. We were ready for the step up or, at least, we all felt we were. The previous year, England lost a World Cup semi-final against Germany on a penalty shoot-out and expectations among the team were high. Taylor had taken over from Bobby Robson when the World Cup campaign in Italy ended with that dramatic defeat and he had made some high-profile changes to the squad. Peter Shilton, capped 125 times by his country, announced his retirement straight after the tournament and Bryan Robson, dubbed Captain Marvel by the manager, Bobby Robson, was later discarded by Taylor.

It was a daunting task for anyone to replace the England captain and his departure left a huge void in the centre of midfield. At the time, he was regarded as one of the finest box-to-box midfielders in the world and there were not many players around who could hold a candle to him when he was on his game. He partnered Paul Gascoigne in Italy and England needed another terrier alongside Gascoigne to fill Robson's boots. David Platt made a name for himself at the World Cup when he came on as a substitute to score the last-minute winner against Belgium and he was already well known to Taylor.

Taylor had managed Platt when he was at Aston Villa and it was obvious that he wanted him to play a key role in the new England set-up. Villa finished third in Taylor's final season at the club and Platt's ability to score crucial goals was a big part of that. Taylor also had a special talent in the shape of Gascoigne, but he was unpredictable and Platt gave him that little bit of reassurance in the centre of the park.

Taylor was expected to lead England through a comfortable qualifying group before the European Championships in Sweden in 1992. In March 1991, I was picked to start the qualifying tie away to Turkey. Along with Dennis Wise, who was also making his first senior start for his country, we got caught up in the razzmatazz that surrounds the national team. We were the new kids on the block and we were desperate to make an impression. The photographers asked us to wear a fez for the pictures and we were only too happy to oblige.

It was exciting: we had made it into the England squad and we wanted to stay there. Taylor had shown, as he did when he selected Wright for the 2–0 victory over Cameroon at Wembley in January, that he was prepared to give players a chance at international level. Wright acquitted himself well alongside Gary Lineker, and there were suggestions that they might be able to form England's first-choice strike partner-

What a team: Ian Whittell, Neil Ashton, me, Robbie Duncan and Matt Lawton (*all photos in this section © Dave West*)

(*above*) Neil looks forward to another long day in the saddle

Ian, strong as an ox, kept the team going whenever we found it tough

Happy days, early in the t

Matt prepares for his heroic climb to Courcheval

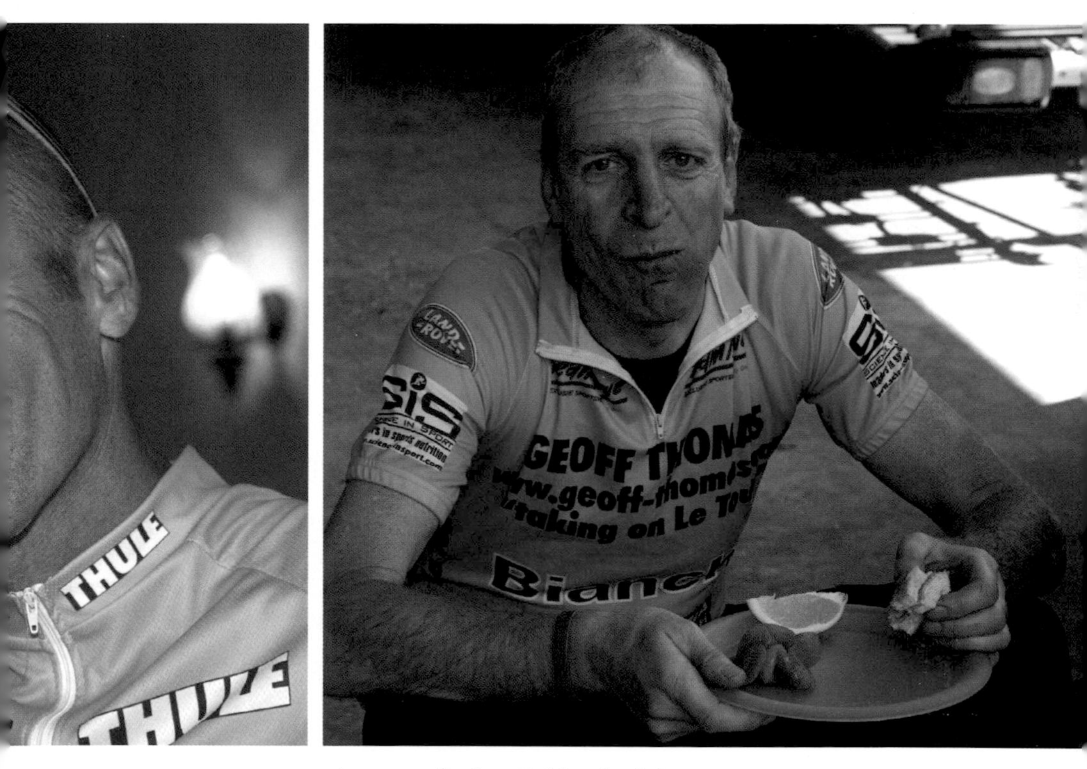

A piece of cake: Robbie had forty years
of cycling behind him, and it showed

The beginning of a dramatic descent down the Galibier in freezing temperatures and snow

(*inset*) Even during the toughest days, nothing could take away from my looks

Touched by angels: Andrea Smith (left) and Hayley Cullum brightened up our days on the road with their cheery support

We did it

Charlie Craddock at the finishing line

Charlie, with my mum, Renee (centre) and sister Kay

With my wife Julie, and Madison and Georgia (front)

It was Lance Armstrong who convinced me I could beat leukaemia

ship. His elevation to the England stage was fully merited and it gave players outside the top clubs in the country the chance to reach out.

I was one of those players. We drew 1–1 in Turkey – Wise scored on his debut – and I was happy with my performance. I was a little surprised when the manager told me he was substituting me at half-time because I was playing well, but I wasn't in a position to complain. His reasoning, and I still wonder about it, was that it was because it was my first game for my country. I couldn't understand the logic. What was that supposed to mean? As far as I was concerned I had performed well in the opening 45 minutes and I was certain I could do just as well after the break.

I was certainly surprised, but, as a junior member of the team, I had no right to voice my concerns. I returned to Palace and we eventually finished third in the old First Division, beating Manchester United 3–0 in our final game of the season. It was an extraordinary achievement for a side that had only been promoted, via the play-offs, two years before. There was more recognition at the end of the season when Taylor selected me for the England tour of Australasia. It was a mini-tour, designed to give some fringe players the chance to shine in the absence of some of the leading lights.

Despite the absence of Robson, the England captain, Gary Lineker, was still on the trip, although he flew off to Japan to negotiate his transfer to Grampus Eight midway through the tour. John Salako had also been selected and we were determined to make the most of the opportunity. I'd already added to my England caps after playing Argentina and Russia and, at the time, I didn't feel there was a better player than me in the country in my position. Gascoigne was by far the most skilful, but his career-threatening injury in the 1991 FA Cup final against Nottingham Forest forced Taylor to look at alternatives.

I was one of them – alongside Platt, David Batty, Neil Webb and Steve Hodge. I knew that the summer tour would give me the chance to force my way into Taylor's plans for the European Championships. I was the kind of midfielder who never gave up. Even when everyone was having a tough time on the pitch, I would roll up my sleeves and substitute skill for sheer strength. Those qualities earned me my chance to play for England and I was determined to make the most of it. I never felt out of place in an England squad and I always felt part of the team atmosphere.

Taylor employed Steve Harrison as his coach and he certainly had an individual approach to international get-togethers. He was a very good coach, but his performances off the pitch used to have the players in stitches. I can remember Taylor taking the team to a show. With so many people sat down for a screening it was easy for us to get restless and, with footballers' notoriously short attention spans, we would need something to lighten the mood. That invariably came when Harrison was around. As the curtains came down to mark the beginning of the interlude, the lights came on and he was just sitting there stark naked. He didn't even cover up his modesty.

He was absolutely mad and, although Taylor had a fairly good idea of the sort of things he used to get up to, he turned a blind eye to most of it. Another time, Harrison disappeared for half an hour while the England team were being shown round a stately home. It was incredibly boring, but suddenly this character came walking down the stairs in full chain mail. It was Harrison – he had gone upstairs, found a mannequin decked out in the armour and put it on. The rest of the guests were horrified.

The moment Harrison walked into a hotel, he would trip over a flight of stairs. Clothes would spill out of his suitcases and he would be lapping up all the attention from old ladies, who would struggle over to him with their walking sticks to make sure he was OK. The humour was childish, but when you are with a big group of lads, it becomes a way of life. Taylor recognised the fact that international footballers need a diversion when they spend time away from their families and I thought it was a masterstroke to employ him.

Ultimately he was sacked by England after a 'toilet' prank was leaked to the press. The players would get a note passed under their doors to be in one of the hotel rooms just after dinner and we all knew what it was for. Steve would close the curtains, dim the lights in his room and, at the appointed time, the lads would file in. It would be very dark, but we would be able to see a figure, with a towel wrapped around him like a cape, perched on top of a wardrobe. We would crowd round and he would beckon one of the lads over. He'd place a plastic cup on the floor and shine a light on it, and then, with the accuracy of a heat-seeking missile, he would empty his guts into it from the top of the wardrobe.

Those were mad times and, although it was very embarrassing when the story appeared in the newspapers, he didn't have any trouble getting work. He is an excellent football coach and his sessions were of the highest order. They were innovative, never boring and always at a high tempo. The lads absolutely loved him because he didn't take life too seriously. As a footballer, you need that from the coaching staff. Managers are under the microscope and under a lot of pressure to pick a winning team, but a good coach can relieve the tension. He was perfect for the role.

He had a spell at Palace under Steve Coppell and he clearly impressed Gareth Southgate because he has since employed him at Middlesbrough as his first-team coach. It is a shame that his England career came to an abrupt halt, but players can be selfish: all they want to know is whether they are in the team when it is announced for the next international. It was always a relief for me to know that I had been selected but for others, it was automatic.

I admired players with more skill than me, but I was never in awe of them. Chris Waddle, then at Marseille, was a phenomenal player and so was Lineker. He was the biggest name in English football at the time, but he never got carried away with success. He was such a unique talent that he mapped out his entire career. He made everyone feel a part of the England set-up and that helped during the tour down under. It had been widely criticised by the press and, although it was effectively a 'B Tour', it was still a chance to represent our country. We got off to a poor start and only squeezed past Australia in our first game 1–0.

The honeymoon period was coming to an end for Taylor and he was under pressure for the team to impress when we played New Zealand for a second time. This led to a bewildering moment.

Taylor sat on the bus on the way to the game against New Zealand

and was giving us a pre-match pep talk. He was shadowed, as he always was, by the assistant manager, Lawrie McMenemy, but Graham was doing all the talking. We were on a tight schedule. After the game, we were going straight back to our hotels to pick up our luggage before flying to the next leg of the tour in Malaysia.

Taylor was demanding an improved performance and he felt that now that we had become acclimatised following the long-haul flight to the other side of the world, we should be able to perform better. He was saying things like: 'Come on, Geoff, you've shown you're a good player for Palace, now I need you to step up and show that you can do it on a bigger stage.

'This is your chance, lads, to make a name for yourselves. We all know that you can play, you've proved that for your clubs, now let's see if you can perform at a higher level.

'You've had time to get used to being in the squad. Now let's get stuck into them and prove to people that you have a right to wear the shirt.'

Then Graham turned to his assistant, as he often did, and said: 'Do you want to add anything, Lawrie?'

McMenemy looked up and, in that booming Sunderland accent of his, he replied: 'Yes. Right, lads, remember to tidy your rooms.'

OO

When things were going well on the pitch, it masked everything else that is going on in your life. I had been married to my first wife, Cath, for seven years and she made huge sacrifices in her personal life to be with me in the early years of my career. We met when I was 17 and married, as childhood sweethearts, when I was 21. She was brilliant at the start of my career. I was a trainee electrician while I was playing for Rochdale and her job helped to keep us afloat financially.

She made sacrifices in her own professional life when I moved to London to play for Palace but, as my career took off, we began to drift apart. I was headstrong, selfish and looking forward to playing for England in the European Championships when we had a trial separation at Christmas 1991. Cath went to Australia to spend some time with friends and to give us both space while we contemplated our futures. We didn't hate each other and there was no animosity, but I think we accepted that we had drifted apart. At the turn of the year, the only thing I was concentrating on was playing for England at Euro 92.

I neglected my home life and was getting my kicks by performing well for Palace in the build-up to Euro 92 in Sweden. I knew that any dip in form would be noted by the press, the fans and, above all, the England manager, and that would be all the excuse he needed to cull my name from the squad list. I was still flying and, as a friendly international against France approached in February, I felt I was an established member of the England squad. Sweden was on my mind, as it was for every other player in the squad at the time. I wondered whether I had done enough to earn a starting place alongside Platt.

The newspapers were full of speculation and many of them were predicting Taylor's squad for Euro 92. Fortunately I was in most of them and Bobby Moore, England's World Cup-winning captain in 1966, even claimed that I should be leading my country. It was an enormous honour to read that and, as far as I was concerned, it strengthened my hand. I had won eight caps for my country and never been on the losing side. I didn't feel out of place alongside England's finest footballers and my next ambition was to get on the scoresheet. I had a good record for Palace – I scored around once every eight games – but I hadn't got off the mark for England yet.

Lineker was always a threat up front, but Taylor wanted more players to chip in with goals. Platt was always likely to assist in that area with his trademark late runs and I felt that if I could score my first England goal, it would cement my place in Taylor's thoughts as we approached Euro 92. It wasn't preying on my mind as we approached the game against France, but I knew that it would help my cause. When the squad met up at Burnham Beeches, the hotel and leisure complex in Berkshire which England used before their matches at Wembley, Taylor took Platt and me to one side.

Gascoigne was still struggling to recover from his cruciate ligament injury and Taylor told us, as we strolled through the leafy grounds, that we were his first-choice midfield partnership. Platt and I had played together against Russia and Argentina, and we had both done well, but we knew we didn't have the flair of Gascoigne. We lacked his creativity, his spark and his genius, but we felt – and, more importantly, Taylor felt – that we were his best alternative. It was in an era when the likes of Glenn Hoddle and Bryan Robson were no longer around, but I was never out of my depth. I was looking forward to the France game, even though they arrived at Wembley boasting a 13-game unbeaten run and they were feared opponents.

Managed by the legendary France striker Michel Platini, they were renowned for their ability on the ball and they had won all eight games during qualification for Euro 92. It was always going to be a tough game. Jean-Pierre Papin, the best striker in the world at the time, was playing alongside Eric Cantona up front. At the back, Basile Boli and Laurent Blanc were two of the best central defenders in the world and their midfield, including the likes of Didier Deschamps and Christian Perez, was formidable opposition. I remember Taylor going through the tactics at Wembley before the game and he told me that I would be marking Boli, a brute of a man, at set-pieces.

Now I'm 6 ft 1 inch and weighed 11 stone 4 lb during my playing days, but one look at Boli was enough to put anyone on edge and he gained a certain notoriety when he went on to head-butt Stuart Pearce during England's draw with them in the group game at Euro 92. He was my only concern as I went into the game because he was as strong as an ox and I thought to myself: 'If he gets a run on me here, I won't have a chance.' There was a fear factor, but it was good because it kept me on my toes.

France, under the guidance of Platini and his assistant, Gérard Houllier, were an impressive team. It was always likely to be tight and, even though they were a superior technical side, we took our chances. Alan Shearer, making his England debut, and Lineker scored our goals and, for one moment, I thought I might get on the scoresheet. It is fair to say that I was not having my best game that night, but I had the chance to open my England account midway through the second half. I laid the ball into Lineker in the centre circle and, when he returned the pass, I found the defence opening up in front of me with only the keeper, Gilles Roussett, to beat.

'He wants you to chip him. Go on, Geoff ... he wants you to try the chip.'

I was more than 30 yards out and I had a lot of time on my hands. Too much time. And that can be fatal. There were alternatives. I could have tried to round the keeper, or even slip the ball past him and inside either one of the white Wembley posts. I was surprised I was in so much space and I thought Roussett was on the edge of his 18-yard box.

If it had gone in, it would have been replayed a thousand times over on television. It would have been up there as one of the greatest goals that has been witnessed by the famous old stadium and would have gone down in history.

It did go down in history, but for all the wrong reasons. I shanked the effort to the right and I knew instantly that I had made a ricket. There is an air of expectation whenever a player has a goal-scoring opportunity and I could tell by the groans ringing around the stadium that it was a bad miss. I stood there, with my hands on top of my head and, if the vast Wembley pitch could have opened up and swallowed me there and then, that's what I would've wished.

There were 59,000 England supporters inside Wembley that night and millions more watching at home. No question, I was embarrassed. Who wouldn't be? Playing for England on the world stage is the highest honour in the game and this would prey on anyone's mind. I learned a harsh lesson, but it wasn't a question of being cocky. By the time we played France, I was an established England international. I was a familiar face in the newspapers and on the television. I had a right to that chip. It was a mistake because I should have carried on until I reached the edge of the area; but I still didn't know the effect it would have on my international career.

I was faced with a similar situation when I was at Wolves later on in my career and both times I ran through and placed the ball around the keeper. You live and learn. There is not a football fan in the country who has not seen that effort at Wembley, but I'm not embarrassed about it any more. I've still got the newspapers from the following day, when acres of newsprint were dedicated to the game, and hardly any of it mentions the effort. Instead, they reflected on the result, which we felt was significant in terms of our chances in Sweden that summer. The *Sun* even claimed it was the result that 'shook the rest of Europe'.

I had a good relationship with the press throughout my career, but a lot of the reporters were staring at their shoes when I walked past them. I expected a grilling after the game, but most of them didn't even bring up the subject. I think they felt sorry for me. I was certainly feeling sorry for myself and I got a taste of things to come when I left Wembley that evening.

The Football Association always put on a chauffeur-driven car to take players home after internationals. I was feeling pretty shattered by the time I left Wembley that evening – it was a wonderful place to play football, full of history and passion, but it was always such a draining experience. After the long build-up to internationals, the pressure, the support and the game itself, it was always a bit of a come-down on the way home. The next day, we were expected to return to our club sides and begin preparing for that weekend's match.

The journey to South London usually took about an hour and a half from Wembley, but I didn't feel like making it with my driver after he introduced himself to me after loading the boot with my kit.

'Hello, Mr Thomas,' he said.

'Hi, you OK?'

'Good, thanks. Good result tonight.'

'Yeah, very pleased.'

'I was listening to it on the radio in the car. I heard you missed a sitter, didn't you ...'

That was just the beginning. The real problems began when *The Mary Whitehouse Experience* started on television – the first programme to start making fun of footballers. I had chosen the wrong time and the wrong place to make such a high-profile blunder, but Frank Skinner really brought it into the public domain with his endless gags.

That's when the stick really started flying. I was the butt of endless cheap jokes and mickey-taking. I was nominated in every supporters' poll going as the worst player to ever represent my country. I was getting battered. It hurt, and it hurt like hell. Danny Baker hosted a phone-in programme on Radio Five and he was constantly urging me to get in touch.

'Come on, Geoff, tell us what you were up to with that chip,' he would demand.

When I did, I could never get through, but I wish I had. By the time I returned to club football with Palace, I was getting abuse from the terraces and my form really started to dip as we approached the end of the season. When we played West Ham, their supporters were even singing: 'If Thomas can play for England, so can I.'

It was the first time I had ever really taken any notice of supporters' chants during a game and that told me that I was not concentrating properly. Palace had sold Ian Wright to Arsenal and, although he was scoring a lot of goals under George Graham, he was on the outside as well. I was still selected for the England squads in the build-up to the European Championships, but my form at Palace had dipped dramatically.

Taylor selected me to play for the 'B' team in Russia in April and I could tell that he was edging away from me. I still thought I would travel to Sweden, but Carlton Palmer's form at Sheffield Wednesday had convinced Taylor to take a chance on him.

To be left out of the squad was hard. There was no escaping the France game. It had got to me, no question, and the fact I missed out on Euro 92 after being a part of the England squad for so long affected my game. I went on holiday to Cyprus that summer and found myself in the same hotel as Colin Hendry, the former Blackburn and Scotland defender, and Kerry Dixon, the Chelsea and England striker. We would play cards by the pool for hours. There was still no escape. One night I was talking to a Scouse lad at the bar. We had been talking for an hour or so and bought each other a couple of drinks before we finally asked each other's names.

'Oh, mine's Geoff,' I said.

'Pleased to meet you, Geoff,' he replied. 'Geoff who?'

'Geoff Thomas.'

'Oh, Geoff Thomas. Well, at least you're not that prick who missed that chance at Wembley.'

'Well, actually …'

People still bring up that chip and now I just ask the same question. 'Where was it?'

'Wembley,' they respond in a flash and then they realise what they have just said.

No matter what anyone says about that night at Wembley, I can proudly point to the nine caps and the fact I was never once on the losing side. I enjoyed playing for England at every level, including the seemingly insignificant 'B' team games. My only disappointment was the way my England career ended. Unless you are someone with the stature of Gary Lineker or Alan Shearer, players do not pick the time when they retire from international football. Instead, they are simply cast aside and rarely given a reason by the manager. Perhaps they want to leave the door ajar in case they are forced to recall you at some point, or perhaps they don't have the nerve to tell you that they no longer feel you are good enough for the job.

Either way, Taylor never said a word. I went through hell after the France game and it was at its height that summer when Skinner and his sidekick, David Baddiel, hosted their *Fantasy Football* programme. Despite my bitterness, I sympathised with Taylor when he was going through hell in Sweden. His decision to replace Lineker with Alan Smith cost him the respect of the country and the Turnip that was imprinted on the top of his head on the back page of the *Sun* when they lost to Sweden was ten times worse than any criticism levelled at me.

I get on well with him now, though. We spoke about it when he became my manager at Wolves two years later, but we never really went into any great detail. He called me into his office when he arrived at Molineux and there was a wry smile on his face as if to say, 'Geoff, we meet again.' He knew what I had been through, but he went through far worse in the period leading up to his dismissal. I couldn't bury the memories, though. He told me I was a permanent fixture in his England team and within weeks I had been cast adrift and left to deal with the devastation in my own way. Who wouldn't be sour about that?

He was the manager and he was paid to make some big decisions. That's fair enough and, despite the way my international career tailed off, I still have enormous respect for Taylor. When I was first diagnosed with leukaemia, he was regularly on the phone to check on my progress and he still calls. I am touched by that. Now I hear from friends in the game that he uses my name as an example whenever people question the reasons why he capped so many unfashionable players.

His response – 'If you don't pick people, you will never find out if they are good enough' – fills me with a warm glow. Taylor was bold enough and brave enough to select me when I was playing for a club outside the established order. He felt he saw enough in me. I was a fighter; I could run all day long but I could also play a bit. There were other players around at the same time who were similar to me – Batty and Hodge were among that number – and when we were playing well, we would stand out.

When our form dipped, we would appear average and that always went against us as far as England was concerned. Taylor took a lot of flak after the experience of Sweden and his failure to qualify for the World Cup two years later, but I didn't enjoy the way it ended for him. I just wish I could have been out in Sweden and, although I might not have been able to make a difference to the result, I never went hiding when I was playing. When he took Lineker off in his last game, it was the beginning of the end for him. By then, I knew that I would never play for my country again.

Just to walk out at Wembley wearing my England shirt filled me with immense pride and it is a feeling I will never let go. Why should I? I'm the man who missed at Wembley, but I've seen players miss easier chances than that. I just did it on the big stage and I suppose I will always be remembered for that.

Still, it could have been worse. On Saturday, 22 February 1992, I met Julie.

14

Agde-Ax 3 Domaines, 220.5 km

I first met Mark Miller in the haematology unit at the Queen Elizabeth Hospital in the early stages of my illness. We always seemed to be there at the same time and his lovely girlfriend, Dawn, first approached me. Mark had also been diagnosed with chronic myeloid leukaemia and we often sat in the same waiting room, whiling away the hours by talking about our troubles. You need friendships when you are going through tough times and this one was built on solid foundations.

Dawn is a fanatical Wolves supporter and, despite my hollow features, she still recognised me from my playing days at Molineux. Dawn introduced Mark to me as her boyfriend and we shared a unique bond as we struggled to beat this deadly disease. His knowledge and support were invaluable and he would give me an insight from a patient's unique perspective about coping with cancer. He spoke about my first steps towards beating this horrific illness and he always lent a sympathetic ear.

I had my first proper chat with him when his blood counts were being taken in the Queen Elizabeth Hospital. He was squeamish and didn't like needles, so he would have to lie down on the hospital bed to avoid the sight of a syringe. Dawn raised her eyebrows at me because she knew, as I did, that he had already been through considerably worse. They met shortly before he was diagnosed with CML and, despite her own domestic situation – she had two children from her first marriage – she supported him through the crisis.

I always admired Dawn for that. She had only known Mark for a very short time and it was a huge commitment on her part. They met on a blind date in Whitby, where they were both on a scooter rally, in April 2002. Within two months, Mark had moved into her home in Wolverhampton. She was a care assistant in an old people's home and Mark, who was originally from York, had taken a job with a removals company. He dreamed of the day when he would be able to take Dawn away on his scooter again, but CML is a debilitating disease. It was slightly easier for Julie and me. We had been together for more than 13 years and we had already been through so much. Julie was always there for me.

I admired the way Dawn was prepared to roll up her sleeves and support her boyfriend. She had lost her mother through cancer when she was only 21 and she was nursing Mark through the illness. It was a difficult time for her and she did her best to juggle her time between Mark and her children. She was always there and she listened intently and compassionately whenever Mark and I talked. It was heartening to know what was lying in wait for me and, although I knew he had been through many difficult times during the course of his treatment, it was reassuring to know that he made it through the other side.

He warned me that my hair would start falling out in clumps within days of my bone-marrow transplant. I would only have to touch the hair on my head and it would be literally falling to the floor. Mark told me he had scabs forming in his mouth from the total body irradiation treatment and, sure enough, I soon got them. His advice was invaluable and he showed immense resolve. He was a tough, doughty character and I admired his resilience. There is so much heartache and pain associated with this disease that it affects everyone's emotional state. Whenever we grew tired of talking about our treatments, we would explore each other's lives.

Our backgrounds were so different and yet we shared similar dreams. He harboured strong hopes that he would make a full recovery and his determination spurred me on. He was clearly struggling to combat the effects of the illness, but he was a fighter and I admired his enormous courage. When Mark was diagnosed with CML, he was already in the accelerated phase of the disease and things were critical. Like so many others, he had ignored the classic symptoms of the disease.

He told me that he had felt unwell for several months. His ankles were swollen, he felt nauseous and tired, and he had stomach cramps. I knew exactly what he had gone through. Just like my wife, Mark's girlfriend, Dawn, had urged him to visit the doctor and eventually he swallowed his pride and booked an appointment.

He went one morning in July 2002 and, the very same afternoon, the doctor knocked on his door and told him he was at risk of a stroke if he did not go to hospital. His platelet levels were through the roof and the specialists put him on the 'washer' to bring his levels back down again. By the time Mark was admitted to hospital for a stem-cell transplant in late July, he was already in 'blast', which is the final stage of the disease's development. The typical response is to have extremely high dosages of chemotherapy followed by a bone-marrow transplant but the chances of survival are slim.

I was often sat in the haematology unit at the Queen Elizabeth when Mark and Dawn came in and we would talk in between consultations with the surgeons. His transplant had taken place around six months before mine, but none of his family had been a suitable stem cell match. He had been fortunate enough to find a match through a bone marrow register and was making good progress. Like me, Mark would have days when things were not going his way but, in general, the doctors were pleased with the progress he was making and they were confident he would be able to make a recovery. I would see him in the out-patients department almost every Wednesday and we would have long conversations about our progress. Any life-threatening illness is a rough ride and his relationship with Dawn was difficult while he was concentrating on beating the disease.

His hair was growing back – even the sideburns that he was so fond of were showing through – but we were both having problems with graft-versus-host disease (GVHD). I had been warned by Professor Craddock that this was one of the side-effects of the stem-cell transplant and Mark and I were both on some fairly heavy-duty anti-rejection drugs called Cyclosporin to try and combat the problem. Although the transplant is a relatively simple procedure, there is always a significant risk that the body will not accept the new cells.

GVHD occurs when the immune system from the donor doesn't recognise your skin, your liver, mouth or eyes and mounts an inflammatory reaction. Jaundice, diarrhoea, rashes and shingles can all be fatal and the doctors monitor their patients on a daily basis when they are in isolation. At some stages, Mark was fighting all of them. The first three months after the transplant are crucial. That is when infection is most likely because the chemotherapy has killed off all the normal cells. People feel nauseous, have intense stomach pains, lose their hair and become infertile. GVHD occurs in around 50 per cent of the people who have stem-cell transplants, but the risk of dying is only 10 per cent. I felt pretty rough when I was going through it – it feels like you have been beaten up.

Mark was having a real fight with GVHD. His energy levels were low, he had severe stomach cramps and problems with his liver. He was admitted for a second stem-cell transplant, but his condition continued to deteriorate. He caught CMV – the shingles virus – in January and was in and out of hospital for months. One day when I saw him, he was jaundiced, he had lumps and blemishes all over his skin and things were looking bleak.

OO

I wondered why the crew consistently referred to Stages Fourteen and Fifteen as the '48 hours from hell' but, from the moment we arrived in Agde, I fully understood. Over the next two days, we would take on some of the toughest climbs in the Tour as we made our way through the Pyrenees. I was pleased that Matt had recovered in time to ride with us.

He eased back into the saddle when we rode the flat stage between

Miramas and Montpellier the previous day, but the trip to Ax 3 Domaines gave him the chance to conquer the mountain climbs again.

Although progress out of Agde was expected to be fairly steady, we knew that the 16 km climb to the 2,000-metre summit of the Port de Pailhères, at an average gradient of 8 per cent, was waiting for us towards the end of the stage. Even the prospect of the 20 km descent on the other side did little to raise spirits because, after that, we faced the relentless climb to the ski station, at 1,372 metres, at the top of Ax 3 Domaines.

The following day, we were to suffer again, but I couldn't think that far ahead. In fact, I wasn't even sure I could think beyond the evening we would be spending in Agde. In the six months' build-up to the Tour, we operated on a strict budget and our choice of hotels, especially in terms of quality, was heavily restricted.

On most days, we sacrificed quality and instead booked the rooms on the basis of their proximity to the start line. Aside from the occasional indulgence, such as our stay in the opulent surroundings of a medieval hotel in Troyes, we mainly chose single- or two-star hotels. It was basic, but it was a bed for the night and we were usually so tired that the comfort factor was of little consequence. I wish I could say the same after our stay in Agde. According to our planning, the hotel in Agde was less than 500 metres from the start of Stage Fourteen. For us, after regularly sitting with our knees bent up by our ears in the back of the Land Rovers as we drove to the start line each morning, this should have been manna from heaven. Instead, it was the start of the 48 hours from hell.

As we approached Agde, just before midnight, we realised that our hotel was in the middle of a carnival that would last until the early hours. After parking the support vehicles outside, we negotiated our way past acrobats, clowns and what seemed like an entire French town just to get to the reception area. Robbie was already getting stuck into them.

'Is this a joke?'

'*Pardon*, monsieur?'

'Is this a joke?'

'*Parlez-vous Français*, monsieur?'

'I don't believe this.'

'*Pardon*?'

'We've got no fucking chance with this racket on.'

As we began the grind of unloading the vehicles and packing our bikes into the hotel's storage area, our worst nightmare was unfolding in front of our very eyes. High-spirited locals were dancing within feet of us and a concert stage was being erected beside the hotel. The music was already deafening and now there was the prospect of a rock band striking up on the streets when we should be getting some precious sleep.

After the dramas of the arguments involving Ian, Matt, Chris, Neil and me, everyone was emotionally drained and this only added to the sense of despair. By now, we were all on autopilot. We were tired and the thought of starting again at 6 a.m. filled us with dread. When we were handed our room keys, it was almost as if someone had deliberately intervened to make the Tour as mentally, as well as physically, taxing as possible. I began to envy the professionals for the first time because everything is done for them by the team *soigneurs*.

When they finish a stage, they are taken straight to the team's tour bus for a shower and, within minutes, they are on their way to the hotel. They certainly wouldn't have to worry about rock bands and their bass guitars when they arrived in Agde in three days' time. The pros have the evenings free to relax before they start the next day's stage.

Time was always against us but we were on the point of despair after this. We were rarely in bed before midnight and, because of the time constraints, we would often be awake by 6 a.m. and on the road by 7 a.m.

Sure, we would stop for coffee and a croissant a couple of times a day but, more often than not, we rode for more than 12 hours a day every day for 21 days. That took its toll: on me, on Ian, on Robbie, Matt, Neil and everyone involved with the support.

The sleep deprivation was hard to get used to. Aside from the team time-trial on Stage Four, when we only had 67.5 km to ride, I cannot remember getting a full night's sleep throughout the whole Tour.

Even six hours was considered a bonus but this was not enough time for our muscles to recover. Often I would be locked up with cramp before I went to bed and Westie would have to come into my hotel room to give me a rub-down. On some days I was so sore that he would come in before I got out of bed to try and encourage my stiff muscles to wake up. I knew there would be big problems before the start of this stage because I didn't anticipate getting any sleep at all.

The building was like a secret garden and, typically, our rooms were located several flights of stairs away – there were no lifts – from the reception area. My room, which could only just fit a double bed inside it, was like a sweat-box. Even though it was mid-July, the hotel's heating system was on; there was no air-conditioning and opening the window was not an option. Outside, the party was in full swing and no sooner had my head hit the pillow than the band began to strum their guitars. The rest of the guys couldn't sleep either and we were in and out of each other's rooms all night.

Poor Robbie could snore his way through most things – he was so loud that one night Ian came and slept on the floor of my room – but even he couldn't get to sleep through this din.

'I don't even like fucking rock music,' Robbie complained.

OO

That morning, I believe I was close to my lowest point. I believe we all were. We still had 48 hours in front of us that would determine our fate, but we would be doing it on empty. Of the ten people on the Tour – the five riders and five crew – I don't believe any of us slept for more than an hour that night. The party carried on until around 4 a.m. and the next thing I remember was Hayley banging on my door, demanding to know whether I was decent.

Hayley or Andrea served coffee every morning and it made my day, but this morning I struggled to raise the faintest smile. Instead, I trudged wearily around the room and contemplated the next 48 hours.

For the first 180 km, we would ride on the flat and simply wait for the Port de Pailhères to appear on the horizon. Although the Alpine climbs are the more celebrated sections of the Tour, the Pyrenees are unquestionably tougher. They are steeper and the descents on the narrow, winding roads are considerably more dangerous.

I knew that the 15.2 km to the top of the Port de Pailhères would be a struggle and it took more than two hours before I finally made it to the top. Even then, I knew that the climb to the ski station finish at Ax 3 Domaines was lying in wait down the other side. By the time we reached the foot of that climb, we had been on the road for more than 13 hours and we still had at least another two in front of us. My eyes were sore, a legacy of my leukaemia treatment, and I was constantly having to stop in order to administer more eye drops.

I wore contact lenses when I was a player, but the effects of my treatment means that I no longer produce enough tears to keep them moist. I had some sunglasses specially made up for the Tour, but they couldn't prevent the sweat rolling into my eyes. We were losing so much salt through sweating that we were replacing our bodies' stores with vast quantities in our food in the evenings. At times, that meant that I was overloaded with salt and my body would pump it out through my sweat glands.

Sweat consistently dripped into my eyes and they flared up at any moment. They were red raw on the climb to Ax 3 Domaines but I was determined not to give up. A combination of my deteriorating eye condition and the fact that dusk was fast approaching meant I could barely see on the final sections. Neil was by my side throughout the climb, but his words of encouragement meant little to me by then.

I was in my own world and I was just determined somehow to complete the stage. When I decided to ride the Tour de France back in January, I did it for myself. I wanted to prove to myself that I had beaten the illness, but, as the months wore on, I realised I was doing it for vastly different reasons. I wanted to be a symbol of hope for people with leukaemia. If you believe in something enough, there is a chance of achieving it.

I wanted to raise money for the vital research that goes into leukaemia treatments and it became a burning ambition to help raise funds to find a cure. If there is no cure, I wanted to find a way of making people more comfortable with the disease. I met so many people along the way with similar symptoms to myself. I often had conversations with total strangers when I was waiting for my weekly meeting with Professor Craddock. We would be sat, patiently waiting our turn, but we knew we were in the club. Our pale features and bald heads ensured our continued membership.

I thought of the hours I spent talking to fellow leukaemia patients during my treatment when Neil asked if I was OK to carry on as we approached the steepest sections of the climb. By now, my face was contorted, I was in my lowest gear and I was nearly at my lowest ebb.

'There are a million reasons why I could stop right now,' I told him, 'but I'm never going to.'

I finally finished the stage at 9 p.m. The only thing on my mind was my friend Mark Miller. Two months before the Tour – on 22 May 2005 – he passed away at the age of 34 and this one was for him. God bless you, Mark.

15

Lézat-sur-Lèze–Saint-Lary Soulan (Pla d'Adet), 205.5 km

I rarely opened up to my team-mates while we were on the Tour. Most of the time we were too tired to talk at any great length, and it was hard enough finding the energy to battle through another day of climbing. My mind meandered through all sorts of things when we were turning the pedals for hours at a time, but Mark Miller was with me all the way through this traumatic stage. I knew that, no matter how hard it was to fight my way to the top of the climbs, he would have been fighting just as hard as me. I have met so many people who have succumbed to leukaemia, but Mark is always my example because it shows how cruel the disease can be. We both had CML and yet I'm here and he is not. How does that happen? No-one can tell me that it is just down to chance. There must be a reason and that is why I will commit the rest of my life to raising funds to find the answers.

We had speculated on Stages Fourteen and Fifteen being the hardest days of the Tour ever since the organisers had released the details of the gruelling schedules. The team referred to it as the '48 hours from hell' and it gnawed away at us for months. We knew it was coming, and here it was – in all its glory. Even looking at the mountain profiles on the Tour maps made us wince and, when I woke up that morning, I just wanted to roll over and go back to sleep.

Someone always had a snippet of information when we sat down for breakfast. Maybe one of the girls would tell us about the weather, or one of the team would be reading one of the many Tour de France guides we had with us. Whatever, it was rarely cheery, and today we were told that, in 1975, 43 riders in the pro Tour had finished outside the time limit when they were climbing Pla d'Adet. The route included four long first-category climbs and, after a 16 km stretch across the Spanish border, there was an 11 km climb to the top of Pla d'Adet. Without question, the 205 km slog from Lézat-sur-Lèze to the mountain-top finish at Saint-Lary Soulan was the toughest day of riding in the entire Tour and I found it difficult to keep up any kind of momentum.

Even when the roads were flat, I did not have the energy in my legs to maintain our target speed and the looming spectre of another day in the mountains was causing me a lot of distress. We were all fairly solemn when we stopped at the monument erected on the Portet d'Aspet in honour of Fabio Casartelli, who died in a crash on the descent during the 1995 Tour, and I left a red Leukaemia Research wristband among the dozens of other tributes. After paying our respects to the Italian, we set off on the downhill stretch but, for once, none of us were in the mood for racing. Evidence of those mountain-top tragedies hit all of us in different ways and we were touched by the ghostly grave that sits by the side of the road.

From the moment we set off at 7.30 a.m., we knew it was a battle against the clock. My team-mates had seen me through some rough days, but when I climb mountains it's just me and the road ahead. Someone always stayed with me, spurred me on and encouraged me to keep turning the pedals, and that was a great source of comfort. With six steep Pyrenean mountains to climb – each with an average gradient of between 7 and 8 per cent – there were concerns even early in the day that we might not be able to finish the stage. Progress was achingly slow and, when I approached the summit of the fourth col that day, some of the crew were talking about returning to finish the stage the next day.

Dusk was approaching and the support team were concerned

whether we would be able to finish the stage before it became too dangerous to cycle on the road. I was distraught that they had even discussed it, but it simply made me more determined and I told them that I would ride on, with or without them. By the time I got to the top of the 7.5 km climb to the top of the Col de Peyresourde, there was a 50:50 split among the crew about whether to stop and return the next day to finish the stage. Every time we reached the top of a mountain climb, we would always high-five each other but this time there was an air of doom and gloom. Ian came over and told me that there was no chance of finishing while it was still light, and he didn't want to take the risk of making our final descent of the day – the Col de Val Louron-Azet – in total darkness.

The whole purpose of the Tour was to ride the stages in 21 days just like the professionals. To me, the notion of returning the next day would be an admission that the Tour had beaten us. The idea hadn't even crossed my mind. Hayley came over with a concerned look on her face and handed me a sticky bun – my favourite way of celebrating another conquered climb – but I didn't stop to talk. I just set off down the other side of the mountain and let the others follow me. While I might not be fast, I'm not a flake and I was prepared to ride in the darkness if it meant finishing the stage that day. The mountains are tough, they are relentless, but as I sped down the other side towards the town of Saint-Lary Soulan, I was more determined than ever to complete the stage.

I have never been a good climber, but I set off up the fifth mountain, the Val Louron-Azet, with a renewed sense of purpose. Robbie caught me and told me to ease off because he was worried that I would burn myself out, but I didn't listen. We approached the final climb of the day at around 9 p.m., as the French celebrated Bastille Day. The lights mounted on our support vehicles guided us up the 10 km climb to the summit of Saint-Lary Soulan. By that time, after 13 hours on the road, the 8 per cent gradient seemed impossibly steep.

It was an incredible night. We were lifted when hundreds of tourists, who were parked in their camper vans on the side of the road, emerged from their bunks to cheer us up the mountain. The support seemed to grow as we continued to climb. To begin with, a few people emerged from their motor homes to see what all the fuss was about but, as we continued to climb, more and more people began to salute us. They must have thought we were crazy as we climbed, sometimes as slowly as 8 km per hour, but as they read our Leukaemia Research jerseys, they cheered even louder.

'*Allez, allez, allez*!'

'*Allez,* Geoff!'

It made me feel incredibly proud whenever supporters sang my name, but this was something special. They knew I was in trouble; they could see how tough I was finding it even to finish the stage and I think it began to dawn on many of them that we were planning to ride every kilometre. It gave me an extra incentive to finish this incredible day at the ski-station high up in the Pyrenees. As we rose through the mountains, the support tapered off, and soon we were left with nothing but our support crew to guide us home. It was cold, but to add more layers would mean stopping and that would lose momentum. During the day, we would often be drenched in sun, as we made our way up one side of a climb and freezing on the other, as we made our descents in the shade. Tonight, it was ice cold as made our way towards the top. Other than nodding our heads at people as we passed them by, there was no way to thank them for their terrific roadside support.

We carried on climbing through the night and, although I was struggling on the steep slopes, I knew that the end of two tortuous days was in sight.

Two kilometres from the top, a barrier prevented vehicles going any further, but the guy manning it simply swung it open for us. When he did that, I felt like I could ride for ever.

It was a magical feeling when we got there. It was 10.30 p.m. when we finished and, after we our traditional group hug, we peered over the mountain's edge. Down in the town, there was a firework display to celebrate Bastille Day.

I could swear they put it on just for us.

16

Mourenx-Pau, 180.5 km

A few turns on the big chain ring, a couple of clicks down through the gearing and suddenly the momentum is carrying me down the mountainside. The lactic acid that has been steadily building up in my thighs for the past two hours is released from my burning muscles and the spasm subsides. It is this moment that I look forward to – the moment of freedom, where there is just me, my bike and the sloping track that leads down the mountain.

I know it is only temporary. Soon – too soon – there will be yet another excruciating reminder that the next climb is close by, but I take the respite all the same. Cyclists quickly learn to seize on any small mercy that happens to come their way, and, after seven hours or more in the saddle each day, I am no different.

A few more strokes on the pedals, a few more seconds, and I am cruising at about 20 kph. Soon it is 30, then 40 kph and then, if I'm feeling brave enough, I might resist the temptation to feather the brakes and let the wheels spin to 50, which will soon become the gateway to 60 and beyond. Sweat drips into my eyes as I freefall; they are so red raw and swollen that I can barely see, but this is not the time to stop and administer the eye drops. The tree-lined roads provide shelter from the sun, my legs are enjoying the rest and, as always, there is the temptation to go even faster. But I temper myself this time

– when you are supported by a bicycle with wheels an inch wide and it is hoovering up the miles at this rate, a brief glance at the speedo could mean losing contact, even momentarily, with the road ahead.

Knowing this still does not stop me from wanting to peer over the mountain's edge to admire the view or spy out the roads below to try and calculate how much longer I will be freewheeling before my legs are required to pump the wheels for 90 revolutions a minute as a precursor to the next climb. I don't look, though; a descent of any kind demands concentration, but when it is 15 km or more of a mountain road, the only thing that counts is staying in one piece and making it to the bottom in the quickest possible time. The professionals adopt an aerodynamic tuck when they reach top speed and it had not taken me long to appreciate the benefits. It allows your body to slice through the air that much quicker and increases the rate of acceleration.

Stretch out across the frame, lock arms on the drops, rest the chin close to the top of the handle bars and let the gradient take care of the rest. The lower you are, the faster the bike will travel. This is a million miles away from my former career as a professional footballer; my 550 professional appearances for seven different clubs over 20 years seemed like they were in another lifetime. And if you talk to the doctors and nurses who helped bring me back to life, they will tell you that it was.

As I descended the glorious roads of the Pyrenees, the only thing on my mind was holding the racing line on the next bend before releasing the brakes and opening up another gap from the man behind. Sometimes, against the whirr of the back wheel spinning at 100 revolutions a minute, I can hear the distant sound of one of my team-mates as they race me down the mountain. Those competitive, but friendly rivalries were moments to cherish because, any minute, the descent will taper off and we will be pedalling like billy-o through the next town and away to the next mountain. Come on, Geoff, concentrate on the road ahead. If you keep still and do not deviate from the imaginary straight line that you have drawn in the middle of the hot, sticky tarmac, it is possible to ratchet up another couple of kilometres an hour or, if you are really going for it, maybe more.

Only when a road is long and straight can I check my speed, otherwise all I have is my experience to tell me whether I'm going too fast. My eyes are fixed firmly on the road ahead, watching the man in front select his line as he sweeps around another hairpin, releases the brakes and blisters his way down a section that is so steep there is no margin for error. I think that I might have time for a quick swig of drink to quench the unrelenting thirst, but then there's another twist and turn to keep me on my toes. It is just me and the bike and we have to believe in each other. Over time, I have learned to trust it. I know how it handles. I know that the brakes are so sharp that if I pull on the levers too hard I will be sent skidding into a ditch or, even worse, over the edge.

I know just how forgiving it is on the tight hairpin bends and constant switchbacks that snake their way down the mountains. At these speeds, anything can happen and if it did, there would be very little I could do about it. A car could overtake coming the other way, I could pitch into a pot-hole, under-steer a corner and be catapulted from the frame, or a tyre could puncture – and if that happened I could only hope I would be lucky enough to keep my composure and brake safely to stop at the side of the road.

These things happen all the time. The Tour de France has frequent casualties as the professionals take their chances on the narrow roads. Some are under pressure from their team to win a stage, others just to stay within the time limit and remain in the race, but most are seduced by the speed. Some unfortunate souls, such as Lance Armstrong's former team-mate Fabio Casartelli, lose their lives in pursuit of excellence.

The only time I came to a halt on a downhill during 21 days riding the Tour de France was to pay my respects at the monument that has been erected in the Italian's honour. All I knew about him before the Tour was that he died, in tragic circumstances, doing something he loved. And, despite the dangers, I loved it too. Casartelli was an exceptional young rider, but the mountains claimed his life when he careered off his bike travelling at more than 90 kph during Stage Fifteen of the 1995 Tour. He was making the 1,219-metre descent from the Col de Portet d'Aspet in the Pyrenees when a stack of riders in front of him lost control and were sent sliding off their bikes.

Casartelli could not avoid the crash and, as he was launched from his frame, his head took the full impact of the concrete blocks at the side of the road, designed to prevent cars running off the edge and into the ravine below.

I loved the thrill of the descents even though I knew that, ultimately, they led to another two hours of torture before I reached the top of the next climb. I even learned to acclimatise to the biting cold that gnawed at my battered body whenever I stopped pedalling and my body cooled off.

I would pull the zip on my jersey right to the top to prevent wind chill, hunch my shoulders to protect my ears from the flow of air and spin my legs to step up the heart rate, get the blood pumping and increase my body temperature. Soon enough, everything is in order and the only thing I can hear for miles is the constant whirr of my wheels spinning as I wend my way down towards the foothills. There is fear, but there is also the buzz, the adrenalin rush, the release and then, of course, there is the lure of taking the next bend with a bit more bravado.

It is not a time for nerves. The exhilaration and excitement of haring down a mountain pass takes care of that and, even as the days roll on, the satisfaction never subsides and the desire for another downhill never diminishes. With experience, you learn to look as far into the distance as the eye will allow. If there is no oncoming traffic, you cut the corner, avoid braking too sharply and, by extension, avoid sacrificing too much speed. For me, each descent was another chance to run up the flag of freedom. You learn quickly, you read the signals and watch out for the danger.

It is living life on the edge, knowing that you are on the cusp of another mountain-top catastrophe, but I did not give a second's thought to any of those potential hazards when I went over the famous Tour climbs of the Galibier, the Aubisque or the Marie Blanque. Instead, I could empty my mind of all the depressing thoughts that had occupied it for the past two years and enjoy, maybe for as much as 45 minutes if the descent was favourable, the flush of freedom: freedom from my screaming thighs, freedom from the daily diet of climbing for hours and hours on end and freedom, above all, from leukaemia. It had taken over for two years and now I was having some time to myself, released from the constrictions of a life consumed by cancer for the first time since I had been diagnosed.

It had been with me, like an old friend, every hour of every day since I was told, on 4 July 2003, that I had a 30 per cent chance of living beyond the age of 41. The doctors had informed me that, without treatment, I probably had three years left to live: three years, 36 months, three more birthdays, three more wedding anniversaries, three more Christmases, three more years with my beautiful children, Georgia and Madison. And that was if I was lucky.

My team-mates on the Tour were often astonished at the speed I descended but, for me, the downhill stretches were rich reward for the spells of two hours or more that I had spent crawling up the other side. It is payment for pedalling up mountain passes that are so steep and so unforgiving that the pain is no longer an issue and all that counts is making the next pedal stroke. If you can make that one, and the next, and the next ... finally you reach the summit, slap your team-mates on the back to salute another minor victory and tumble over the top.

I had only got on my bike for the first time in February but, within weeks, it felt as if it was welded to my body. In time, it became an extension of myself. I no longer had to think about which gear to use, when to brake or how to corner. It became second nature and I learned to love it. Although they were often short and sharp, the descents on my training runs fuelled my enthusiasm for a sport that I knew very little about before I was diagnosed. I wanted to know everything. I trained virtually every day for five months in the build-up to the Tour and, when I was not on the bike, I was looking up everything there is to know about the toughest sport in the world.

I knew all about Armstrong, the brusque Texan who had survived cancer to become, at that time, the six-time winner of the Tour de France, but I wanted to know more. The more I learned, the more warnings I got. The more people I told about my attempt to ride the 3,584 km Tour route in 21 days, the more motivated I became by their response.

'Do you seriously think you can do it?'

I had never been so serious about anything in my life.

OO

Climbing, climbing, climbing ... until we climbed through the clouds. Sometimes it's all we seemed to do on the Tour. Stage Sixteen, our last day in the Pyrenees before we turned inland towards the Massif Central and then on to Paris and the finish line, promised nothing different. By then, I was accustomed to the daily grind. Each night I would consult the Tour's official magazine and look at the stage profiles for the day ahead. I never looked beyond the following day. I didn't want to know. I literally took one day at time, but the mountain profiles for our last serious day of climbing looked especially tough.

Although the Alps are prettier, the Pyrenees are considerably tougher. The climbs are often short and sharp and they punished my legs as I tried to turn over the pedals until we reached the top. As we rolled out of Mourenx that morning, I knew that six mountains were on the menu and that no sooner had we warmed up by reaching the top of the 674-metre summit of the Col d'Ichère than we would be starting the struggle all the way to the 1,035-metre-high Col de Marie Blanque.

After reaching the top of the Marie Blanque, we flew down the other side before climbing the 1,677-metre Col d'Aubisque and then the 1,475-metre Col du Solour. The Tour spent three days based in Pau, tucked away in the south-west corner of France, and we saw it as a good opportunity for many of our family and friends to come and find out what it was all about. However, the 177 km trip from Mourenx proved to be among the toughest we had encountered. Matt Dickinson, the chief footballer writer with *The Times*, had joined us for the weekend and he decided to ride with us on the final mountain stage.

He knew the other three journalists riding the Tour and had written about my fundraising efforts several times in the build-up to the event. I had even ridden with him a few times as part of my training and he is a strong lad. He rowed for Cambridge when he was at university and, although he was in his late 30s, he still had a solid fitness base and was in physically great shape. Although we expected a difficult day in the saddle, our spirits had improved with the news that the website had broken the £100,000 barrier over the weekend.

Although I was aiming to raise double that, it was uplifting to hear that we had broken the six-figure barrier. I was always encouraged whenever I heard news from the Leukaemia Research team about our progress, but it wasn't always easy to keep in touch with them during the Tour. Back in London, they were busy setting up interviews with various media outlets and often there wasn't time to tell me that I was expected on air. Sometimes I would just be riding along, drafting behind Ian's back wheel, when one of the support vehicles would pull up alongside and hand me my mobile phone. On average, I took three or four of those calls every day and, even though it broke my rhythm, it was important to let people know how they could donate money. Most of it was done through my website, but there were some significant donations made directly to Leukaemia Research while we were away in France.

The £200,000 target was still some way off but the fact we had reached the halfway stage was another breakthrough and we were full of good spirits as we left Mourenx that morning. Dicko borrowed one of the spare bikes for the stage and I think he got a fairly good taste for the Tour that day. In the space of ten hours he crashed, fought a battle with Ian to be the first to the top of the Col d'Aubisque and then, along with the rest of us, went into autopilot as, typically, we went several kilometres off course. Since Matt and Robbie's accident on the first long stage of the Tour, we had been far more conscientious. We often rode for long periods in a five-man paceline, but Dicko's arrival meant making a small adjustment to accommodate an extra body.

After riding together for so long, it shouldn't have made a difference, but cycling is a sport where you have to keep your wits about you at all times. If anyone switches off, even momentarily, it can lead to an accident and it is fortunate that Dicko took the precaution of wearing a helmet when he left Mourenx that morning. With Ian leading the way, and Dicko holding his wheel at just over 32 kph, there was plenty of good-natured banter as we made our way to the first climb of the day.

That changed in a stroke when Dicko clipped Ian's back wheel and was sprung from his pedals and into a ditch by the side of the road. The sound of the clash of metal as the bikes collide, together with that sickening thud when someone lands on the tarmac, always sends the shivers through me. It could have been much more serious, but Dicko was lucky: although he had grazes scattered across his body, a ripped cycling jersey and a sore backside, he was able to continue.

There is a thin line between danger and disaster, but someone was smiling on us that day. The accident brought back memories of the potentially fatal accident on Stage Two and there was a certain nervousness as we headed toward Col d'Ichère. When cyclists are confident in each other's company, they ride within a couple of inches of their back wheel. I often rode behind Neil in our five-man paceline, and I picked up his riding habits so that I was prepared for anything.

If he got too close to Ian, he would freewheel for a while until he was off the back of his wheel and I would shout at him to close the gap. Sometimes it annoyed me because it meant working harder to get back in his draft, but much of it is down to anticipation. When I rode behind Ian, I had to watch out for his sudden bursts of acceleration. He could ride for hours at 32 kph and I would just sit in behind his wheel to take full advantage. If we were all feeling fresh and we were on a relatively flat stage, we would give Ian a nudge to step on the gas. The only problem was that no sooner had you said that than he would be 100 metres down the road, leaving everyone else trailing in his wake. He had tremendous acceleration, but I learned to listen for the gear changes.

As soon as I heard him drop down a couple, I knew I should be doing the same and, in time, we learned to live with him on those flat stages. No-one could live with him on the climbs, though. He would just pull away as soon as the roads started pointing uphill. Within seconds he was a dot in the distance and, within minutes, he would be around the next bend and there would be several hundred metres between us. As soon as we reached the Marie Blanque he was away, but Dicko, who had trained specifically to ride with him all day, matched him to the top. I watched as they peeled off into the distance, but I was soon having a battle of my own.

Although the road to the top of the Marie Blanque is only a few kilometres, the last three are brutal. The girls knew that it would be tough to reach the top but, in true Tour tradition, they made my day by painting my name in the road. It might only seem like a small gesture, but I was touched whenever they did it. Those little things, like handing me jelly babies as I struggled to navigate the notoriously steep hairpin bends that dominate the mountains, always improved my morale. Sometimes I was too focused on clawing away at the next few metres even to acknowledge Andrea or Hayley for the gesture, but they played a huge part in the event.

They were always looking for ways to improve our morale – one day they went to a toy shop to buy face masks and they drove up and down the mountain wearing them – but today it was just me against the Marie Blanque when I made my last desperate turns towards the top. The last 3 km average 12.5 per cent and it was a battle to beat the heat and the gradient as we rode through the cloud cover. For the first time on a climb, I even snapped at Neil when he was trying to take my mind off it by making me laugh.

'Never meet your heroes' was one of his favourite expressions, but I wasn't in the mood for it.

He was usually there to offer me words of encouragement and we would always have a few breathless conversations during a climb, but the Marie Blanque is a beast.

When I watched the Tour on television the following year, I saw the professionals retrace our steps over that mountain and even they struggled towards the top. They set off like an express train on the lower slopes, but the final section catches them every time: they know it's coming, but there is nothing they can do about it. There is a certain gratification in watching the experts struggle to conquer a climb – and they would have winced if they had seen me. At the top, it was a wonderful feeling to see so many family and friends waiting for us, but we didn't stay long. There was the danger of catching a cold if we paused too long. Soon, I was on my way, hammering it down the other side.

There was little respite, though, and the climbs to the 488-metre summit of the Blana and then the Col d'Aubisque, the jewel in the crown of the 2005 Tour, were soon upon us. After spending most of the morning climbing the Marie Blanque, I was dreading our arrival at the Aubisque. At 16.5 km, with an average gradient of 7 per cent, it was a formidable obstacle. Robbie had ridden it once before and warned us of its reputation, but I had an overwhelming feeling of well-being as I made my way to the top. It was tough, no question, and it called for the iPod and the comforting sounds of Kraftwerk's *Tour de France* album as I struggled up the steepest sections. Perhaps it was the feeling that we had beaten the Alps and almost made it through the Pyrenees that spurred me on. I knew that the Aubisque was the toughest climb left on the Tour; once I had conquered this one, nothing could stop me reaching the finish line on the cobblestones of the Champs-Élysées in a few days' time.

From the moment I rolled over the top of the Aubisque, I expected it to be downhill all the way to Paris. Provided we didn't have an accident, I could look forward to seeing my wife, Julie, Georgia and Maddy, and my mother Rene when we reached Paris. Throughout the Tour, I had never forgotten David Duffield's words – 'be prepared to walk up some of the climbs' – but I had used his warning to inspire me. Every time I climbed, I asked myself whether I could keep pedalling if it got steeper and the answer was always the same. Even on some of the steepest sections of the Pyrenees, like the 20 per cent climb to Saint-Lary Soulan, I never thought I could be beaten. When I was down to my last gear – the granny gear – I thought of the people who have touched me during the dark days and used them to pull me all the way to the top.

In all, there were 62 climbs on the Tour, but the Aubisque was the last that is considered by the organisers to be 'beyond classification'. I didn't even notice the countless switchbacks as we made our way upwards, but the sensation of reaching the top will live with me for a long time. Once again, we had climbed our way out of the mist, through the clouds and reached another barren wasteland. Some of the team's families had come to Pau that weekend, and had driven up there. I think it was only when they made their way to the top of the Aubisque that they began to have an understanding of the Tour. By the time we reached Paris, we would have intimate knowledge of the demands that are made on the professionals as they make their way across 21 stages.

By the time we finished, we could even argue that we had ridden 22 stages, because we took so many detours that we had added another 150 km to the official route. Another 8 km were added on towards the end of this stage, when Westie made the wrong call at a T-junction, but after surviving the Marie Blanque and then the Aubisque, I had long since stopped complaining.

17

Pau-Revel, 239.5 km

I have never found it easy to say goodbye. My sister, Kay, and I were close as children and there was a part of me that left with her when she decided to travel up to Paris in time to cheer us over the finishing line. She had travelled out to France with her husband, Bryan, and they spent the weekend with us as we slogged our way through the Pyrenees. It was fitting that she was there for some of the toughest climbs of the Tour.

They knew what I had been through, and seeing the expression on her face whenever her car pulled alongside me on the road gave me an idea of the suffering she had been through during my illness. In the old days, when I was so selfish that I wouldn't even let Julie wrench the remote control away from me, I would never have given it a second's thought, but now I recognised the contribution Kay had made to my recovery. Without her, I probably wouldn't be here.

We were close as kids growing up in Littleborough, on the outskirts of Manchester, but now there is an unbreakable bond. Life-threatening illnesses affect so many people around you, but it is easy to forget their contribution. I can't ever forget Kay's. From the moment she heard that I had been diagnosed with leukaemia, she was with me every step of the way. Sometimes she was downright annoying. Like the times when she would phone so often that I would dread the ring. I knew who it would be and I would send Julie to answer the phone. Kay's a nurse and she is a worrier; that combination can be combustible. She was only doing it because she cared, but I had a completely different attitude towards my illness. She would call on the pretext that she was asking about my condition, but it didn't matter what I said because she would be back on an hour later to start quizzing me all over again. I would tell her to relax, but she would surf the internet looking for answers, prepare a list of questions for the doctor or call my mother, and that would only increase the concerns in our family.

She constantly voiced her opinion, but I always remained positive and relaxed. I knew that the medication would take its course and, soon enough, we would find out whether I would survive. Sometimes she was beside herself with worry. When she found out she was a bone-marrow match, she broke down in floods of tears, but then the panic set in.

What if her stem cells were not a good enough match? What if my body rejected her bone marrow? What if I caught an infection before her immune system started to work?

It was questions, questions, questions. She felt responsible for my future and, although her concerns were understandable, it clearly would be no fault of hers if I didn't survive. Unfortunately, she didn't see it that way. Before the transplant, she felt that people were putting her under the microscope. In the end, she struggled to sleep at night and she ended up signing herself off work. She is a practising nurse and she had first-hand knowledge of leukaemia treatments.

Despite Professor Craddock's positive prognosis, she had so many fears that I even offered to try and find another bone-marrow match. At times she felt helpless and there was nothing that I could say to put her at ease. I recognised what an incredible gesture she was making, but she was not liable in any way for the results. She would break down at work, but she was fortunate to have many friends, family and colleagues who were able to help her through her own private ordeal. She found the period between the results that revealed that she was a perfect match and the moment I went into hospital especially difficult. It was a waiting game and, although I began to prepare myself mentally for the months ahead, Kay could barely cope from day to day.

It didn't help when our friends Clive and Jan stayed at our house for the weekend and Clive inadvertently caused Kay to burst into tears when he joked: 'So, it's all down to you now.'

It was an innocent remark and he certainly didn't mean to cause any offence, but it added to the tension and nagged away at her confidence. She thought people would judge her if the transplant was not a success, but I had a very different approach to the process. It was a fraught period and my mother's heart attack didn't help. My mother and I would sit together joking that we were both going to die, but Kay took it too literally. She was so distraught that Julie and I didn't know what to say to her on the telephone at times.

She suffered anxiety attacks when she couldn't produce enough stem cells for the hospital to harvest on the first day and spent a sleepless night at my house before returning the following day. That was a success, but she was traumatised by the whole experience. I can remember her staring through the windows of the isolation unit while I lay motionless on my bed, struggling to stay awake after another dose of radiation. I was helpless and so was she. It was out of our hands, but she didn't see it that way. As my elder sister, she felt responsible for my welfare.

Even when I went home to convalesce, she was forever on the phone. Although I had been told that my immune system was low and that I would be prone to potentially life-threatening infections, I ignored Professor Craddock's advice and bought two dogs.

Kay was angry, but I knew that my recovery would take a long time and I wanted some company while I sat at home in a blur. After that, I couldn't bring myself to tell her that I had also adopted a cat. In her professional role as a nurse, she knew that it was irresponsible to bring in pets, but I wanted something to focus on. Julie spent hours with her on the phone and they just wanted to wrap me up in cotton wool when I first came back from hospital.

It was a critical time in my recovery, but Julie was incredibly resilient. She wasn't a natural nurse and, although she was always very good with our children, she found it harder to cope with her husband being at home all day.

Julie is far removed from the WAGs lifestyle that we see today. She never once courted the limelight during my career and she let me make the decisions about my future. We met through my sister, Kay, when my marriage to Cath was on the verge of collapsing. Kay had told me about Julie, who used to cut my mother's hair in Rochdale, but it took me a while before I could find a chance to go home for the weekend. When I did, it was certainly worth it because we hit it off straight away. Unfortunately, she didn't tell me that she had a boyfriend and, in towns like Littleborough, news travels fast. A little bit too fast for my liking.

After our first date, I was sitting in the car outside her house when this hulking great figure emerged from nowhere and began striding towards the car.

I turned to Julie and said: 'Who's that?'

She just said: 'Drive!'

I didn't hesitate because he was a pretty big lad. It was certainly an experience. From that moment on, Julie and I have hardly spent any time apart.

We married in 1997 and she still hasn't forgiven me. Although Julie wasn't in favour of a big white wedding, I think she expected something a little bit more lavish than a Portakabin in a makeshift car park in Worcester. It was down to circumstances more than anything else: the registry office in Worcester had burnt down and the Portakabin was the only option available. It was low-key affair and, after dropping Maddy and Georgia off at the nursery, Julie and I travelled to Worcester for our nuptials. It only cost £70 for the marriage certificate – without doubt the best £70 I have ever spent.

Much to Neil's annoyance, I phoned Julie every night from our hotel room. I knew it irritated him because he would start throwing the covers around and giving me looks, but I pretended not to notice. Those 20-minute chats gave me the chance to catch up and try to put the Tour into perspective. Julie has been with me every step of the way since we first met, a few days after my infamous chip against France in 1992, and she has certainly put up with a lot. She let me make my own decisions when it came to my football career, but we always took them together when it came to our clothes shops.

We have been a close family, but my illness has changed my outlook on my children and wife. I didn't necessarily take them for granted, but the illness definitely brought us together.

She was used to me being injured and the many operations during my career meant I spent a lot of time at home, but she got used to the frequent moans from her footballer husband. Sometimes I wonder how she put up with me. When I signed for Wolves, she was out shopping with Maddy, who had only just been born. I left a note on the lounge floor to tell her that we were moving and drove up to Molineux that afternoon to complete the transfer. She took it all in her stride. I found us a house to live in for a few months until we found somewhere permanent, and Julie just got on with things.

She knows exactly how to handle me. I used to get irritable and nasty if my team was winning without me and that really upset her. I still maintain that it used to upset me more. I got really angry when I was out injured and Julie put up with a lot because I was frequently on the treatment table. Leukaemia was different, though. I could barely move and it was hard to even hold a conversation. My mum often came to stay to help relieve the burden and I took advantage because she waited on me hand and foot. It allowed Julie to concentrate on the children while I began the slow process of recovery. If my mum was around to look after me, Julie ran the children to school.

For a long time we never spoke about her ordeal. I knew that, behind her tough exterior, she was suffering, but we used all our energy on beating the disease. Despite the constant phone calls from friends and family, the offers of help and people dropping in to ask if we needed anything from the shops, she was very alone. The hospitals offer all the support they can for their patients, but at the time there was very little available for the people in the background. It is a harsh reality, but Julie had to fend for herself and deal with the situation as best she could.

That has changed and now there is a support network available for families and friends. There is also a counsellor available, but what is there to say?

People always ask if they can help, but there is precious little that they can do in these situations. Sometimes we wanted to barricade ourselves in and fight the disease together. People would ask how I was and the answer was always the same:

'Yes, he's fine.'

It was very matter of fact, but behind the curtain I knew that my wife was hurting more than anyone.

When I was in hospital, it was tough for Julie because she would come into the room, take one look at me and wonder whether I was dying. I can't imagine what it must have been like for her, but she always came over and gave me a hug. It was comforting to have her there and, even though she was looking after our children throughout the ordeal, she offered constant support.

We have been together for so long that she knows when to leave me alone with my thoughts and when not to. Of course it is a great source of comfort to know that people care so much, but the situation makes everyone feel helpless. Julie rarely got upset in front of me, but there were times when she broke down in tears in front of people she barely even knew. Just after my diagnosis, she went to see the headmistress at Georgia and Maddy's school to let them know that I was suffering from leukaemia and to ask them to keep a special eye on our children to make sure that they were not affected too much. Julie had shown so much strength during the first few weeks, but the moment she started to tell the headmistress, she was uncontrollable. There was nothing I could say to her to help relieve the tension. I never thought about the worst-case scenario because I knew that if I did, it would have finished me.

When I was in the isolation unit at the Queen Elizabeth I could see the anguish on her face and the night she was told by a nurse, just a few days after my bone-marrow transplant, to prepare for the worst still haunts me. Professor Craddock would try to put her mind at rest by explaining what could happen next, but it doesn't take away the pain. It was reassuring, but it would heighten the tension and increase anxiety as I bounced from one illness to the next.

OO

I always looked forward to my daily bulletin via text message from Magnus Backstedt's mobile phone, but I began to realise just how difficult it is to finish the Tour after the end of the 240 km stretch from Pau to Revel. Not only did we have our own problems after Ian was thrown from his bike when he hit the lip of a roundabout on a breakneck descent, but Magnus hinted that he might have to retire from the pro Tour after picking up a bronchial infection during a Pyrenean stage.

There is so little margin for error in top-level sport and I began to appreciate how that can be applied to cycling after his latest bulletin. He was riding the Tour for real as part of Liquigas-Bianchi team and I had got to know him quite well through our link-up with the Italian bike manufacturer.

The Tour imposes a strict time limit on the backmarkers and Backstedt had been struggling to stay in the race after picking up a chest infection. In the Pyrenees, he was sick four times on his bike as he tried to stay in touch with the race leaders. After 16 days on the road, we undoubtedly appreciated the rigours of the race and I knew that there was probably no way back for him after he picked up that illness. To stay in touch with a professional *peloton* skimming through French villages for five or six hours at a time and averaging more than 40 kph places enormous demands on the human anatomy.

We saw something similar with Matt when his immune system was so low after that courageous climb to the top of Courchevel and the food poisoning was so serious that he had to sit out two of the stages, but the professionals didn't have that option. They could either pull up at the side of the road or try and ride through it. Despite the scorching temperatures in France, Armstrong had set a blistering pace during the Tour and it was up to the rest of the field to try and stay on his wheel.

It was his last professional race and he was determined to triumph. He eventually brought his fabulous career to a conclusion when he crossed the finishing line on the Champs-Élysées on 24 July, 4 minutes and 40 seconds ahead of his nearest rival, Ivan Basso. By then, Backstedt had long since been forced to retire. By the time we began the longest stage of the Tour, turning east out of Pau to ride the 239.5 km to Revel, Magnus was on his knees. The *peloton* pushed ahead and left him at the foot of every climb. Although he somehow summoned the strength to complete the brutal 15th stage, which takes in six monster ascents from Lézat-sur-Lèze to Saint-Lary Soulan, he didn't sound confident that he would be able to continue. Despite his enormous physical strength, he was almost out of energy. His infection was becoming more severe and he was having difficulty breathing on some of the tougher sections.

I didn't think Ian would be given a choice either after his high-speed crash towards the end of our 17th day in the saddle. After leaving a particularly tough weekend in Pau behind, our team had been full of banter as we eased our way towards the Massif Central and headed for the home straight towards Paris. Although there was still a lot of ground to cover, we had broken the back of the Tour and only unforeseen circumstances would prevent any of us riding triumphantly into Paris. That nearly occurred when Ian began his pursuit of Neil after he sped off on a solo burst. Often, the stronger riders would put their foot down for half an hour and speed into the distance to try and burn off some of the frustration of riding in formation for long periods of time. Ian and Robbie would often break off, but Neil had taken to flying out of his saddle from time to time to test himself as well. As long as we knew the route, no-one had a problem with this, and our team was riding at such high speeds on the flat that a solo rider could never get too far in front.

We knew we were on the Tour's homeward stretch and there was definitely a different attitude among the team as we headed towards the middle of France. Despite another hard day in the sun, we were more relaxed and a little bit more carefree. The stresses and strains of the mountains had been forgotten and we were looking forward to partying in Paris. Even though we were due another ten-hour shift on the road, we enjoyed the company of some Wolves supporters for an hour as we passed through a small town called Trie-sur-Baise. They anticipated our arrival by holding a quiz evening in two of the town's cafés and raised around £900 for Leukaemia Research. Some of them were waiting in the road, resplendent in their old gold Wolves shirts, as we approached the town centre and they flagged me down before directing me to one of the bars – the Bar du Sport and Le Bar l'Ancien – where they had held their quiz. It was incredibly moving and, even though time was against us again, their support was all the excuse I needed to stop for another round of lattes.

They explained that they were all ex-pat Wolves supporters living in the area and I was deeply touched that they had gone to such special lengths for me. The whole town knew of my exploits and I was happy to sit down with them and share a few stories about my days at Molineux. In fact, I could have sat down all day, but the boys were soon pushing me on.

Robbie, Matt and I were happy to tick over and keep taking a turn in the front until we eventually caught up with Ian and Neil, but as we rode over the brow of a hill, we came on a scene that looked as if there had been a fatality. Ian was lying motionless on the road with Neil standing beside him. There was blood everywhere and Ian's bike was a buckled mess on the other side of the roundabout. Ian didn't realise it at the time, but Neil had almost come off his bike during the high-speed descent when a roundabout suddenly appeared at the foot of the climb. He braked sharply and avoided the lip of the roundabout but it had shaken him up so badly that he stopped to talk with Andrea and Hayley on the other side of the roundabout.

It was a dangerous descent, with no warning of any impending danger: there was likely to be carnage on the official Tour a couple of days later. When Ian came off his bike, Neil had only one concern. He unclipped from his pedals and sprinted in his cleats to Ian, who was unable to move, his face embedded in the hot tarmac. His bike was buckled in several places too, but the only concern was Ian's safety. Cars were already grinding to a halt and there was so much confusion that we didn't spot a French camera crew, who were covering the professional Tour, suddenly draw up alongside us.

Westie was soon on hand to administer first aid, but the camera crew was shoving their lenses in Ian's face. It took some fairly strong words to get them to back off. Someone had called for an ambulance, which was on the scene within minutes, but Ian had incredible determination – although everyone felt that he should go to hospital for scans, he refused to leave the team. He viewed climbing into the back of an ambulance as an admission of failure and he knew that there might not be another opportunity for him to ride the Tour.

He ignored our advice and gingerly made his way into the back of one of the support vehicles. We took refuge in a local bar so that Westie could attend to his various ailments. He had cuts and bruises all over his body and he was clearly shaken up. I still didn't think he would ride again that day but I should have known better; within the hour, he had taken a spare bike off the rack and was urging us to get going for the final 112 km of the stage.

This was met with groans from the team. We were on our third cup of coffee and we had been captivated by the progress of the professionals. It was the first time that we had been able to watch the Tour unfold live and, although my French was pretty poor, I had a fair idea of what was happening. It seemed that Magnus, whose condition had deteriorated overnight, was struggling to complete the stage.

Later that night, I got the text that I know would have hurt like hell for him to send: 'Geoff, the Tour is over. Keep going.'

18

Albi-Mende, 189 km

I enjoyed the adulation as a player, but I never considered myself to be a celebrity. If a supporter asked for my autograph or wanted a picture with me, I never had a problem with that. Footballers didn't have the same appeal in my era and the closest I ever got to a spread in *Hello* magazine came when the Wolves match-day programme asked Julie and me to take part in a feature called 'At home with the Thomases'. I didn't mind and I used to make sure I enjoyed the media side. Some players regard interviews as a hazard of the job, but I always thought of it as a privilege and a bit of an honour that someone had an interest in something I had to say.

It might sound crazy in today's climate, but that's how I viewed it. Perhaps as captain of Crystal Palace and later Wolves I regarded it as one of my responsibilities, but I rarely found it to be a chore.

My father logged my whole career in a scrapbook and I love to flick through it from time to time. There was never a period during my career when I would say I was in the full glare of the media spotlight, but neither did I want to be. I had my own life and I enjoyed the fact that I could leave training in the afternoon and go back to see my wife, spend some time with the children or concentrate on my clothing business.

I can certainly be quite protective of my privacy, and that is probably to do with a period of events that began just after Palace reached the FA Cup final.

As Palace became more successful, the interest in the team inevitably increased. Unfortunately, some of it centred on me and it was a little bit too much for my liking. Supporters often wrote to me at the club and my mail would be passed on to me to read at our training ground in Mitcham. People usually wrote asking for a signed photograph or some other request, and I always tried to be accommodating, but a pattern began to emerge as we began the 1990–91 season.

I received a couple of letters from a supporter called Betty, but she was beginning to get a little over-familiar. She began writing occasionally at first, but she seemed to know a little bit too much about my life. They were only little things, but she obviously took a great deal of interest in my career. She was a mad Palace fan and she told me that she used to travel up from her home in Brighton to come and watch all our games.

She had the most beautiful handwriting and it was obvious that she spent a great deal of time crafting her letters to me. I was a little unnerved at first, but the lads in the dressing room got used to reading her regular correspondence. I would sit and read them through to myself, while the rest of the lads would be desperate for me to read them out loud. It was harmless at first. When she was saying how well I was playing and that it was nice to see me on Saturday, I took it that she meant seeing me on the pitch. But then it began to get a little bit more personal.

She wrote to tell me that she saw me looking at her in the crowd, and the letters began to get stronger and stronger. Tickets for the ballet began arriving in the post, with a note to tell me where to meet her and at what time. I was beginning to think that she was convinced we were some kind of item, but nothing could be further from the truth. I had never even met her and had no idea what she looked like. That changed when Andy Thorn, our mischievous central defender, met her at the Palace Christmas party a year later.

Supporters could buy tickets so that they could meet the players at a very informal function at Selhurst Park. This year, there was one introduction I wasn't expecting. Out of the corner of my eye, I could see a middle-aged woman staring at me and I knew that she wanted me to look at her. I didn't know who it was, but she was trembling as she began to approach me and there was a kind of frenzied, nervous excitement in her voice as she introduced herself.

'Hello Geoff.'

'Hello.'

'I'm Betty.'

It was like my worst nightmare. She was shaking as she spoke to me and she introduced me to her son. I didn't know what to do, but I politely told her that I didn't understand what was going on but it had to stop.

I thought that would be the end of it and I told some of my team-mates that she was in the room. Some were genuinely worried, but Thorny took it as an opportunity to create some mayhem.

He went up to Betty, introduced himself and asked her for a dance. She immediately stepped on to the dancefloor with him and that was when he took his chance. He was a real joker in the team but this wasn't a laughing matter. He was speaking in her ear and it was only afterwards that I found out what he had been saying.

He was encouraging her pursuit by saying things like: 'Oh, Geoff's just shy, don't worry. We'll get you and him sorted.'

That was exactly what she wanted to hear. 'Don't worry, Betty. He talks about you a lot. Don't you worry – it's just his way.'

It sparked off an incredible period in my life. She started sending knickers in the post and all sorts after that, and more tickets for concerts at the Fairfield Halls in Croydon.

Of course I ignored it, but then I would feel the full force of her anger a couple of days later. A letter would arrive at the training ground and I could see her fury in her handwriting. She would write so hard that the pen would go through the paper. But, as the letter continued, her handwriting would return to normal and the deep, dark blue ink that she used would fade.

It was an incredible obsession, but I tried not to let it affect me. I didn't consider myself to be in any danger and I used to have a laugh with my team-mates about it.

She told me she worked in the City and she even sent her bank statement to me with about £60,000 in it to prove that she wasn't after me for money. She sent pictures of herself in a bikini 'to prove that I don't have any scars' and was at pains to point out that, at 50 years of age, she could still have children.

I didn't feel particularly threatened at first, but when the letters began to turn sinister, I started to have a few more concerns. She used to talk about a black man she had been seeing and would warn me that 'if you make me angry, I can't explain what the repercussions will be'. I took this to mean that she would stab me if I ever had the misfortune to meet her again because she had mentioned that in a previous letter.

It was all so bizarre. She started to send packages through the post – birthday cakes, tapes of her singing about me and cassettes of her talking to me. Then she followed me home from training one day and found out my address, at Kenley, five or six miles away from Palace's ground at Selhurst Park. She stepped up her activities another notch when Julie, who was pregnant with our first daughter, Maddy, came to live with me.

I had a gravel drive with a five-bar gate at the top and I could hear whenever someone was walking down it. On a few occasions, at around 2 a.m., I heard footsteps in the gravel and a package would be shoved through the letterbox from her. She sent notes saying she would pick me up at 5 p.m. She was absolutely crackers, but I continued to ignore it. That was a mistake because eventually I had to call the police when she backed her car into my drive.

She had suitcases in the back seats and she was unloading them because, in her deluded state, she had decided that she was moving in with me. Despite my protests she refused to move and I had no choice but to call the police. Eventually she went away, but not for long.

At the end of the 1992 season, Palace were asked to play exhibition games against two South African teams. The apartheid system that had been in place since 1948 was just coming to an end and it was a big honour for an English team to be invited there to play games against the Orlando Pirates and the Kaiser Chiefs – the first such games for over 40 years.

They were great games, with packed stadiums and it was one of the best experiences I have ever had. The supporters were singing throughout and it was actually quite haunting to listen to the crowd during the games. We won convincingly and there was a lot of coverage because of the changes that were taking place in South Africa.

I was keen to gauge the amount of interest being generated by our presence and I walked into the newsagent's to browse through the newspapers. I was standing with my back turned to the entrance, flicking through the papers when I heard a chilling voice behind me.

'Hi, Geoff.'

I turned round and Betty was stood there. It frightened the life out of me. I couldn't believe she had flown all that way for Palace's end-of-season tour. After that I just didn't know what to do.

The letters kept coming, even when I moved to Wolves. I was holding our second daughter, Maddy, in my arms in the players' lounge after I made my debut against Bristol City and this woman came running up to me screaming.

She was shouting: 'Whose baby is that? Whose baby is that?'

She had somehow convinced the doorman at Molineux that she had something to do with the players and he had allowed her in. Julie and my mum were sat down close by when she came running over and it was bedlam until she was eventually bundled away.

She was crazy, but it stopped all of a sudden. Nothing. No more cards, no more birthday cakes and no more knickers.

Mind you, that incident at Wolves didn't stop her finding another weird fascination. Years later, as I got to know Barnsley keeper Kevin Miller, who had also played at Palace, he told me about a fixation one of the supporters had with him.

Her name? Yes, you guessed it.

oo

Even if I had coveted it, I'm not sure the celebrity lifestyle would have suited me. When I was with my first wife, Cath, she invited some friends to stay with us and I decided to show them the bright lights of London. I used to shop in a boutique called Apparel in Croydon and the two girls, Christine and Mel, who worked there recommended Langan's, the famous restaurant in Green Park which is part-owned by Michael Caine, for a night out.

They knew the manager and they organised a table for us. I didn't know too much about the place but I knew that if you were someone, they would put you on a table by the window. I've never been one for recognising faces, but we were all very excited to be in a nice restaurant and in such a lovely setting. I was trying not to make too much of it, but the next thing I knew there was a tap on my shoulder. I looked up and Bill Wyman, a Palace supporter, was standing there. I didn't really know what to say to him.

He just shook my hand and said: 'Well done, keep it up, Geoff, you're having a fantastic season.'

I just said thanks and carried on eating my dinner, while the others sat, open-mouthed around the table. This was in complete contrast to the first time Julie came down to London.

We had only just met and I was feeling all chivalrous, going to meet her off the train at Euston. We had just walked out of the main entrance when I saw a chap on a motorbike do a double-take. I was desperately trying to impress Julie, who had no interest in football whatsoever, and I just casually dropped it into our conversation. 'See that guy? I think he recognises me.'

He realised I had spotted him and that's when he decided to come round again. He slowed down to take a good look at my face, looked at Julie, looked at me, and then said: 'You're shit, anyway!'

The landscape of British football has certainly changed since I played. In my era, dressing rooms had mainly British players and that nucleus created the dressing-room banter. Now there are players of all different nationalities and I don't think the dressing rooms would be the same. With the amount of money that is involved, there is bound to be some resentment in the dressing room when things aren't going well. At Palace, Forest, Wolves and Barnsley we were all in a similar wage structure so there were few grievances on that side.

I certainly don't begrudge modern-day players earning that money. If someone is daft enough to pay them, they can't be faulted for signing the contract. Some players aren't worth the money, but it's not for them to decide how much they are being paid.

In some ways, though, I would love to have played now because the stadiums and the pitches are so much better. There are always a lot of positives that come out of a negative. Obviously it took massive disasters – Hillsborough and Bradford – for football to take a good look at itself; since then things have improved and safety is paramount in a lot of football grounds. Even the smaller clubs are building new stadiums. I played in the days when people were sandwiched into terraces.

When I look back, Eric Cantona was the standard-bearer. Before his arrival, people would say that English teams had the work ethic and would win matches through sheer determination but he changed those attitudes. Suddenly teams were being noted for their skill. He brought his game into English football and he influenced the Premiership. Now we see the best players, like Thierry Henry, in the English league instead of them going to Italy or Spain to play.

We have never seen Henry's like in this country. Cantona was an accident, he was thrown out of France. Leeds were pondering a bit, but give Fergie credit, because he built a team around him. The likes of Beckham, Giggs and Scholes took advantage of being around such a great player because his enthusiasm and his standards rubbed off on them.

The influence of foreign players has affected the English national team. There are players who won't get a game in the top flight and, to some extent the lower divisions, because there are so many foreign players in the game.

Players have a limited shelf-life and if you don't make it by a certain age you shuffle down the divisions. The best example of that is David Platt. If he had stayed at Manchester United he would never have had the chance to play in the first team. Instead, he was persuaded to sign for Dario Gradi and that gave him the opportunity to develop and mature at a lower level and he flourished. I have to admire Platt for having the confidence to play at that level and it worked for him because he went on to have a great career with England, Aston Villa and Juventus.

When I watch Arsenal, Chelsea and Manchester United now, they are teams with the kind of quality we have never seen before. They combine skill with the best fitness schedules and they can hold their own in any competition in the world. I would love to know whether I could have done the same.

OO

I admired our backroom team on the Tour for their resilience, but their propensity to send us on the wrong road – often for an hour or more before they realised their error – would leave us frustrated, angry and agitated. Despite nearly three weeks of practice, they didn't disappoint when they sent us to the top of a 9 km climb at an average of 5 per cent.

Despite the constant questions from the riders – 'Are you sure this is the right climb?' – they would nod their heads and drive off into the distance. We knew there were problems whenever we saw one of the Land Rovers driving past us the other way with whoever was in the passenger seat – Richard, Chris, Andrea or Hayley – staring at a map with a quizzical look on their faces. At times, I think they were almost scared to tell us they had made a mistake. They knew it would be met with groans and the usual string of expletives and this stage was no different. That mistake cost us another couple of hours and it ruined what had been a magnificent start to the day as we approached Millau. The French town is home to the highest bridge in the world. The stunning Millau Viaduct, which was designed by British engineer Sir Norman Foster, is over 343 metres above the town in places and is 2.5 km long – and we could see the sprawling project in front of us as we made our approach.

It has been built to connect the motorways between the south of France and Barcelona and it is a truly awesome sight. Before it was built, traffic would converge at the foot of the valley, causing long tailbacks in the holiday season. The viaduct bypasses the town and has solved the problem. It is a truly impressive sight, but it was about the only highlight of another depressing day in the saddle.

Although we knew that the stage was always likely to be fairly arduous, locked away in the back of our mind was the potentially tortuous climb into Mende at the very end. Although the road to the small heliport at the top of the Côte de la Croix Neuve was only 3 km, it averaged 10.1 per cent and rose to 14 per cent at its steepest pitch.

We knew that, after a long day in the saddle, it would be especially tough and none of us were looking forward to it. Typically, it started with a gradual climb on the lower slopes, but, after a couple of switchbacks, we were soon grinding our way to the top. In many ways, it reminded me of Winnat's Pass, back in the days when I was training for the Tour, and it was a measure of my progress as a cyclist that I managed to stay on my bike all the way to the top.

Progress was slow, but I rarely worried about the clock. I was only ever interested in making it to the top and I took a lot of satisfaction from reaching the summit of such a difficult climb. It was late and we had been on the road for more than ten hours again, but I had long since got used to the daily grind. We were tired – we always were – but somehow our support team always found a way to put a smile back on our faces. They didn't disappoint when we reached the airfield at Mende; I can't tell you how much it meant when they brought out dozens of pizzas and pre-packed pasta from their car the moment we got off our bikes. Usually we would waste a lot of time finding somewhere to eat in the evenings, but Andrea and Hayley came up trumps that evening. Then again, they always did.

19

Issoire–Le Puy-en-Velay, 153.5 km

I don't have any regrets about my football career, but I regret the fact that my father, Gordon, will not be in Paris to cheer me across the finishing line. Julie, Georgia and Maddy, my mother and Kay will all be waiting for me when I make my way down the Champs-Élysées after 21 days on the road. They will be bursting with pride and I know that if my dad was there he would be too.

He died, within the space of a few short weeks, in 1993. It was the month before Crystal Palace were relegated from the Premiership and my mind, as well as my life, was in turmoil. When I look back on my dad's life, I sometimes wish I had fulfilled an ambition by playing for Manchester City when I had the chance. They were my team growing up as we lived in a terraced house in the shadows of their fabulous old stadium, Maine Road.

Dad was a City fan and, even though he worked as a van driver for a Manchester company called Corthaulds, we couldn't afford to watch their matches. We would just play football in the streets surrounding the ground until 20 minutes from time. That was when the gates would open and we would sneak into the stadium to watch our heroes – Colin Bell, Mike Summerbee and Franny Lee – in action. I can remember the first game I went to with my father because City lost 5–1 against West Ham. It was a bitterly cold day and Dad was trying to keep warm. I remember it for Ronnie Boyce's incredible goal more than anything else. Jimmy Greaves was making his debut for West Ham and that was part of the appeal but Boyce stole the show.

It was a really boggy pitch, but, when the City keeper, Joe Corrigan, kicked the ball out of his area, Boyce caught it first time on the volley from the halfway line and sent it straight past him. That was my first memory of a professional football match and it gave me a taste. Dad played as an amateur, but he had more interest in watching me as I made my way into local teams. By the time I was 15, I was playing four games at the weekend. I played for my school first thing on a Saturday and then Littleborough Parish, an adult side, in the afternoon.

The following day I would turn out for a local Sunday pub side and then play an under-18s game in the afternoon. I'm sure it wouldn't be allowed now but, back then, there were no rules or regulations in place. I was a left-winger in my youth and I just wanted to play as often as possible. Dad often came to watch me play, but I didn't like it. I got nervous if he came to watch and I even sent him home from a school match when I spotted him hiding behind a tree. I learned to relax a bit more when I became a professional and Dad became my biggest fan.

When I was being ripped to shreds by David Baddiel and Frank Skinner on the *Fantasy Football League*, he recorded the programme and sent the tapes down to me in London. Even though he lived in Manchester, he kept a close watch on my career and he had urged me to sign for Blackburn when they offered Palace £2.5m for me when they were promoted to the Premiership in 1992.

It was a lot of money for a player at the time, but they had big plans. They had beaten Palace to sign Alan Shearer and their owner, Sir Jack Walker, was bankrolling the club to try to win the Premiership title. As the negotiations continued, it became clear that Palace were not prepared to sell me unless Blackburn paid the 15 per cent sell-on clause that was due to my previous club, Crewe. I was very disappointed with Ron Noades, the Palace chairman, because I felt I had been incredibly loyal to them over the years. They signed me from Crewe for £50,000 in 1987 and now they were being offered 50 times that amount. It was a profit of £2.45m on a player they had taken a gamble on when they were trying to get out of the old Second Division.

I didn't know it at the time, but Steve Coppell had told Noades that he would resign if I was sold and that made it very difficult for the club to sell me. They still held my contract and if they wanted to keep me, they were entitled to. The negotiations dragged on into the start of the season and it didn't help that Blackburn were due to play Palace on the first day. I had expected it to be my last game for the club and we scrambled a 3–3 draw when Simon Osborn, who later became a team-mate at Wolves, equalised for Palace in the last minute. Ominously, Shearer scored twice and I could sense that they were building something special. Instead, my dreams of moving to Blackburn were shattered over the weekend and I don't think I recovered until I moved from Palace the following summer. The miss against France had knocked my confidence and I was no longer an England international.

Coppell resigned in the wake of relegation and his assistant, Alan Smith, had been promoted to the role of manager. I liked Alan, but I hadn't been able to forgive him for some insensitive comments towards the end of my father's life. Dad became ill very suddenly. He was only 60 and he should have been looking forward to his retirement. He was work-conscious and he never took his holiday entitlement. Instead, he worked right through the year and we never went abroad on holiday as a family. My parents split up for a while when I was about 12 and, for a period, Dad and Kay were the only people there for me.

We were very close and I shot up the motorway the moment I heard he was ill. He started to have pains in his head when he was driving and he booked an appointment with an optician to find out what the problem was. They ran some tests and sent him to hospital where they saw what appeared to be a growth behind his eye. From then on, everything happened very quickly. The tumour behind his eye was a side-effect of something far more serious. He had lung cancer. He was a heavy smoker and his condition was almost certainly a result of spending more than 40 years puffing away on cigarettes. I drove up to the hospital in Rochdale straight away, but I didn't get the answers I wanted. The specialists were skirting around the issue and they didn't seem to be armed with enough knowledge to put my family and me in the picture.

It didn't compare with my own experience, when everything was black and white and matter of fact. With me, it was blunt but this was hazy. With my father, things changed in a very short space of time. They were not sure of his survival prospects and it seemed like there was nothing for him to hold on to. I can vividly recall going into a meeting with the doctors at the Rochdale Infirmary and asking what they could do.

They just replied: 'We can't really say.'

He was immediately sent for radiotherapy, but the treatment affected him more than the illness. It made him very tired and, even when he came home, he just had to sit down. Shortly after, he became bed-ridden and I knew then that he didn't have long left to live. The Macmillan nurses got involved and, when that happens, you know time is running short. They do a fantastic job to make people comfortable and ensure that they can die with a bit of dignity. Mum found it particularly distressing because it was sinking in that he was close to the end. I was up and down the motorway, making the 360-mile round trip three times a week so that I could be there for my family.

Steve Coppell was very understanding and he told me to come back when I was ready. I didn't train at all in the last week of my father's life. His condition was rapidly deteriorating and I slept in the same room as him to make sure that he was OK. We played Leeds on 17 April 1993 and it broke my heart to leave him that day. Palace were in the middle of a battle against relegation and I arranged to meet the team at a hotel in Yorkshire before the game.

I had just put a toiletry bag together before I left our house and Dad asked me a question.

'Who are you playing today, son?'

'Leeds away, but I'll be back a bit later.'

I left the room, but came back a minute later to say goodbye.

He looked up at me from his bed and said: 'Hi, son. How did you get on?'

OO

That game – a 0–0 draw – was a haze. I was in a world of my own when I was waiting for the rest of the squad at the hotel and my mood didn't improve on the pitch. Palace were struggling to stay in the Premiership, and I had a chance to win the game near the end but their keeper, John Lukic, pushed the shot around the post. It has gnawed away at me for a long time that Alan Smith, who frequently spoke to the press if Coppell didn't want to talk after a game, criticised me for missing the opportunity. He felt I should have put it away and, although my father's illness wasn't an excuse, I didn't need the criticism at the time. That still jars with me because I never put in less than 100 per cent effort during my whole time at Palace. I was the captain of the club and honoured to be the figurehead.

After the game, I drove back to Manchester to be with Dad, but he only lasted another couple of days. I was there when he eventually passed away and it is something of a paradox that it comforts me to think that I was holding his hand when that moment arrived. Julie, who was heavily pregnant with Maddy at the time, was there and so too was my ex-wife.

In a small house, it was a very uncomfortable and distressing time for everyone involved. Cathy had been very close to my father and she felt, quite rightly, that she should be there. Julie took it all in her stride. I missed Palace's midweek defeat at home to Manchester United, but I wasn't interested in football at that time. I was so preoccupied with Dad's funeral that I didn't even think to check the result and I didn't hear about it until the following day. I couldn't believe my father had been taken away at such an early age. I knew it would happen at some time, but it was sad he didn't get to enjoy his retirement. A few weeks later, Palace were relegated when we were beaten 3–0 at Arsenal on the final day of the season.

I was courted by City all summer, but I resisted the temptation to sign for them. Trevor Francis, who was Sheffield Wednesday manager at the time and was trying to persuade me to make a move to Hillsborough, did a fairly good job of convincing me not to go to Maine Road and, even though I was a Manchester lad and had blue blood running through my veins, I decided not to join them. Although Trevor told me City were one of the best clubs he had played for, he also warned me there was a lot of boardroom upheavel there, and he was later proved spot on. After losing my father so suddenly, there would be a lot of pressure on me if I returned to the area. My whole family were City fans and I wasn't sure that I was ready mentally to cope with the pressure of living life in the Manchester goldfish bowl so soon after losing Dad.

Yes, it was my dream to play for them, but timing is everything and Wolves simply swept me away when they agreed a £1m fee with Palace. They would be in the same division as Palace that season, but they were showing a lot of determination to get promoted. Sir Jack Hayward was pouring money into the club and they were using the same template as Blackburn the previous year. They had the same mentality and they were throwing money around to build a new stadium at Molineux and a team equipped for the Premiership. That turned my head and I went to meet their manager, Graham Turner. I got caught up in the vision, the dream and the prospect of winning promotion to the Premiership with this famous old club. After six years at Palace, I felt that this was a unique challenge and it was one that I relished.

I was disappointed with the way my career at Molineux ended. I made a flying start when I joined them and scored four times in the first 12 games. But disaster struck when we played Sunderland at their old Roker Park stadium in the September. We were winning 1–0 and hanging on when I scored a decisive second. It was a memorable goal for me because I buried a few demons from the infamous miss against France that day. I was clean through with only the keeper to beat and this time I made the right decision. We finished Sunderland off with that goal and I went up to the Wolves fans behind the goal to celebrate.

Mark Rankine, the Wolves midfielder, was having some fun with the crowd as we ran back to the centre circle. He was gesturing to the Wolves fans to show their appreciation and they were lapping it up, but then he turned to the Sunderland supporters and was giving them the thumbs down and pretending to have a sad face. It infuriated them and it raised the temperature inside the stadium. Unfortunately, I didn't get to see the game out. The moment Sunderland kicked off, they lost the ball. As I knocked it past Lee Howey, who had just come on as a substitute for Sunderland, he came through me unexpectedly. It was a bad challenge but I couldn't get out of the way and it ripped my shin open.

I thought the impact had broken my leg and those fears seemed to be confirmed when our striker, Dave Kelly, went running away with his head in his hands. I was in agony, and I was surprised when Don Goodman, then at Sunderland, came running over and pointed a finger in my face: 'You deserved that, you fucking wanker.' Lying on the ground, knowing that my season was probably over, I wasn't in a position to argue. There was a deep gouge in my shin and the surgeon stitched the skin together to try and knit the wound. They originally felt that I would be out for around six weeks, but when I played a reserve team game against Derby, I knew my knee wasn't right.

I went to run for the ball on the edge of the area and I have never experienced pain quite like the feeling I had in my right knee that night. My knee was bent the wrong way, to the point where my foot was right in front of my nose, and I knew it was serious. Tom Bennett, who was just returning from a cruciate ligament injury, was in the dressing room after the game and he knew what I was going through. That was the start of a period when I felt that I was always struggling with injury. In the time that I was on the sidelines, the club sacked Graham Turner and Graham Taylor, my manager when I was an England regular, replaced him.

'So, my friend, we meet again,' were the words he used when I met him in his office, but I wasn't sure I would ever play for him.

My knee had been reconstructed but, even though I returned to the Wolves side, I wasn't the same. The following season, as part of my rehabilitation, I came on as a substitute at Sunderland but I had a different agenda to the rest of the team. I wanted revenge on Howey for the tackle that could have ended my career. My chance came at a corner. I was so frustrated because I knew I was not the player who was super-fit and back at the top of his game when I had scored there at the start of the previous season. Now I felt I was lucky even to be playing.

I tried to throw an elbow in Lee's face when the corner was swung in but I missed him by a mile and ended up getting in a ruck with their striker on the ground. The referee thought I stamped on him, even though I didn't, and he sent me off. My condition didn't improve and I ended up having another reconstruction at the Droitwich Knee Clinic on the outskirts of Birmingham. The cruciate was the sort of injury that used to finish careers, but the surgeon was very positive about my chances of playing again.

Despite his claims, he warned me that I would be on the sidelines for another six to 12 months. I had already missed a huge chunk of my Wolves career and, when I look back on that time, I wonder what could have been. The chairman, Sir Jack Hayward, was spending part of his vast personal fortune to try and achieve promotion to the Premiership and I felt guilty about spending so much time on the sidelines. Turner had paid the price for his failure to win promotion the previous season and Graham Taylor was struggling to match the weight of expectation.

Wolves are a huge club and everything about the place, from the facilities and the stadium to their supporters, was first rate. I just wanted to be on the pitch. I became good friends with Billy Wright, their legendary wing-half, and I was choked when he passed away in 1994 with stomach cancer. He had played more than 100 times for England and I was touched when I received a letter of encouragement from him during my rehab. I always had a good relationship with the Wolves supporters and I think they appreciated my hard work when I was on the pitch. It took me two years to regain my fitness and I eventually played against Palace in the play-off semi-finals.

By then, McGhee was the manager and, even though we lost, he lifted the spirits of everyone in the dressing room by telling them that their contracts would be renewed. I was in the final year of my contract at the club and I took him at face value, as did all the other players who would be free agents that summer. I can still see them going home to their families, wives or partners after the disappointment of the play-off defeat. 'We lost the game, love, but don't worry, the manager says I will be getting a new deal tomorrow.'

It would hardly mask the disappointment, but at least they would be certain of their livelihoods. The next day, all the players came in and it quickly became apparent by the order of the names on the list that certain people, including myself, would not be staying. I lost a lot of respect for McGhee over that. Personally, I was fortunate that the club stuck by me throughout the four years I was there and I was in no position to argue. The ones I felt for were the younger players. They went home after the Palace game believing they were safe, but the next day the rug was pulled from underneath them.

Throughout my career, I was never interested in signing for clubs that expected to win trophies. I played for teams that had to earn the right and that pattern followed me during my entire career. I had that outlook when I played for my first junior team, Littleborough. Other teams in the area would try to entice the best players away, but I was fiercely loyal and I stayed at Littleborough when I could have played for better teams. I was the same when I was at Palace and Arsenal tried to sign me. George Graham wanted me to join Ian Wright at Highbury, but I felt that Palace had just as much ambition and I didn't consider Arsenal to be that much better than us at the time.

They had the history, the infrastructure and infinitely more money than Palace, but they were not much better than us when we played them in the 1990–91 season. The difference between the two clubs was the investment. George Graham carried on building his team but, when Wright left, Palace fell apart. That is why I needed a new challenge and Wolves represented it. I would rather play for the second-best team in the league and earn my corn than play for the best and expect to win it. I would get a lot more satisfaction winning matches that way and that's why I always played for the underdog.

oo

Dave Bassett gave me a fresh start at Forest. He was a chirpy Cockney and he revelled in the banter with the players. I admired him because he was always so honest. To him, everything was always black and white and players respect that kind of manager. If you wanted to know why you weren't in the team, he would tell you. He wouldn't skirt around the issue, and he would tell you exactly what you needed to do to get back in the team. If that meant telling you that you weren't good enough, that's what he would do.

Forest had just been relegated from the Premiership when I left Wolves in the summer of 1996, but they were an established club and most people expected them to bounce straight back. Stuart Pearce had been caretaker manager, but he had been unable to save them from the drop.

I didn't know Stuart very well, but he introduced himself to me in my first training session. It was a special welcome. No sooner had we started a five-a-side to wind up than he came straight through the back of me and raked his studs down the back of my calves. He followed it up with that familiar icy glare. I thought it was an unusual way to familiarise himself with a new team-mate. Although I played in the same England team as Pearce, I didn't really get to know him. The Forest lads – Pearce, Nigel Clough and Des Walker – all stuck together in their own little clique and made it fairly obvious that they didn't really want to socialise with the rest of the players.

It was a different attitude and a different philosophy to anything I had been used to, but Pearce probably saw me as one of Bassett's boys. He had come in as the new manager at the City Ground and my recruitment was his statement of intent. Despite that extraordinary introduction, we had a good season. With Pierre van Hooijdonk and Kevin Campbell scoring goals, we won the First Division championship. With myself and Andy Johnson in the middle of the park and Steve Stone on the wing, we were too strong for the other sides in the division. We had the makings of a good side, but it soured at the City Ground when van Hooijdonk went on strike.

He claimed that he was frustrated by the lack of signings and he had even presented the club with a list of potential players. I was gobsmacked by his attitude and it affected our preparations ahead of our return to the top flight. There was talk of him coming back on the eve of the season, and this provoked a memorable response from Dave Bassett when he was asked what he would do if van Hooijdonk offered an olive branch.

'I tell you what I'd do,' he replied. 'I'd stick it up his arse!'

That was the feeling among most of the players at Forest and he was anything but welcome when he did finally return to the City Ground after his self-imposed exile. He had taken the gloss off our promotion back to the Premiership and, instead of the focus being on the team, everything centred around Pierre. To me that kind of attitude was disruptive and made him appear incredibly arrogant.

I always thought Alan Rogers was a pretty solid player for Forest, but Pierre would shout to him, 'Alan, we're playing in red,' if he misplaced a pass. Things were never good enough for Pierre; if you argued white, he would argue black. He had a different take on absolutely everything and it used to irritate the other players.

It was a shame because Pierre was a very, very good player, though not half as good as he thought he was. He lacked pace and that's what stopped him from being a really top player. That said, he was one of the best strikers of a ball I have ever seen, but there were aspects to his game that I could never fathom.

He was 6 foot 3 inches and, if he was in the mood, you couldn't get near him, yet he insisted on taking every corner. He would have been far better off in the box, but he just couldn't understand it.

He had some extreme views on the game and the fact that he made it clear that he wasn't buying into the team ethic stopped him from fulfilling his potential at any of the clubs he played for.

He scored 34 goals in our promotion season and he enjoyed a prolific partnership with Kevin Campbell. I felt sorry for Kevin throughout this time because he had worked hard to win over the Forest supporters and Pierre had lifted some of the pressure off his shoulders. They were both more than capable of scoring goals, but Kevin thrived when he was in the team. Without him, Kevin had too much responsibility and we really suffered in our first few months back in the top flight.

It was a slap in the face for the rest of the players when Pierre didn't turn up for pre-season training and there was a lot of uncertainty because Bassett, quite rightly, didn't want him back at the club under any circumstances.

When he eventually showed up, he didn't exactly do anything to endear himself to his team-mates. We had not seen him since we won promotion – he didn't even come on our end-of-season tour to Miami. His attitude was summed up for me when he walked into a restaurant in Nottingham the night before his comeback. Mark Crossley was there with his wife and, when they saw Pierre approaching their table, they assumed he would at least stop to say hello and shake hands, but he just carried on walking.

Mark left it at the time because he didn't want to cause a scene, but at training the next day it was carnage. There were hundreds of photographers and reporters waiting for Pierre to show up and we didn't let them down when he arrived. As soon as he got to the ground, Mark had a slanging match with him over the incident in the restaurant, telling him that he was a 'disgrace'.

I couldn't disagree and neither did anyone else. He had let us down and it was difficult even to be sat in the same room as him. He made his comeback against Wimbledon in November and, two weeks later, when he scored his first goal in the Premiership against Derby, the fact he celebrated on his own said it all.

Despite van Hooijdonk's attitude, we made a reasonable start to the season. I scored the best goal of my career at Arsenal on the opening day. I started the move on the edge of our own area before nutmegging Patrick Vieira and Tony Adams and beating David Seaman from the edge of the box. We still lost 2–1, but Seaman came up to me at the end of the game and said: 'Bloody hell! Where did you learn to do that?' I wasn't sure myself, but I was enjoying myself back in the limelight. I was fit again, but I suffered another blow at Stamford Bridge the following month.

We were losing 2–0 when I rashly challenged the Chelsea keeper, Ed de Goey, from a Steve Stone cross at the start of the second half. De Goey is a massive bloke and I was always going to be hurt. The moment I landed on the floor, I knew the impact was serious. It was my left knee this time and, as I tried to stand up, it buckled. I told the physio straight away that it was the cruciate, but he wasn't so sure. I was behind the goal, being stretchered off, and a Forest fan shouted at me: 'See you next season, Thomas.'

He didn't. I never played for Forest again.

20

Saint-Étienne–Saint-Étienne, 55 km Time-Trial

There were times during the Tour when I wondered whether I could have made a career out of cycling. At 42 years of age, it was too late to be talking about taking up the sport competitively, but I frequently asked myself whether I could have made it as a professional cyclist before I embarked on my football career. By the time the Tour ended, I lived and breathed the sport. If a cyclist came past us, I would check the make of his bike, his shoes, his clothes and his riding style and I could tell, within seconds, just how proficient he was likely to be.

I loved the sport. I loved everything about it – despite the frequent drug scandals that threaten to rip the soul out of it. I still marvel at the procession of riders who fly through the French towns every summer. I can watch the Tour for hours on television and even find myself mimicking the distinctive voice of Sean Yates, the Eurosport commentator and former Ireland champion, as I walk around my house.

These days, I read the cycling press from cover to cover. I don't have to walk to the village shops every Thursday morning because I've taken out subscriptions.

There were times when I felt that way about football. During my playing days, I watched anything: Premiership, Italian football, Spanish football – whatever was going, I would be glued to it. I still love the game, but I no longer get wound up by it. I feel as though I have done my time after more than 20 years as a professional. All the tension, the hatred for other teams and other players, as well as the passion, has drained away over the past couple of years.

Certain players weren't interested in any banter on the pitch, but I used to love that side of the game. Others, like Dennis Wise at Chelsea or David Batty at Leeds, loved the physical side and I really looked forward to those clashes. We were all very similar because, although we weren't the most talented players in our respective teams, we had a point to prove. I didn't like to give an inch against those kinds of players and a lot of people thought I was a nasty bastard on the pitch. But I preferred the verbal exchanges to anything else.

I can remember Vinny Jones sidling up to me when Palace were playing up at Sheffield United in 1991. It was around the time that I had split up from Cath and Vinny just came over and said: 'All right, Geoff? I saw your missus out on the town in Sheffield last night.'

He gave me 90 minutes of grief after that, but I used to take it on the chin. That kind of talk would fly straight over my head but sometimes you have to become a bit more philosophical. When we played at Norwich, their striker Lee Power came up to me and said: 'You know what you are, don't you? You're the most hated man in football.'

Those are the moments when I questioned myself, but I never let it affect me for long. I wasn't playing football to make friends. I had a spirit and a will to win that might have set me apart from other players at times, but I don't think that Lee's view was universal. At least I hope not.

I enjoyed playing the better teams, probably because I always regarded myself as an underdog. There was always plenty of needle when we shared our ground with Wimbledon and Charlton, but the games against the likes of Liverpool, Arsenal and Manchester United were the real tests. I didn't have any difficulty winding myself up for those matches, but it is one of my biggest regrets that I never won at Highbury. At Palace we couldn't get near them and I never came away from their ground thinking that we could have got a result. I scored there for Forest the season after we got promoted, but I still ended up on the losing team.

Too much has happened in my life for football to touch me in the way that it once did. I'm not even sure, after the highs of leading Crystal Palace to the FA Cup final and going on to represent my country, that I would ever want to go back. I have wonderful memories of my playing career and nothing will ever take the shine off some of the more precious moments.

I seldom watch matches now, but when I do I don't jump and down in front of the television. It's a game and I don't show the emotion that characterised my playing career. When I watched England during the World Cup in Germany, it was very much matter of fact and I didn't feel the pain so many supporters did. Like everyone else, I was disappointed with their performance, but it doesn't hurt and it certainly doesn't eat away at me. It's a game for me now – nothing else. Towards the end of the football season, when the Sky cameras are panning around empty stadiums and focusing on supporters who are crying their season away, I can understand their feelings but I can't ever imagine having that passion for the game again. I'm too detached from it now.

Sometimes I consider returning to the game, but it would have to be for the right reasons and under the right circumstances. The dream scenario would be to return to Palace and revive their fortunes, but I don't know whether it can ever happen. After everything I have been through over the past three years, I often can't see beyond my fundraising efforts. I remember the days when football dominated my existence, but I don't live and breathe the sport any more. Perceptions change and so do feelings.

Now there is something new to fight for and it doesn't revolve around a Saturday afternoon. I was always taught never to say never, but with each passing day, I doubt whether I will return to the game.

I cried like a baby when we lost the 1990 FA Cup final replay at Wembley, but I don't think I will ever cry again over a football match. Other things mean too much to me these days and I have a different perspective and a different outlook to the one I adopted when I was a professional footballer. During my playing days, I had a win-at-all-costs mentality. Nothing else mattered. I wanted three points in the bag and then we would move on to the next game. I felt ruthless at times, but I don't feel that way any more. I look back on the 550 matches I played with seven different clubs and I am proud to say that I gave my all in every one of them, but it seems like a lifetime ago. For the doctors and nurses who wished me happy birthday by telling me, 'You're zero,' when I had my bone-marrow transplant, it probably is.

In my youth, I had a raw determination and an arrogance about me even when I was a Sunday league player. It wasn't that I felt I was necessarily the best player, but I had an approach to the game which said, 'I'm going to do something out here today.'

I had a desire to win games, win challenges and score goals. Even when I was 16, when I was as skinny as a rake, I used to relish the challenge of playing against men. When I look at professionals now, I wonder whether they still enjoy the game as much as they used to. In years gone by, when money wasn't such a big factor, players used to drop down the divisions and be paid pocket money. Now players drop down the divisions for an easy ride and still pick up big contracts and that gets to me because I'm not sure they still merit them. I was a well-paid footballer, but it was only when I moved to Wolves that I really noticed the difference. Even when Palace became an established top-flight club, I struggled to live well in London.

When I went to Wolves and earned a far bigger salary, I never got cocky with the money. Someone once advised me to be nice to people on the way up because they won't be as nice on the way down if you have been a bastard. It's difficult to know when the time is right to retire, but I have no regrets about the decision.

At the end of the 2001 season, I was thinking about retiring to concentrate on my clothing business, but I had a chat with Dario Gradi, my old manager at Crewe, and he asked me to train with them over the summer.

Dario gave me my first full-time professional contract. I was only part-time at Rochdale and, although I had been pushing their manager Jimmy Greenhoff for a contract, he told me I would be better off looking elsewhere. Jimmy didn't think he would be at the club much longer and he advised me to move to Crewe.

I scored for Rochdale against Crewe on my debut for the club and Dario made a mental note of me in that game, but he didn't seem that keen on signing me when we agreed to meet at a service station on the M6. He had got lost in the Lake District on the way up and kept me waiting for hours.

I was earning £125 a week and training to be an electrician when I met Dario, but I dropped it all for the chance to go full time at Gresty Road. Crewe were in the old Fourth Division, but my first big test was the huge drop in wages. I am sure he offered me less than I was earning at the time to see just how much I wanted a career in football. I didn't hesitate. He was an excellent coach and was grooming the likes of me, David Platt and John Pemberton for better things when I joined the club.

I was only at the club for three years, but I began to make a bit of a name for myself in the lower leagues. Liverpool were regularly watching me; I was also asked for a trial at Everton by Howard Kendall. They had to make a choice between Kevin Langley and me. Dario thought that signing for Everton would be too big a step and, although he had once been sacked as the Palace manager, he recommended the club to me when they began showing some interest.

Dario wanted to build a conveyor belt of talent at Crewe that he could sell on to enable him to develop more talent and it was just beginning to pay off. Dave Waller had left for Shrewsbury, Gary Blissett had been sold to Brentford – both for decent transfer fees – and I was the next to leave.

Wolves, who were trying to get out of the Fourth Division, offered £100,000 for me and Platt, but Dario said no and insisted that I went to Palace.

It was a great finish to my career. It was always a small friendly club and there were a lot of familiar faces when I returned in the summer of 2001. Dario always wanted the best facilities for his players and he had training pitches that were the envy of some Premiership sides.

Dario has certainly mellowed from the manager who first signed me as a skinny, 20-year-old apprentice electrician in 1984. He used to rant at players, he would play every pass and he would grimace with every mistake, but he has changed. He has also refined his style of football and now everyone who comes up against Crewe knows that they will get the ball down and play a certain way.

He is still bringing players through the system and he must be especially proud when he sees the likes of Dean Ashton, who was initially sold to Norwich for £3m in 2005 and moved to West Ham a year later for £7.25m, being called into the England squad.

I played with Dean for a season and he was a very talented player.

Dario knows exactly how to get the best out of his players. When we won, we would often be given a rollicking but he was the exact opposite when we lost. Defeats brought the best out of him because he would pat players on the back, give them a few quiet words of advice and that would motivate them for training the following Monday morning.

It was refreshing to play under him at the age of 37 because he was in it for the love of the game.

After I was released by Barnsley in March 2001, I spent two months at Notts County and it was the only time in my career where I actually fell out of love with the game. I enjoyed my first couple of games under their manager Jocky Scott and, considering I was an ex-Forest player, I was actually made to feel welcome by the supporters. I was expecting a few groans when my name was read out before my debut against Peterborough, but I soon began to wonder what I was actually doing there. I was an experienced professional but, for the first time in my career, I started to lose the belief and confidence that had characterised me at Palace, Wolves and Forest.

Even though I was 36, I was playing at a lower level and I thought I should still be dictating games, but I was quickly losing my energy, my enthusiasm and my appetite. I had a couple of particularly average games at the beginning and Jocky could see the signs. He told me that he would be resting me for a game at Swindon and I just picked the family up and took them to LegoLand in Windsor for the day to try and forget about the problems. I wasn't enjoying training, I didn't think I was up to it physically any more and I didn't think I could play the game.

Mentally, I was drained, but I didn't realise just how much my role at Barnsley had affected my fitness. As player coach, I hadn't been training as hard as the other players and it really showed when I moved to Notts County. I couldn't put my finger on it at the time and I was seriously thinking about packing the game in when I left the club that summer.

Instead, my enthusiasm was reignited when I got a call from Dario. I really enjoyed the pre-season and I had done enough to earn a season-long contract when I stood on the ball in training and cracked my ankle. I was out for weeks, but by February I was in full flow and, although I knew I was in the twilight of my career, I was really looking forward to an FA Cup fourth-round tie against Rotherham United. In the end it turned out to be a day of mixed emotions because, although I set up two goals for Dean Ashton and scored myself in our 4–2 victory, it also turned out to be the last game of my career. I was so fit going into that game but my knees, after 27 operations, couldn't sustain it. I went into a challenge towards the end of the game, similar to the one I had made against Ed de Goey when I was playing for Forest, and I knew that was it.

It wasn't a major injury, but it was the first time that I had felt bone against bone. When I ruptured my cruciate, I didn't have problems with the cartilage, but other players had warned me about it and I knew straight away that my career was over. There was only a minute of the game left and I just tried to get through it without anyone noticing. Afterwards, the *Match of the Day* team interviewed me and it seemed a fitting end because I was enjoying my game so much.

I have wonderful memories to look back on. When I say the name 'Liverpool', it still sends a chill down my spine because I just think of that amazing day when Palace beat one of the finest teams of that era in the FA Cup semi-final at Villa Park. Many people don't even realise that I played in that game – but I can assure them that it was one of the proudest moments of my career. Some of the Palace team from that era – Ian Wright, Mark Bright and Alan Pardew – are still household names, but I left the public eye when I ended my playing career. There were plenty of lows, too, and the feeling of rejection when I was left out of the England squad for the European Championships in 1992 will never leave me. The feeling of embarrassment haunts me because I had set my heart on representing my country in Sweden that summer. When I look back at the press cuttings from that era, I wasn't omitted from a single newspaper's squad. Even after the humiliation of the chip against France, I was still expected to travel to Sweden and it was a massive shock to be left out.

Those were the lowest moments of my career, but I learned to take the rough with the smooth. I was involved in football for more than 20 years and it is the only way to survive. Although I loved playing in matches, I miss training – and the banter that goes with it – more than anything else. The bond between the manager and players at Palace was something I have never experienced at any other club. Many of them – such as Alan Pardew, Chris Coleman and Gareth Southgate – have gone on to become managers in their own right.

I briefly managed Barnsley's reserves when Harry was at the club, but I left the club shortly after he resigned. It gave me my first real experience of running a football club and I used to go into Dave's office after training to talk about tactics and transfers. He convinced me that I could be a successful manager and I even started to take my coaching badges, but I put that on the back-burner when I was diagnosed with leukaemia.

I had an excellent relationship with Harry Bassett and he showed tremendous faith by signing me for Barnsley when I was still struggling to recover from the cruciate ligament injury that finished me at Nottingham Forest. At times, I did things for Dave that I wouldn't have done for any other manager in my career. He was the kind of guy who commanded so much respect. He wasn't a conventional manager in any respect, but his methods brought success. He was a motivator and would make sure that his teams were prepared mentally, as well as physically, for any game. He didn't take any nonsense, but he treated his players with respect. He is an excellent manager and he doesn't give his players any flannel. As a player, you can't ask for much more than that.

In a 30-year management career he won seven promotions with Wimbledon, Sheffield United and Forest. He is also one of the game's characters. I can remember Simon Jordan, shortly after taking over at Palace, referring to Harry as a 'dinosaur'. That was just the sort of thing to get up Harry's nose, but he thrived on it too. I knocked on the door to the manager's office that afternoon and he was just finishing off a letter that just had the words 'Fuck off, you prick', ready to send to Simon at his office at Selhurst Park. He loved the banter almost as much he loved being a manager.

We made it to the play-off final in 2000, but my ankle was so badly swollen that I should not have played. Harry wanted experience in the dressing room against a very good Ipswich team and I decided to have a jab ahead of the game so that I could come on as a substitute if they needed me. In the end we lost 4–2, but I was grateful to Harry for resurrecting my career with two different clubs. He knew what I was going through when I was injured at Nottingham Forest, but he also realised that I was desperate to play football again and he knew I wouldn't waste the chance.

He is the sort of manager who made his mark in the game because he would rather rely on characters for the spine of his team than skill. His methods attracted a lot of criticism, but I thought he was an exceptional man-manager. He gave me the opportunity to take over the reserves at Barnsley and I was surprised how quickly I made the transition from being one of the lads in the changing room to being regarded as a manager.

On one occasion, Glynn Hodges, my assistant with the reserves team, took the youngsters to a hotel in Aberystwyth as part of our pre-season preparations. We had only just settled into our rooms when we were summoned to see the hotel manager in reception because of complaints from members of the public. Some of the young players had never been away before and they were clearly excitable because it transpired that a few of them had been throwing wet toilet rolls from the top window, aiming them at the old people sat on the benches on the prom. One of the ladies had come into the reception with soggy toilet roll stuck in her permed hair and she claimed to have seen the perpetrators.

Glynn and I disciplined the players, but, as soon as we walked out of the room, we couldn't stop laughing. They were young kids – maybe 17 or 18 – and it was the sort of thing players at any club do. It doesn't mean that I condone it, but there was a funny side to the situation. I certainly enjoyed my time there, but I left the club when Dave resigned and Nigel Spackman took over. He was from a different school of thought to me and I knew he wanted to make changes. That was his right and I couldn't argue.

I don't think anyone who saw me play for Rochdale in the early 1980s would have predicted that I would go on to play Premiership and international football. Sometimes I could hardly believe it myself.

OO

Leukaemia touches people in so many different ways. I watched helplessly as my own family tried to deal with the traumas of my illness, and I know how it affects other people: Julie, my daughters, my mum and Kay went through so many emotions during my treatment. But I saw another side to it when Alastair Campbell came out to ride the penultimate stage with us. During our first couple of weeks in France, Leukaemia Research had been in regular contact and they told me that the Prime Minister's former director of communications and strategy would be coming out to ride a stage.

It seemed increasingly unlikely as we made our way through the Massif Central and headed up towards Paris, but there was a story behind his decision to come out from London to ride the 55 km time-trial around Saint-Étienne. He was a colourful and controversial character, and I had tremendous respect for his fundraising achievements. Despite the high-profile nature of his role with the government, he is also an ambassador for Leukaemia Research, and it was only when I met him for the first time when he arrived in France that I found out the driving force behind his charity work.

Leukaemia had claimed the life of his best friend, the *Observer* journalist John Merritt, in 1992, and it was obvious that he was still traumatised by the experience. They were close friends during Campbell's early career as a political reporter with the *Daily Mirror* and then *Today*. Merritt had helped Campbell overcome his own demons when he suffered a nervous breakdown resulting from years of alcohol abuse in the mid-1980s and their two families were very close. They grew even closer when the disease claimed the life of Merritt's daughter Ellie two years later, and I could see that was one of the motivations behind his incredible fundraising efforts.

It always amazes me how people react in adversity. Alastair is on a crusade for Leukaemia Research and I couldn't help but admire the amount of time he devotes to the cause. The bigger the challenge, the harder he works and I admire that. He showed incredible resilience during his career as both a newspaper executive and one of Blair's trusted aides, but he also demonstrated those qualities away from his working life. He raised around £400,000 by running the London Marathon, which included a significant donation from the US President George W. Bush, but he didn't stop there. He went on to complete the Great North Run and the Great Ethiopian Run before taking part in the 2004 London Triathlon.

Campbell leads a busy life and he had only just returned from his controversial assignment as the public relations manager for the British and Irish Lions Tour of New Zealand when he joined us in France. He certainly helped to raise the profile of our event. As we had breakfast in our hotel before we set off for the start line, he was already conducting interviews with various television and radio outlets and he even received a telephone call from Sir Alex Ferguson before we left. The Manchester United manager had been listening to Radio Five Live in his car and, after talking to Campbell on the phone, he sent a message of support. That was a fantastic gesture and it meant a lot to know that people of Ferguson's standing in football were taking such an interest.

Although I barely knew him, I played his team many times in my career and he can be incredibly warm-hearted. It gave me another lift as we prepared our bikes for the two-hour trip around the Saint-Étienne countryside and we were determined to enjoy what was likely to be a fairly comfortable trip for us. Campbell was still fit when he arrived, but he didn't have the benefit of riding over 3,000 km in three weeks, as we did.

The professionals were aiming to ride the undulating course in just over an hour and, although we wouldn't be riding at their speeds, I wanted to give Campbell an idea of what we had been through over the past three weeks.

I had become accustomed to the elements. If it was raining, I would put my cape on, put my head down and ignore the spray that acts like a jet stream off the back wheel and up my backside. If it was windy, I put on an extra layer and took refuge behind Ian and the rest of the guys. If it was hot, I applied some more sun cream and rattled out the miles. Campbell had ridden his bike on the London Triathlon, but he wanted to get a real feel for the Tour de France. He flew out to interview Lance Armstrong for his column in *The Times* and they had become friends as a result. He was certainly a welcome addition to the team, but I think we all wanted to prove a point to him when we set off from Saint-Étienne. After riding solidly for three weeks, we were all so much stronger and there was a great deal of bonhomie as we left the start line.

Although he suffers from asthma, he made a valiant attempt to stay with our team on the first climb out of Saint-Étienne, but we dropped him. He was struggling on the first few climbs, not least because he was riding in the big chain ring, but we eased off when we reached the top. He is a charming and engaging character and I remain indebted to him for coming out. He was surprised when we dropped him on the climb, but it gave him a flavour of what we had been through.

Having watched Ian fly up 62 climbs, I knew exactly how he was feeling.

21

Corbeil-Essonnes-Paris, 144 km

Every so often I get a flashback. Sometimes I'm sitting in Doctor Taylor's surgery in Barnt Green on the day that I was diagnosed with leukaemia; sometimes I'm sitting in the Cancer Unit at the Queen Elizabeth Hospital, surrounded by the little children who are pumped full of chemotherapy. Or I go back to the times when I was in the isolation unit after another dose of radiation and could barely make it to the sink before I was sick. On some days during my treatment, especially when I was lying in my hospital bed and trying to focus on my life through the fog, I could feel my life slipping away. I wanted to fight, in the same way that I fought for everything throughout my career, but there were undoubtedly times when I felt helpless.

It upsets me even now to think of the times when Julie would walk into the ward and the sister would warn her that my condition had deteriorated through the night. I don't know why I fought and fought and fought, but I knew that if I ever gave up then that would be it. I made a resolution from the moment I was diagnosed that I would fight until the bitter end, but I don't think that is the reason I got lucky. And I am lucky, I know that. For every person who comes out the other side, there are two who don't; it's a game of chance. I owe my life to people like Charlie Craddock. I've met many people over the last four years who adopted the same attitude as me. When I was playing football, if we were 1–0 down with five minutes to go I always believed there was a chance that we could grab an equaliser. It might be tough physically, but everyone has that little bit extra hidden away. I'm not sure that counted for much in my battle against leukaemia, but it certainly gave me a way of focusing on my goals.

That attitude doesn't offer any guarantees. I've watched too many people slip away for me to believe that survival has anything to do with character. I meet a lot of patients through my charity work and I can see in their faces that they have been through it. All that counts is making it through another day. I didn't know from one day until the next, as I drifted in and out of consciousness, whether I would make it. When I talk about the treatment, I can feel my face tightening up and my palms begin to sweat. The cocktail of chemicals to help reduce swelling, pain, sickness and diarrhoea are so severe, and the feeling after being 'cooked' for 12 minutes at a time in the radiation room will never leave me.

In some ways, I don't want it to. It is a memory, a constant reminder of what I went through to beat the disease. I imagine there are worse feelings in life than this, but I've never come close to anything like it. As part of my work for Cure Leukaemia, the Birmingham haematology centre pioneered by Professor Craddock, I often speak to people who are about to go through the transplant procedure.

It is almost impossible to prepare someone for the night sweats, the nausea and the nerves, but I try to tell them that there are only a few bad days. I know what it's like – I've been there – and I never want to go back. Even now, three years on, the memories are so recent that I can reach out and touch them. It is easier to tell people what they will get through, but their questions always choke me.

'How do you feel after the irradiation treatment?'

'What is the transplant like?'

'How long did you stay in hospital?'

'When did you start to feel better?'

And then, the one question that always has me fighting to hold back the tears.

'Geoff, do you think I will make it through?'

oo

From the moment our five-man team slipped off the starting ramp in Fromentine, I dreamed of riding triumphantly past my family and friends on the Champs-Élysées and heading up towards the Arc de Triomphe before throwing down my bike and hugging Julie for the first time in more than three weeks.

I wanted that feeling of euphoria, the surge of adrenalin that kicks in whenever you reach defining moments in your life; I wanted to feel the emotion after 21 days on the road. I envisaged the tears streaming down my face when I saw Julie and my two children waiting for me on the side of the road. It was meant to signal the end of the dark days, the days when I was fighting for my life in hospital, and the start of something new. It was meant to leave me fulfilled and allow me to close a chapter on my life.

I felt uneasy as I packed my day bag for the final time. The previous night, my team – Ian Whittell, Matt Lawton, Robbie Duncan, Neil Ashton, David West, Chris Haynes, Richard Chessor, Andrea Smith and Hayley Cullum – sat together in the hotel bar for the final time. When we reached Paris, we had plans to throw a party for our family and friends, but that night in the bar was the last time we would be together as a team.

We were ten people, thrown together from different walks of life, but we had built a unique bond after three weeks on the road together. Our Tour was not without its moments – Matt's heroic climb to the top of Courchevel was truly inspirational, and it is only now that I can finally laugh about the time we sat in the rain when we were hopelessly lost in Germany – but it was *our* Tour. I sat back and relaxed with a couple of glasses of beer that night and tried to take in everything we had achieved. I knew that, barring a catastrophe, I would ride into Paris the following day and complete the 3,500 km route in exactly the same way as the professionals.

Now, I wasn't sure how I would feel. There were times during the Tour, especially when I was out of sight of my team-mates, when I could feel myself breaking up. I vividly recall being in the shower the night we got off our bikes at 10 p.m. in Pla d'Adet, struggling to hold myself together. I rarely let my emotion show, though. Most of the time I would head it off with a laugh and a joke with the rest of the team, but inside I could be hurting. The thought of some of those Alpine and Pyrenean climbs can drain the colour from my face and, when I was really struggling to turn the pedals, I can remember pleading with my team-mates: 'Don't leave me.'

The fact they never did fills me with a sense of pride. We achieved something special and I can look back on those 21 days with enormous satisfaction. I wanted our 144 km trip into Paris to be a celebration, but it was tinged with sadness as well. Before we left England, our kit sponsor had provided me with a yellow jersey, the colour worn by the leader of the Tour de France, to wear on the final day and I kept it in my suitcase throughout. Every so often I took it out and thought about some of the legendary Tour riders who have worn the *maillot jaune* – people such as Lance Armstrong, Eddie Merckx, Miguel Indurain or Greg LeMond – and I knew I would be privileged to wear it. At the same time, I wanted my team-mates to be wearing the same shirt. They had ridden every step of the way and, although they had not been through the same traumatic experience, they supported me for three weeks solid on the road. They deserved to be wearing it just as much as me. I wanted them to feel what it was like to wear the yellow jersey and ride into Paris to be greeted like heroes by family and friends. It was an honour to put it on for those final 144 km, but I also knew that this was the end of the road.

The following day, after the celebrations, we would all drift off back to our homes in England. Ian and Robbie would return to Manchester on the first ferry; Matt would travel back to England to pick up his family before returning to the south of France for a holiday; and Neil would return to his home in Buckinghamshire to prepare for the new football season. On the outskirts of Paris, as we reached the brow of a hill, we found ourselves staring at the Eiffel Tower in the distance. We were probably still 50 km away from the Champs-Élysées, but I knew that we were coming to the end of a journey. It was a strange day. I didn't want it to end, but we nearly didn't make it after a typically disastrous stunt to mark the final stretch.

Traditionally, the final leg of the Tour is full of high spirits and plenty of high jinks and we wanted to be no different. Previous Tour winners are pictured with their team-mates clinking champagne glasses as they cycled towards Paris and we wanted to emulate them. Although we sensibly bought plastic champagne flutes for the occasion, we underestimated just how difficult it would be for five riders to line up abreast as we hurtled down a dual carriageway at 30 kph. Haynesy was driving one of the Land Rovers and Westie was hanging out of the back window with his camera, bellowing instructions as we wavered all over the road. It was difficult to hear him and it was so dangerous with cars speeding past us at 100 kph that we abandoned the idea. Ian thought we were trying to kill ourselves, and I don't think Matt and Robbie were too impressed either.

Unfortunately, we never did get those pictures.

OO

I expected to burst into tears when we reached Paris. I thought about it a lot during the three weeks away from my family and I expected that the final turn down the Place de la Concorde, as we fought our way through the city-centre traffic and into the grid-lock of the Champs-Élysées, would be my undoing. Instead, I felt empty. By the time we reached the cobblestones and headed towards the Arc de Triomphe to meet our families and friends, all I had was memories. I would no longer wake up every morning wondering whether my legs had recovered enough to ride for another ten hours, or whether I could make it up the ten climbs of the Madelaine, or whether I could survive the snow-capped peaks of the Galibier.

Now I knew I could do it. I had proved it to myself. I survived the mountains, but there was something about them that made me want to go back there again and again. They were the true challenge of the Tour. I can remember being at the bottom of the Galibier. Our bodies were battered by the rain and we couldn't even see the summit past the black clouds that had enveloped the area. Those were the memories that made the Tour. I knew that if I could beat the rain, beat the gradient and keep turning the pedals, then I would make it to the top. After our final climb of the Tour, I knew we couldn't be beaten. We had conquered every challenge the organisers of the 2005 Tour de France had thrown at us.

All the emotion had been drained long before I got to Paris. The last couple of stages had been long, rolling hills and, although they could hurt you, they were not categorised. We hadn't been expecting that and we paid for switching off after we left the Pyrenees a little bit.

I was fitter, stronger and more resilient than ever. When we left the mountains behind, I felt as though I was leaving leukaemia behind. During some of the climbs, I went through unimaginable suffering – in my mind, in my legs – but I never gave up. I couldn't. When I thought of characters like Mark Miller, I had to keep turning the pedals. During my playing career, I always had that little bit extra in the tank in the final ten minutes of a match, but I didn't realise just how far it was possible to push the human body. I'm sure, particularly on the Galibier and during some of the Pyrenean climbs, that my body was close to shutting down and I struggle to describe how I could even make one more rotation, let alone do it for hour upon hour.

A part of me never wanted to leave the mountains. That spell across the Alps, into the Pyrenees and then across the Massif Central is the true test of the Tour de France. At times on those climbs I realised that I had slipped 20 metres behind the person I was supposed to be riding with and I had to call out for them to slow down and wait for me. Some of the Pyrenean climbs were so tough – especially the Marie Blanque – but I was driven by the fear of failure. Once I completed one climb, I began preparing myself mentally for another. When I got to the top of the climbs, the raw emotion would hit me. The year before, I was struggling to take my dogs for a walk without getting out of breath and now I was conquering the toughest climbs on the Tour. It's a mental battle because no-one else can help you climb and sometimes I had to think about everything I had been through to make sure I kept turning over the pedals.

It hurt like hell, but it was a reminder of the days when I was lying in my hospital bed wondering whether I would soon be another leukaemia statistic. Instead, our arrival in Paris marked the end of a journey and the start of another. I was nervous about riding down the Champs-Élysées, but that was more to do with the traffic than anything else. The professionals complete 20 laps on the cobblestones but there was never any chance of us being able to do that. Instead, we added 30 km on to the start of the day and completed a victory lap by riding up to the Arc de Triomphe before fighting our way past hundreds of bewildered motorists to greet our family and friends. The scenes were chaotic and I was relieved finally to get off my bike and off what has to be one of the most dangerous roads in the world.

We had been killing time for the past couple of days and, although we had been steadily building ourselves up to the final stage, it wasn't what I had hoped for. When I went past my family and friends for the first time, I was bursting with excitement but we had already lost the support cars on the Champs-Élysées. They were caught up in the traffic and, as we meandered our way through it heading up towards the Arc, I thought there was a danger that, after 3,500 km, we might end up being knocked down by a motorist.

The moment I put my Bianchi down on the side of the road I spotted Julie waiting among a crowd of around 50 people. I'll never be allowed to forget the first thing I said to her.

'Christ Julie, I forgot how gorgeous my wife is.'

It just came out, but she reminds me of it whenever she wants some new clothes or something for the house. My team-mates haven't forgotten it either and, whenever we meet for a beer, they always remind me of the moment I finished the Tour de France. I was struck by how many people had come out to see me. Apart from my close family, some Palace supporters had made the trip to Paris and they unfurled a banner 'England's Lance Armstrong' as we made our way down the Champs-Élysées. To this day, I regret the fact that I didn't spend some more time with them to thank them for their truly amazing gesture by coming out to France for the final leg.

The finish line was one of those moments that passed by in a haze.

There were so many handshakes, so much champagne and so many pictures that it was impossible to keep track of everything that was going on around me. I wanted to talk to everyone individually and share some special moments with them, but it proved to be impossible. It was especially disappointing as we had arranged a family party that night at the Radisson Hotel just off the Champs-Élysées and many of the people who came to Paris for the day would not be able to come. I felt guilty after everyone had made so much of an effort, but I'm sure they understood.

In the past, I always celebrated winning big matches, such as semi-finals or promotions, by going out with my team-mates for the night, but we decided to spend it with our families in Paris. We wanted them to share the experience after being away for such a long time. If it had been a football team, in the days when I was so selfish that I did whatever I wanted, we would have had a lads' night out. We would have really let our hair down and been hitting bars and clubs and dancing the night away. That's how footballers work. In those days, I wouldn't have given anyone else a second thought. When you are playing professionally, you get close to other people, especially when you are achieving things and a bond starts to form. You work together and you work as a team.

It only ever happened to me at Palace and, for a time, it seemed that nothing would get in our way. At times, Wrighty, Brighty, Andy Gray and I would be at loggerheads, but we had such respect for each other that, the moment we crossed the white line, we would do anything for each other. I hadn't seen Andy for nearly ten years when he came into the dressing room for my testimonial against Manchester United in March 2006 and we greeted each other like long-lost brothers. I barely knew Ian, Robbie or Matt before we took on the Tour, but it would be the same if I saw them now. We would go and sit at the bar for a beer and things would be the same. During the World Cup in Germany, I was asked to be a guest of the All-Parliamentary football team against the England Press team and, when I sat at the bar after the game with Matt and Neil, we recalled our endless days on the roads around France.

When you share something so personal, when you really have to grind something out, you see different sides to people. They change when they are at their lowest point, but that's when people show their true colours and that's when they earn respect. When any team works together for a long period of time, it drains away all the façades that you see in the workplace. It breaks you down. I will never forget the time Neil threw a pair of cycling socks that probably hadn't been washed for a week at his girlfriend, Andrea. Despite his apologies, they barely exchanged a word for another week after that, but at least those moments brought some sanity to the Tour. When Andrea and Hayley arrived towards the end of our first week in France, they brought the warmth that had been missing in the previous few days.

Before that, everything had been very regimented and it was getting to the point where it would have all kicked off if they hadn't come out. They found the halfway point on the Tour and marked the spot on the road – typically it was in the middle of a climb – and they brought humour to the endless days in the saddle. One day they drove the entire stage wearing face masks and another time they admitted they had covered their hotel room in red paint when they were putting our names on an enormous banner that they would hold up on the side of the road from time to time. For me, those are the memories of the Tour and, in truth, I never really wanted it to end. Everyone was ready to do more if it had been asked of them and I know that we could have carried on indefinitely if we had to.

At the very beginning, I worried about what was coming and I read the various Tour magazines every night to try and get a mental image of the next day's stage. By the end, it seemed a long time since Robbie and Matt had their crash, Matt became a victim of food poisoning and Ian came off his bike during a dangerous descent. Until we reached Paris, I never once thought that the job was done.

I would certainly like to feel some of the sensations of the Tour again. Whether they can be recreated, I just don't know. If I think back to Alan Pardew's winning goal for Palace in the 1990 FA Cup semi-final, I never felt like that again in football. Try as hard as you can, but some things can never come back.

Epilogue

Some people seem to have an instinct and they know when they are about to hear bad news, but I can never tell when it's coming. I can be pottering around the house, I can be riding my bike around Birmingham, or indulging in my usual banter with Julie in the kitchen when the phone will ring.

'Hello?'

'Hello, is that Geoff?'

'Geoff, it's Roy – Steve Hayden's dad.'

'Oh, hi Roy, how are you?'

'Listen, Geoff, I have some sad news to tell you.'

And then there is the pause that will trigger a thousand emotions. As I move away from the kitchen table, or leave my bike resting against the pavement, I can feel the anxiety creeping up on me. I have been here before and I know what this feeling is like. My throat will be dry, there will be a knot in my stomach and I can feel the colour draining from my face.

'Geoff, I'm calling to tell you that Steve passed away today.'

Those are the phone calls that never leave me.

OO

One of the last times I saw Steve was at my testimonial game against Manchester United at Selhurst Park on 6 April 2006. He had only just had a bone-marrow transplant, but he was making huge strides. I spent weeks in bed, struggling to even make it to the bathroom, but Steve was incredibly sprightly considering his ordeal. He was a West Bromwich Albion supporter, but I invited him to Palace for the game and I was as proud to have him there as anyone else in the stadium that night. More than 15,000 people were at Selhurst Park, but Steve stood out for me. When I saw him before the game, he appeared to be through the worst phases of the treatment and I was amazed by the speed of his recovery.

I first met him when Professor Craddock asked me to go and see him shortly after he was diagnosed with leukaemia and I was proud to see him sitting in the stands for such a special occasion. Charlie often asks me to go and see patients and it is remarkable how quickly you strike up a bond with people. On another occasion, Charlie asked me to talk to Claire Wadley, a lovely young girl from Birmingham who had been struck by the disease. I got a phone call from her one day and she told me that palliative care was her only option. She wanted someone around her to be positive and all I could offer was my support.

I asked what she wanted to do and she instantly said: 'Fight it.' She had a target to be a bridesmaid for her friend's wedding in 2006 and that was her goal. I'm sure the brain has a major part to play in any illness and I'm convinced that the human body can give up. If the incentives aren't there, things begin to wear you down after a while. I can remember being in the mountains and my body was telling me to get off the bike and walk, but my mind was overriding it. With leukaemia, there are so many things that can happen that the body starts to shut down after a while. That happened with Mark Miller and I will never forget when his girlfriend, Dawn, told me that he was giving up. Everything was going wrong with his treatment and he became disillusioned and despondent. That is when I wanted him to fight, but sometimes you have taken so many punches that you just can't pick yourself up again.

Claire had a different attitude. She wanted to fight, she wanted to survive and she showed so much courage. She made it to her friend's wedding and, although I would like to say that there was a happy ending, I'm sad to say that she too passed away.

When I visit people in hospital, I can see the suffering and sometimes they don't even need to say anything. We both know what they are going through. I know what it is like to be sat in a hospital bed and be told that I would develop shingles. Sure enough, I got it.

Even when I went home, I knew that if I developed a temperature I would have to be admitted to hospital as soon as possible because my immune system was so low that it could develop into something life-threatening. I knew that graft-versus-host disease would affect me at some stage, I just didn't know when and that would send me into a downward spiral of depression and despair. I could knock myself out of it quite quickly, but for some people it is relentless. Sometimes the disease has a bigger grip on them after their transplant and that is when I most admire their fighting qualities. Leukaemia used to drain me, but now I use it as my inspiration. When I see people struggling to cope with their treatment I know, just as they do, that there is every chance they may pass away but I never think about it. When I sit with people who are in their hospital beds, we both know that they are battling just to have another couple of days.

I don't get depressed by that, I get uplifted. I am there for anyone who wants to talk but I don't throw myself in anyone's face. If they want to talk, I'm here for them.

OO

I know leukaemia has changed me. During my football career, I was aggressive on the pitch and could be just the same off it. It might sound churlish, but after I was diagnosed I took a conscious decision to take a step back. Things I never noticed before – such as flowers, trees and fields – suddenly take on a different dimension and I learned to appreciate them. During the Tour, Matt would often turn to me and say: 'Geoff, I can't believe you're so laid-back.'

I assured him that I never used to be that way, but attitudes change. I came close to losing my life – so close that there were times in the isolation unit at the Queen Elizabeth Hospital when I wondered whether I would even wake up the following morning – and that gave me an altogether different perspective. Having spoken to dozens of people who survived leukaemia, I know I am not alone. Many of them feel the same way. My wife tells me that I am a much nicer person now and I'm certainly more relaxed. She sees the occasional signs of the 'old Geoff' returning and she is always quick to remind me. Usually we will be in the outside lane of the motorway and I will be 6 feet away from the rear bumper in front, flashing them to move out of the way.

I don't like myself when I'm like that and neither does my wife, but it shows that I'm returning to normal. I certainly don't have any regrets about my life any more and I look back on the Tour with a tremendous sense of achievement. The football season may be nine months long, but three weeks around France was an incredible slog. I know public perception of me has changed since I rode the Tour. Before, if anyone recognised me in the street, they were more likely to say something unkind about my disastrous chip against France in February 1992. These days, people stop me in the street and tell me that they admire what I have done, but I always feel embarrassed when that happens.

I didn't set out to be an ambassador for Leukaemia Research. I set out on the Tour de France to raise as much money as possible for people who had been placed in the same position as me. I want to find a cure and if my contribution – fundraising or otherwise – helps in any way, then I will die a happy man. We set out to raise £200,000 through the Tour, but we eclipsed that figure after my testimonial game at Palace. It was a wonderful evening, but there was a long-term goal behind the game at Selhurst Park. It was another opportunity for me to raise awareness and I gain satisfaction from knowing that all the money raised that night helped to employ people for research purposes. For me, I am repaying Charlie Craddock a little bit at a time by raising money for his research centre in Birmingham. He wants to build a centre of excellence in haematology and one day I want to be able to say: 'Charlie, here is the money – go do it.'

That will give me a great sense of achievement, but I don't want it to end there. I was proud to be honoured at the BBC Sports Personality of the Year in December 2006, when I was given the Helen Rollason Award for bravery and courage, but I want to use the profile it has given me to continue my fundraising activities.

I know that I will never be able to look at test tubes or stare down microscopes to find a cure, but I will do whatever is necessary to help the research teams. I thought my enthusiasm might wear off after the highs of riding the Tour, but it remains as strong as ever. Lance Armstrong has a charity foundation in America and I am in the process of starting something similar. It would be a tremendous waste if I didn't use my experience for the long-term benefit of others. I'm not as well known as someone like Ian Botham, who has raised millions of pounds for charity through his walks from Land's End to John O'Groats, but I can play my part. Before my illness, I was trying to find a way of keeping my family in the lifestyle that they had become accustomed to during my football career.

I didn't realise it at the time, but I can look back now and see that it gave me all the trappings. The house, the car, the family ... it can give you everything you want, but it doesn't necessarily guarantee happiness and it certainly doesn't guarantee health. I feel grateful to still be here, but I don't dwell on just how sick I was. I can remember vividly just how I felt and I don't really want to be reminded of it too often. It's not exactly great conversation for a dinner party. There are not many times in life when you are so reliant on other people to save it, but I always had 100 per cent faith in whatever Charlie wanted to do. I became like a human guinea pig for him and whichever cocktail of chemicals he wanted to put inside me, I let him do it.

These days, my financial affairs are of secondary importance. My football career gave me a wonderful lifestyle, but I have other priorities. Every charitable cause is worthy, but I have to fly the flag for leukaemia research. I have survived the disease and I want other people to do the same. If they can't, then I want to make life as comfortable for them as possible. It doesn't always have to be about money. Whenever Charlie asks me to give a patient a ring, or asks me to drop into their house for a cup of tea and a chat, I am always happy to help. From my own experience, I know how comforting it is to have someone who has been through the ordeal sitting beside you.

It doesn't take away the pain, but they are a security blanket. I know it is hard for patients, but it is also difficult for their families. At times, Julie will get emotional over certain things, but it's usually when she hears about people's problems.

I've been through so much that I am hardened to the illness now, but occasionally we will see something that makes the tears well up. I always keep a cap on it, but I can never tell when it's coming. Films often set me off and I can't watch *In America*, the story of an Irish family with two little girls who are struggling to settle in New York, without reaching for the handkerchief.

OO

There is always a chance that leukaemia will come back but if it does, the doctors will know before I do. Although I am officially in remission, I still have regular blood tests and they will be able to detect the disease in its early stages. That threat will always be there and there is always a danger that it will tap me on the shoulder again, but I am determined to lead a happy and healthy life. After being told that I had a 30 per cent chance of living beyond the age of 41, it is great to be in this position, but I will never consider myself to be completely cured. There is no point in time when the doctors will tell me to uncork champagne bottles and start to celebrate.

From time to time, I get bitter reminders of the disease. Not so long ago, Julie and I were invited to the opening of a research unit at the Queen Elizabeth Hospital and we met a woman whose daughter had exactly the same type of leukaemia as me. Like me, she had recovered from a bone-marrow transplant and, although she had been in remission for ten years, she eventually succumbed to the disease. That scared the hell out of me and, although Charlie reassured me that the treatments and after-care had moved on significantly in the last decade, it certainly shook me up.

I know I will never be completely cured, but I don't want the disease to be hanging over me like a dark cloud. I will always be prone to infections, but it is up to me to spot the symptoms quickly and take the appropriate action. If it ever comes back, it will show up in one of my regular blood tests before I start to feel the stomach pains that left me crippled in the early stages of my illness. I go back every couple of months for a check-up and they usually have the results within five minutes; then Charlie and I can have a catch-up. We don't talk about my illness any more. Instead we have the sort of conversation that I would have with someone if I met them in the pub for a pint.

People often ask me whether I would go through it all again and the answer is always the same. Do I want to? Never again. Would I? Yes.